Relax. There will be no test.

Museums can ruin a good vacation. Or you can look into the eyes of *David* and see the soul of Renaissance man. Ancient sites can give you goosebumps or heat stroke, depending upon your ability to resurrect the rubble.

Rick Steves' Europe 101 sorts Europe's tangle of people and events—from the pyramids to Picasso—into an orderly and fascinating parade to make your sightseeing more meaningful and fun.

Rick Steves' Europe 101 connects yesterday's Europe with today's sights—art, museums, buildings, and people. Throughout the book, lists of sights tie your new understanding of Europe right into your upcoming trip plans. This unique approach to art and history, supplemented with maps, timelines, and illustrations, makes this "professor in your pocket" an essential tool in any thinking tourist's preparation for Europe.

Beyond their formal university educations in European history, art, and culture, the authors have spent over eighty months roaming Europe, on their own and as tour guides. These two professional tourists understand what you need to know and, just as important, what you don't.

With *Rick Steves' Europe 101*, smart people who slept through their history and art classes before they knew they were Europe-bound can enjoy a fun-to-read, practical book that makes Europe's history, art, and culture come alive.

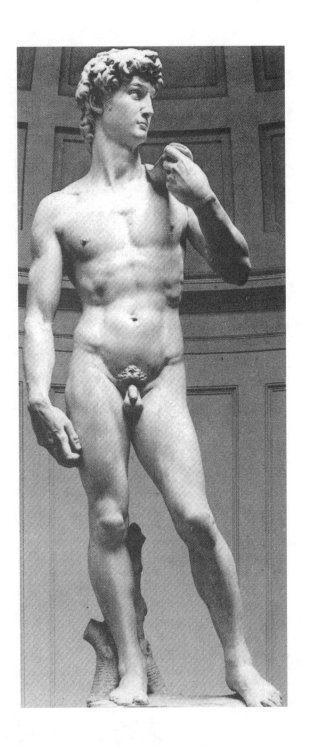

Rick Steves' EUROPE 101

History and Art
for the Traveler

Sixth Edition

Rick Steves
and
Gene Openshaw

Graphics and Maps by
David C. Hoerlein

AVALON
TRAVEL
publishing

Other ATP travel guidebooks by Rick Steves:
Rick Steves' Mona Winks: Self-Guided Tours of Europe's Top Museums (with Gene Openshaw)
Rick Steves' Postcards from Europe
Rick Steves' Europe Through the Back Door
Rick Steves' Best of Europe
Rick Steves' France, Belgium & the Netherlands (with Steve Smith)
Rick Steves' Germany, Austria & Switzerland
Rick Steves' Great Britain & Ireland
Rick Steves' Italy
Rick Steves' Scandinavia
Rick Steves' Spain & Portugal
Rick Steves' London (with Gene Openshaw)
Rick Steves' Paris (with Steve Smith and Gene Openshaw)
Rick Steves' Rome (with Gene Openshaw)
Rick Steves' Phrase Books: French, Italian, German, Spanish/Portuguese, French/Italian/German

Avalon Travel Publishing, 5855 Beaudry Street, Emeryville, CA 94608

Sixth edition. First printing September 2000

Library of Congress Cataloging-in-Publication Data
Steves, Rick, 1955–
Europe 101: history and art for the traveler / Rick Steves and Gene Openshaw.—6th ed.
        p. cm.
Includes index.
ISBN 1-56261-535-1 (pbk.)
1. Europe—Civilization. 2. Europe—Guidebooks.   I. Openshaw, Gene.   II. Title.
CB203.S734   2000
940'.024'91—dc21   00-057598
                                                                                        CIP

Distributed to the book trade by
Publishers Group West
Berkeley, California

Europe Through the Back Door Editor: Risa Laib
Avalon Travel Publishing Editor: Kate Willis
Copy Editor: Donna Leverenz
Production: Kathleen Sparkes, White Hart Design, Albuquerque, NM
Sidebars (on Punic Wars, crusaders, popes, and others): Risa Laib
Photography: Rick Steves, David C. Hoerlein, and others
Text Design: Kathryn Lloyd-Strongin
Cover design: Janine Lehmann
Typesetting: Kathleen Sparkes, White Hart Design, Albuquerque, NM
Printing: Publishers Press

Contents

Appendix 349

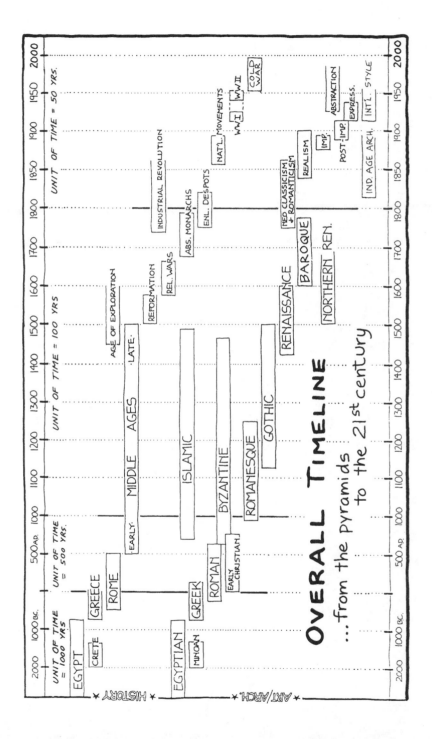

Owner's Manual

Most history is about as exciting as somebody else's high school yearbook—a pile of meaningless faces and names. This history is different. *Rick Steves' Europe 101* throws out the dreary dates and meaningless names. What's left is simple, fast-moving, and essential to your understanding of Europe.

After stripping history naked, *Rick Steves' Europe 101* dresses it up with just the personalities and stories that will be a part of your travels. Take Frederick the Great, for instance. Great as he was, he's just Frederick the So-So to the average tourist, so he isn't mentioned in this book. Louis XIV, however, gets special attention because nearly every traveler visits his palace at Versailles or its many copies throughout Europe. Unprepared, bored tourists will wonder why you are having so much fun at Versailles. When you understand Louis, he becomes a real person who pulls his leotards on one leg at a time just like you and me. And his palace comes alive.

A victim of the Louvre

Art, like history, can be confusing and frustrating. _Rick Steves' Europe 101_ carefully ties each style of art to its historical era and relates it to your trip. You can't appreciate Baroque art through _Better Homes and Gardens_ eyes. You need a Baroque perspective.

Museums can be a drag or they can be unforgettable highlights, depending on what you know. _Europe 101_ prepares you. After reading this book, you'll step into a Gothic cathedral, excitedly nudge your partner, and whisper, "Isn't this a marvelous improvement over Romanesque?" Europe, here you come!

Learn about art and make it fun.

No apologies. This book drives art snobs nuts. Its gross generalizations, sketchy dates, oversimplifications, and shoot-from-the-hip opinions really tweeze art highbrows. Our goal is to give you the practical basics (and no more) to make your sightseeing fun and meaningful.

Take a minute to understand the layout. This book covers the essential story of Europe's history and art chronologically through the prehistoric, ancient, medieval, Renaissance, early modern, and modern times. Each chapter ends with a timeline that helps you visualize how history and art interrelate. The best examples of this art and history are listed throughout the book in "sightseeing highlights" boxes. These lists are based on fame, accessibility, visitor friendliness, and arbitrary whims because, heck, it's our book. Important topics that don't fit into the chronology are covered in Part II–Country Specifics, Part III–Art Specifics, and in the Appendix.

Take notes as you read this book. Keep your travel plans in mind. Now, raise your travel dreams to their upright and locked positions, and get ready for a fascinating story... the story of Europe.

Part I
History and Art of Europe

*Twelve thousand years ago, in caves like these at **Lascaux** in southern France, hunters painted their prey. This art is not decorative, but magically functional . . . art with a purpose.*

Prehistoric Europe

Uncivilized men and women, armed with crude stone tools and fire, survived by hunting wild animals and gathering plants and fruit. Europe was populated by nomads with the munchies. Civilization was born when nomads settled. Before this, there was no tourism.

Paleolithic Art (40,000–8000 B.C.)

Europe's first art goes back over 30,000 years: that's five times as old as the oldest pyramid. Living at the mercy of nature, people worshiped "Mother Nature," who took the form of a fertile woman. The earliest art included fertility symbols, burial artifacts (such as stone tools), and cave paintings. The most famous and finest early cave paintings—at Altamira in Spain and at Lascaux in France—date back to around 12,000 B.C. The startlingly realistic drawings of animals are made with charcoal, ocher, and other natural pigments. In many cases, artists expertly incorporated the pre-existing contours of the stone into their art. Some of these paintings look like modern art, and, in fact, have inspired some modern artists.

The best prehistoric cave painting still open to tourists is the Grotte de

The Venus of Willendorf, *25,000 B.C. (Natural History Museum, Vienna). This 4-inch-high limestone fertility symbol was one of many such statues made by prehistoric Europeans who worshiped Mother Nature. This faceless Pillsbury Dough Girl was found in present-day Austria.*

Font-de-Gaume, near Lascaux, in France's Dordogne region. The Altamira and Lascaux caves are closed due to the heat and humidity generated by modern crowds, but a realistic "copy cave" adjacent to Lascaux is open to sightseers. Made with the same materials and techniques, this is worth a look.

Cave paintings were not simply decorations, but magic symbols that likely played a part in ritual ceremonies. Cave dwellers hoped they could gain control over animals by capturing their likenesses.

This "hunter style" of art is found throughout Europe. Ancient drawings of animals and, occasionally, drawings of the hunters themselves have been chiseled and sanded onto rocks or dug into hillsides.

After Ice Age, Civilization Heats Up

As the ice fields slowly receded from northern Europe (beginning around 9000 B.C.), prehistoric life changed. The frozen plains were replaced by forests and plants. As wandering hunter tribes learned food gathering, farming, and herding, they began to settle down. Europe entered a new era.

Not all of Europe progressed at the same rate. Scandinavia, enveloped in ice long after the Continent had turned to forest, lagged behind the rest of Europe. Many present-day tribes (the bushmen of Africa, Australia's aborigines, the Eskimos, and England's punk rockers) still employ some Stone Age technology.

Gradually, the scrambling of Europe's prehistoric nomads took on a pattern. People saw the advantages of farming their own plants and raising their own animals in a choice spot. Eventually, more people farmed and fewer hunted. By 10,000 B.C., groups began settling in the most fertile and livable areas near rivers. By 7000 B.C., small independent cities had appeared.

This transition from hunter-gatherer to farmer-herder led to cooperation and leisure time, two elements key to the rise of civilization. People living together and dealing with mutual problems need to get along. This cooperation, or social organization, enabled early societies to accomplish giant projects—such as building irrigation and drainage systems—that no one could do alone. This interaction nurtured the formation of governments, a greater exchange of knowledge and ideas, the development of common languages, the rudiments of writing to preserve this new knowledge, and paid vacations.

Domestic people were more productive than nomads. In the off-season, they had time on their hands: time to sing songs, tell stories,

From Hard Rock to Heavy Metal

Historians divide prehistory into ages to show our progression from the use of stone tools (lith = stone) to more sophisticated metals.

Paleolithic	40,000–8000 B.C.
Mesolithic	8000–4500 B.C.
Neolithic	4500–2000 B.C.
Copper Age	3000–1800 B.C.
Bronze Age	1800–500 B.C.

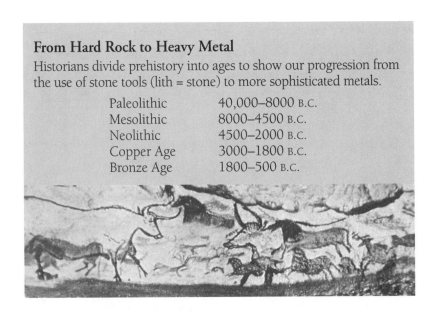

make decorative pottery, organize religion, and construct permanent buildings.

Ideally located with a good climate, Mesopotamia (present-day Iraq, Iran, and the Middle East) was the birthplace of Western civilization. This "Crossroads of the World," where Asia, Europe, and Africa meet, was perfect for receiving and spreading through trade all the world's knowledge. This was the age of Jericho, followed by the kingdoms of Ur, Uruk, Lagash, and Babylon, each in its time the hub of the known world.

Neolithic Art (4500–2000 B.C.)

As art passed from Paleolithic ("Old" Stone Age) to Neolithic ("New" Stone Age), it became less realistic. Figures were simplified and more stylized, used as symbolic stick figures for that society's magic.

This trend is especially evident in the small goddess statues so popular in the ancient world. Paleolithic goddesses were realistic portrayals of a female, but, as time went on, artisans began to exaggerate some of the goddesses' most feminine features: breasts, hips, butt, and genitals. By late Neolithic times, the figures were even more stylized: a goddess might be just a stick with two lumps for breasts.

The most awe-inspiring and mysterious remains of Neolithic culture

Stonehenge, England. *One of Britain's many ancient wonders, Stonehenge is a 4,000-year-old celestial calendar made of giant stones.*

are the massive stone circles such as Stonehenge (2800–1500 B.C.), the most famous of the 300-plus circles that litter Britain. These megalithic ("big stone") structures were calendars on a grand scale. A recent study found they were designed to calculate the movement of the sun, moon, and stars, and even to predict eclipses in order to help early societies know when to plant, harvest, and party. Stonehenge's pillars are placed so that the rising sun on the longest day of the year (the summer solstice) filters through and strikes the altar stones. An avenue of stones that could accommodate huge crowds leads up to the sanctuary.

Made of stones weighing as much as 400 tons, stone circles amazed Europeans of the Middle Ages, who figured they were built by a race of giants. The bluish stones used to build Stonehenge likely came from Wales—240 miles away, close if you're taking a train but far if you're packing a megalith. New Age pilgrims speculate that ancient congregations levitated the mammoth slabs along powerful "ley lines"—lines that connect Britain's prehistoric sights. Stodgy engineers contend that the huge stones were rafted from Wales, then rolled inland on logs.

The two major types of megalithic structures are menhirs and dolmens. Menhirs are upright stones which either stand alone or are arranged in a circle (Stonehenge and Avebury, England) or in lines (Carnac, France). The menhirs that were designed to stand alone like

Sights of Prehistoric Europe

- Stone circles, Stonehenge, Avebury, and Castlerigg (near Keswick), Britain
- Lascaux II (re-creation of cave painting), Les Eyzies, Dordogne, France
- Grotte de Font-de-Gaume (cave painting), near Lascaux, France
- Grotte de Rouffignac (cave roof with etchings of mammoths), Rouffignac, France
- Grotte de Cougnac (cave art), France
- Grotte de Peche Merle (cave art, Cro-Magnon footprint), near Cahors, France
- Abri du Cap-Blanc (subtle sculpture and carving), France
- Menhirs and Dolmens, Carnac, Brittany, France

Additionally, artifacts can be seen in many museums, especially national museums in Copenhagen, Vienna (Venus of Willendorf), and London.

a statue were sometimes decorated with a relief carving of a stylized human being. Dolmens are tombs made of several upright stones topped with a slab for a roof. These became more elaborate with larger chambers over time.

Megalithic tombs, similar in purpose to the pyramids of ancient Egypt, were burial chambers for the great warrior chiefs of the time, carrying them into the next life. Warriors were buried with all their possessions, a boon for modern-day archaeologists. Found throughout Europe, megalithic tombs are most common in western France, which has several thousand.

Prehistoric art, ranging from fist-sized goddesses to Chevrolet-sized megaliths, will always be a shadowy mystery. As we progress farther in time, history and art are thrown in sharper focus.

Age of Metals (3000–500 B.C.)

Copper was first concocted in Anatolia (modern day Turkey) in 6500 B.C., but its practical application took several thousand years to migrate to Europe. New copper tools brought on a new age, leaving stone tools back in the Stone Age.

In about 1800 B.C., armed with the recipe for bronze (copper and tin—found in abundance in England), Europe forged ahead. People learned to specialize, making various tools, cooking pots, figurines, jewelry, keys, and always-popular weapons. You'll see these copper odds and bronze ends throughout museums in Europe. Artisans produced, trade flourished, and cities grew. With the invention of the plow and wheel, things really started rolling...in the East.

While Europe was still figuring out what to put in its new metal pots, Egyptian civilization was already cooking.

The Pyramid of King Zoser at Saqqara, *from about 2600 B.C., is probably the first of Egypt's great pyramids. Unlike later pyramids, King Zoser's is solid with the burial chamber underground. Its designer, Imhotep, who was deified by wowed Egyptians, is the first recorded artist in history.*

Egypt
3000–1000 B.C.

The year 3000 B.C., when writing appeared, marks the beginning of recorded history—a historic event that reached its culmination in this book. But first things first.

Egypt was united in 3000 B.C., establishing a remarkable civilization that thrived for 2,000 years. Egypt is part of *Europe 101* because it influenced Greek culture, its artifacts are scattered throughout Europe today, and it's easy to visit as part of a European trip.

The earliest great civilizations grew up along river valleys: Indus, Tigris, Euphrates, and Nile. Egypt is the Nile. From an airplane, the river looks like a lush green ribbon snaking through an endless sea of sand. By learning to harness the annual flooding of the Nile—its water and its fertilizing silt—ancient Egyptians prospered. The Nile's blessing, combined with relative isolation from enemy civilizations, brought Egyptians contentment and stability.

Except for periodic struggles to unite the two kingdoms of Egypt (upper and lower), Egypt was politically stable. The Egyptian leader, the pharaoh, was believed to be a living god or at least the all-powerful link between the human world and the world of the spirits. To challenge the pharaoh was to challenge everything that held Egyptian society together. Pharaohs ruled a pro–status quo Egypt virtually unchallenged for 2,000 years.

The pharaoh's religion stressed preparation for the afterlife. In those days you could "take it with you." Pyramids, built over a period of decades by hordes of (probably willing) slaves, were giant stone tombs designed to preserve a king's or queen's body and possessions so he or she would arrive safely in the afterlife. Many pharaohs even took their servants with them, alive—for a while. The walls were painted with images of earthly things in case the pharaoh's real goodies didn't make it (a primitive forerunner of baggage insurance).

Egyptian Architecture

The Pyramid of Chephren, or Khafre, (2500 B.C.) is one of the three famous pyramids at Giza, near Cairo. King Chephren was buried inside, and his likeness survives (almost) in the face of the Great Sphinx. With a lion's body, he towers 65 feet high.

One way to keep a pharaoh alive was to remember him or her. While the tomb would be hidden for safety, the temple, such as Queen Hatshepsut's near Luxor, would be high profile for all to see and honor. Today, tourists probably remember the high-pressure merchants more than the queen.

Egypt's art changed little from 3000 through 1000 B.C., reflecting a stable society obsessed with the afterlife. Most Egyptian art is funerary, built for the tombs of the wealthy and found on the Nile's west bank. Since the sun "died" every night on the west bank, it seemed logical for Egyptians to be buried there as well. All the pyramids are on the west bank.

Saqqara, the original pyramid (c. 2600 B.C.), is a "step pyramid," designed as a series of funerary buildings stacked one on top of the other. The three Great Pyramids at Giza (c. 2500 B.C.) are the most visited of the pharaoh's stairways to heaven and well worth seeing. These are far from the only pyramids, however. You'll find dozens of them as you explore the Nile region.

The Hypostyle Hall from the Temple of Amen-Re at Karnak (1280 B.C.), near Luxor, is crowded with a forest of thick columns. Just to have a roof over this huge building was an accomplishment. But a society's architectural sophistication can be measured by the distance it can span without a support. By this measure, Egypt was pretty crude. Later civilizations built more graceful temples with thinner columns spaced farther apart.

(Left) Place de la Concorde, Paris. _Egyptian obelisks_ decorate squares from Rome to London. Two thousand years ago, they were barged across the Mediterranean and given as gifts to (or taken by) emperors. Today, they're the oldest pieces of art many tourists will see in Europe.

Eventually, grave robbers broke into most of the pyramids. Time and time again, pharaohs woke up in heaven with absolutely nothing. Rather than marking their tombs with huge pyramids, rulers decided to hide them in the "Valley of the Kings," near Luxor. Mounted patrols guarded these hidden waiting rooms for the Eternity Express. Many have been opened as recently as the last century, revealing incredible riches and art that looks brand new even though it's more than 3,000 years old. Tutankhamen ("Tut" to his friends) was just a mediocre pharaoh—an ancient Gerry Ford—who achieved fame only because his tomb was discovered intact. Many more unmarked and hidden pharaohs' tombs wait in silence and darkness.

Egypt also built remarkably sturdy temples that still stand today, mainly in and near Luxor. Some were cult temples that housed images of gods (like Luxor Temple) and others were memorials for pharaohs (like Queen Hatshepsut's).

Recipe for a Egyptian temple: Choose a god. Build a monumental doorway and flank it with obelisks and colossal statues. Add a courtyard filled with thick columns, a huge pillared (hypostyle) hall, and the shrine. Sprinkle in a few private rooms for priests.

Rich in clay, Egypt built its temple walls of thick brick, with few windows. Outside walls were etched with hieroglyphics and colorful pictographs. Due to a lack of wood, roofs were made of stone slabs, supported by closely placed stone columns. These immense pillars bulged near their base like buds, narrowed near the top, and opened into papyrus flower capitals.

Egypt invented obelisks, the tapered monoliths which inspired our Washington Monument. Originally gracing temples, obelisks were dedicated to the sun god and incised with hieroglyphic ads for the current pharaoh.

Mummy case, 1290 B.C. (British Museum, London). This mummy case, like much Egyptian art, was funerary: intended for the dead and their baggage back in the days when you could take it with you.

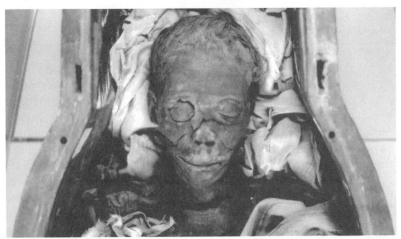

Tombs and mummification preserved corpses and possessions for the afterlife.

Egyptian Art

The distinguishing characteristics of Egyptian art—two-dimensionality, strong outlines, and rigid frontality—are explained by Egyptian religion and politics. Egyptian art was symbolic. It was a pictorial roll call of people and things which would be preserved in the afterlife, and it affirmed the divinity of the pharaoh and the relationships of the gods. It was more important for figures to be easily identifiable caricatures than to be lifelike.

Nobleman Hunting in the Marshes, _1425 B.C. (British Museum, London). Looking as though he was just run over by a pyramid, this 2–D hunter is flat, as is most Egyptian art._

"Good" art is not necessarily lifelike art. Often artists with great technical skill purposely distorted a subject to make an emotional, social, intellectual, or artistic point. It helps to understand the artist's purpose before judging his work.

The Egyptian artist, a master at portraying details realistically, would paint or sculpt only what was necessary to recognize the subject. Egyptian art consists of picture symbols (like our "Deer Crossing" road signs) showing things from their most characteristic and easy-to-recognize angle. For example, while both shoulders may face the viewer, heads are shown in profile.

Painters created unrealistic but recognizable scenes. Fish and birds were shown as if a biologist had stretched them out, trying to capture every identifying trait. This was so effective that scientists today can identify the species of most of the animals found in Egyptian drawings.

When Egyptians died, their souls had to make a long journey to the Egyptian paradise. No normal soul could make this hairy journey without a coffee break. A statue or painting of the deceased qualified as a rest stop. If you were rich, it was worth having your statue on display everywhere you could, to improve your chances of providing your soul with the necessary pit stops on its long journey to salvation.

These were mug shots for eternity, easy to recognize quickly: chin up, no funny faces, nothing fancy. Statues were bold, stiff, frontal, and designed according to a rigid set of proportions. The head might be a third the height of the body and a forearm as long as a shin. This

Egyptian statues and paintings, stiff, unrealistic, and forever standing-at-attention, fill several rooms in the British Museum and Vatican Museum.

"canon of proportions" was considered correct and remained unchanged for centuries.

If any pharaoh made it to heaven, it was Ramses II (the one who wrangled with Moses and the Israelites). Not only did he have more statues than anyone else, but, just in case his soul could read, he even had his name chiseled over the names of many earlier pharaohs' statues.

The one striking exception to Egypt's 2,000 years of political, religious, and artistic rigidity was the reign of the Pharaoh Akhenaton (1350 B.C.). We owe much of our knowledge of this period to the discovery of the tomb of Akhenaton's son-in-law and successor, Tutankhamen. Akhenaton was history's first monotheist. He startled the conservative nobility and priesthood of his time by lumping the countless gods of the Egyptian pantheon into one all-powerful being, Aton the sun god.

In paintings from Akhenaton's reign, we see the royal family painted with a new artistic freedom, with more natural, lifelike, personal settings—such as a family portrait with Akhenaton, his wife Nefertiti, and their children. Ignoring the custom of portraying the most powerful subjects larger, his wife is shown as big as the king. There is a naturalism and gaiety in these pictures that is radically different from the stiff symbolism of earlier years. Yet after this brief period of freedom, the old rigidity returned.

Egypt's artistic legacy to the rising Greek world was the technical mastery of a formal religious style. Herodotus, an ancient Greek historian, said of the Egyptians, "They are religious to excess, far beyond any other race of men." The statues, wall paintings, coffins, mummies, and tombs you'll see in Europe's museums attest to the Egyptians' fixation with their gods, pharaohs, and the afterlife.

A brief rundown of the symbolism will help you identify who's who in Egyptian art. Amen-Ra was the King of the Gods, the god of the sun. He is usually shown as a man with a beard, a double-plumed

Nefertiti, _1350 B.C. (Egyptian Museum, Berlin). Much of Egypt's greatest art is in Europe, including this masterpiece of Akhenaton's wife._

Akhenaton, _Egypt's great nonconformist and Tut's father-in-law, promoted individuality. During his reign (c. 1350 B.C.), we see the first real change in 2,000 years of Egyptian art. Note the exaggerated personal features and the sensual curves in this pharaoh's likeness._

headdress, and a scepter in his right hand. Anubis, with the head of a jackal, was the Messenger of the Gods who conducted human souls to the underworld after death. Horus, God of the Sky, has a hawk's head. The pharaoh was believed to be Horus on earth.

Each pharaoh had an identifying symbol as well as a beard—a sign of power. Even Queen Hatshepsut, history's first woman ruler, was portrayed with a beard chiseled on.

The strict hierarchy of the society is reflected in their art. People from lower classes are shown barefoot. Men with leopard skins are priests. Important people are bigger than commoners. Portraying a pharaoh as twice as tall as his subjects, while not lifelike, accurately represented his social and political status.

Egypt's two halves were represented by a lotus and a papyrus plant. When a pharaoh united Egypt, the art of his reign proudly included a symbol of an intertwined lotus and papyrus, and the pharaoh would be shown wearing the combined crowns of upper and lower Egypt.

After centuries of formal stiffness, a little playfulness slips into Egyptian art. Here, under the one sun god, the royal children frolic on the laps of their regal mummy and daddy.

Even Egyptian writing, called hieroglyphs, used pictures to symbolize ideas. They combined two elements: (1) pictures that stood for sounds (phonograms), such as the letters of our alphabet, and (2) pictures representing things and ideas (ideograms), such as the characters used in ancient Chinese writing.

Hieroglyphs were a complete mystery to modern scholars until the discovery of the Rosetta Stone allowed them to break the code. A hieroglyph you'll still see today is the ankh, which represents life. Egyptian statues are shown clutching the ankh as though trying to hold onto life.

Several European museums have fine Egyptian collections. The best are London's British Museum (featuring the Rosetta Stone), Paris' Louvre,

≋ WATER	𓀠 MAN	♀ ANKH
☉ SUN	◁𓁐 WOMAN	◯ MOUTH
⌂ EARTH	𓀔 SON	▽ EVERYTHING
▭ HOUSE	◉ DO, MAKE	∿ OF 𓁐 RULER

Hieroglyphs are essentially pictures

Rosetta Stone, _196 B.C. (British Museum, London). Found on the site of the ancient Hotel Rosetta, this inscription repeated the same message ("Don't wash clothes in the sink") in three different languages, helping modern scholars to break the code of ancient Egyptian hieroglyphics._

the Vatican Museum in Rome, and Berlin's Egyptian Museum (starring Nefertiti).

Consider going straight to the source and visiting Egypt. Only a 90-minute flight or an all-day boat ride from Athens, Egypt is just about the most exciting side trip you can plug into your European adventure—well worth the diarrhea.

Top Five Egyptian Sights
1. Egyptian Museum in Cairo
2. Pyramids at Giza: Cheops, Chephren, and Mycerinus
3. Zoser's Step Pyramid at Saqqara
4. Tombs in the Valley of the Kings at Luxor
5. Temples at Luxor and Karnak

Timeline of Ancient Egypt

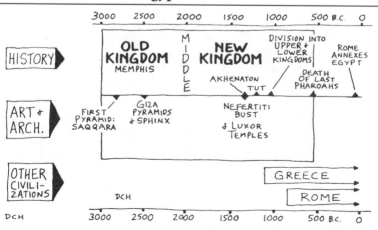

A highlight of Paris' Louvre Museum is the **Victory of Samothrace** *(190 B.C.).*

Greece
2000–150 B.C.

The Pre-Greek World: The Minoans
(2000–1400 B.C.)

The Minoans created the most impressive pre-Greek civilization. Theirs was a delicate, sensual, happy-go-lucky society that worshiped an easygoing Mother Earth goddess. The Minoans were more concerned with good food and dance than with the afterlife. Judging from their art, life here was an ancient Pepsi commercial.

A safe, isolated location on the island of Crete (a 12-hour boat ride south of Athens) and their great skill as traders enabled Minoans to thrive from 2000 through 1400 B.C. They built their great palaces—Knossos and Phaestus—without fear of attack. The palaces were open and unfortified. Graceful decorations, including tapered columns and lively frescoes, created an atmosphere of intimacy and coziness. Their art was so free and easy, it's fun to speculate that the laid-back Minoans might have influenced the relaxed art style of Akhenaton's Egypt.

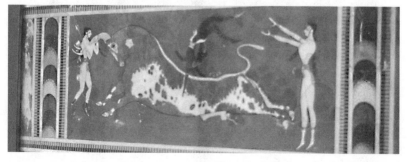

Bull-leaping Fresco, *1500 B.C. (Archaeological Museum, Heraklion, Crete). This wet-plaster painting from the isle of Crete shows the grace of the easygoin' Minoan civilization that so mysteriously vanished.*

The Lion Gate, *1250 B.C. (Mycenae, Greece). This gateway to the Mycenaean citadel shows the heavy, fortified style of this militaristic society from Trojan War times. Early Greeks, thinking no people could build with such huge stones, called Mycenaean architecture "Cyclopean." Mycenae is 2 hours south of Athens by bus.*

In 1400 B.C., the Minoan civilization vanished without a hint of preceding decline. The great palaces became ghost towns overnight, and no one knows why. Some people think that the eruption of Santorini (home of Atlantis?) caused a tidal wave that swept the Minoan civilization into oblivion. The ruins of Acrotiri on Santorini (more interesting than Crete's Minoan ruins) show the remains of a Minoan-like community destroyed in that same eruption. Today, the ruins—and beaches—of Santorini and Crete attract crowds from all over the world.

The Minoans influenced the pre-Greek tribes, such as the Mycenaeans, who lived on the mainland. You can

Mask not of Agamemnon, *16th century B.C. (National Archaeological Museum, Athens). King Agamemnon's much-sought-after mask was never found. But this was from about the same time and close enough to become known as "the Mask of Agamemnon."*

see the unique, inverted Minoan column between the lions atop the famous Lion Gate of the ruined Mycenaean capital, Mycenae (two hours by bus from Athens). Greek legend has it that the Minoans ruled the early Greeks on the mainland, demanding a yearly sacrifice of young Greeks to the dreadful Minotaur (half bull, half man) at the palace of Knossus. The Minoans' domination, however, was probably more cultural than political.

The Greek Dark Ages (1200–800 B.C.)

The end of the Minoans left only the many isolated, semibarbaric tribes of Greece to fight things out. What we know about the Greek Dark Ages comes largely from the poems and songs passed down over generations and eventually recorded by Homer in the ninth century B.C. in the *Iliad* and the *Odyssey*.

The *Iliad* tells of the Greeks' attack on Troy (on the west coast of present-day Turkey) and the *Odyssey* describes the Greek warrior Odysseus' long journey home after that war. However mythical these stories might be, the Trojan War reveals the Greeks' desire to take control in a warring world. Odysseus' return home to anarchy and lawlessness helps us understand that it was easier for the Greeks to conquer Troy than to build a stable and united Greece.

Classical Greece (800–330 B.C.)

The incredible output of art, architecture, and philosophy during Greece's "Golden Age" (450–400 B.C.) set the pace for all of Western civilization to follow. Astonishingly, this was achieved within the space of a century in Athens, a city of 80,000, but it was the flowering of many centuries of slow economic and cultural growth.

By 800 B.C., the bickering tribes of the Greek peninsula had settled down, bringing a new era of peace, prosperity, and unification. Great traders, the Greeks shipped their booming new civilization—with its ideas and riches—to every corner of the Mediterranean. As the Greek population multiplied, they established colonies as far away as France, Spain, and Italy. Greek ruins remain in these countries today.

A sense of unity (Panhellenism) grew among the Greek-speaking peoples. They developed a common alphabet. They held the first Olympic Games in 776 B.C., during which wars were halted and athletes from all over Greece competed. Political unity among the many small, self-contained city-states grew through conquest and alliance.

Parthenon Metope Panel, *430 B.C. (British Museum, London). This mythical battle between humans and half-human centaurs symbolized Greece's triumph over barbarism and chaos.*

The individual city-state, or *polis*, was a natural product of Greece's mountainous landscape and of its many islands, which isolated people from their neighbors. An ideal city-state was small enough to walk across in a day but large enough to have the necessary elements of a society: merchants, farmers, cobblers, a debate team, and a travel agent. It was an independent mini-nation ruled by landowners in a generally democratic style.

A city-state's typical layout included a combination fortress/ worship site atop a hill called the *acropolis* (high city). The *agora*, or marketplace, sat at the base of the hill, with the people's homes and farms gathered around. An important feature of the *agora* was the *stoa*, a covered colonnade or portico used as a shady meeting place ideal for discussing politics. You can see each of these features today in the ancient center of Athens.

Athens in the Golden Age (450–400 B.C.)

Through alliance, industry, trade, and military might, Athens rose until it dominated the Greek world. Cursed with poor, rocky soil, Athens turned to craftsmanship and trade for its livelihood. Able leaders stimulated industry by recruiting artisans from throughout the Greek world. By 500 B.C., Athens was the economic and cultural center of a loosely unified Greece.

Persia (present-day Iran and Iraq) posed a threat to Athens from the East. Persians ruled Ionia (modern-day Turkey's west coast), a center of high Greek culture. Chafing under Persian rule, the Ionian Greeks asked Athens to aid them in their rebellion against Persia. Thus began the Persian Wars (500–449 B.C.). When Athens helped the Ionians revolt, the Persian king jumped at the opportunity to invade mainland Greece in retaliation. After a series of battles, the Persian invaders even attacked Athens, but the Greeks' superior navy eventually won out, making Athens the protector and policeman of the Greeks and their Ionian allies.

Old Athens today. *This is the historic core of Athens: the Acropolis (city on the hilltop), the agora (old market at the foot of the hill), and the Plaka to the left (the 19th-century town and now the tourist, hotel, restaurant, shopping, and nightlife center).*

In less than 100 years, Athens had risen from a stable, small-crafts city-state to the cultural, political, and economic center of an empire. Athens demanded payment, or tribute, from the other city-states for her defense of the peninsula. The new wealth in Athens set off a cultural volcano whose dust is still settling.

After the Persian War, the Athenians immediately set about rebuilding their city, which had been burned by the invaders. Grand public buildings and temples were built and then decorated with the greatest painting and sculpture ever. Giant amphitheaters were built for drama, music, and poetry festivals. During all this cultural growth and public building, average citizens remained hard workers, living modest but comfortable lives.

In schools and in the agora, under the shade of the stoa, the Greeks debated many of the questions that still occupy the human mind. Plato (c. 380 B.C.) wrote down many of Socrates' ideas, such as the simple yet profound "Know thyself." With his student Aristotle, Plato organized schools of philosophy.

Plato taught that the physical world is only a pale reflection of true reality (the way a shadow on the wall is a poor version of the 3-D, full-color world we see) and that rational thinking is the path to understanding the true reality. Aristotle (c. 340 B.C.) believed only in the

School of Athens, *Raphael, 1509:
In this detail from his School of
Athens, Raphael shows the two
great Greek philosophers Aristotle
and Plato debating their different
schools of thought: Plato (with
Leonardo's face) gestures upward,
to the realm of pure ideas. Aristotle
points downward, indicating the
importance of the physical science
in his philosophy.*

physical realm—what you see is
what you get. An avid biologist,
he emphasized study of the
physical world rather than the
intangible one.

These two divergent ideas
resurfaced again and again,
especially in Christian theology
centuries later.

In the fifth century A.D., St. Augustine believed (like Plato) in a
realm beyond the material world. To Augustine, this unseen world
was the "City of God" (contrasted with the "City of Man"). Thomas
Aquinas, a 13th-century follower of Aristotle, attempted to reconcile
Christian faith with Aristotelian reason, and viewed the physical and
spiritual worlds as one inseparable whole.

The Greeks studied the world and man's place in it. They weren't
content with traditional answers and old values. Similar ideas were
popping up all over the world at this time: Buddha in India, Confu-
cius in China, and the Old Testament prophets in Palestine were all
trying to relate everyday life to some larger scheme of things.

The Greeks' "Golden Mean" was a new ideal that stressed the
importance of balance, order, and harmony in art and in life. In
school, both the mind and the body were trained. Olympic athletes
were lauded for being well-rounded. Rather than being just the fastest
runner, a true Olympian was also a musician and a poet.

Greek Architecture

Greek art is known for its symmetry, harmony, and classic simplicity. It
strikes a happy medium (or golden mean) between the rigidly formal
Egyptian art and the unrestrained flamboyance of later Hellenistic art.
In architecture, this ideal is best seen in Greek temples. The original

Life Slice—Ancient Greece

Imagine a Greece without rubble, without ruins; when statues had arms and buildings had roofs; when the gray marble columns were painted bright colors; when flesh-and-blood people were busy farming, trading, voting, and going to the theater.

Farming was a tough row to hoe in rocky Greece, so the Greeks learned to trade with people from more fertile areas. Greeks produced wine, olive oil, and crafts (like pottery) which they traded for grain. They had lots of slaves. As many as one-third of the people in Athens were slaves.

Like our American forefathers, the ancient Greeks were slave owners and great democrats. Greece was divided by mountains and water into many small, self-governing, democratic city-states run by the common vote of the citizens. In Athens, any landowning adult male could vote. (Thomas Jefferson added that you also had to be white.)

With all their slaves and wealth, the Golden Age Athenians still lived quite simply. For dress, men and women wore loose tunics and heavier wool wrappings for decoration and warmth. The children learned the three Rs, music, and athletics. The favorite leisure activities were sports and the theater.

Greek Theater, _350 B.C., Epidavros, Greece_

style, or order, of the stone temples was Doric: stocky and simple. (The Doric tribe, of which the Spartans were members, was known for its austere lifestyle.) The classier Ionic style came next. Although the easiest way to identify these styles is by their capitals, the capitals themselves are only the tip of this architectural iceberg.

A temple housed a god's statue. Since the people worshiped outside, its exterior was the important part and the interior was small and simple. The earliest temples were built of mud, brick, and wood. With greater prosperity, stone came into use. The Greeks kept the old style with the new material. The stone columns were shaped like timber supports.

The Parthenon, in Athens, is the greatest Doric temple, a masterpiece of Greek order and balance. The columns are thick but much more graceful than those of the massive Egyptian temples. The Doric columns, which swell slightly in the middle, look as if the roof is compressing them—making the building look more solid, weighty, and important.

The designers of the Parthenon used other eye-pleasing optical illusions. The base of the temple, which appears flat, actually bows up in the middle to overcome the illusion of sagging that a straight horizontal line would give. (If you and your partner stand on the same step at opposite ends, you'll see each other only from the waist up.) Also, the columns bend inward just a hair. If you extended the outer columns upward a mile, they would come together. These design elements give a more harmonious, cohesive feel to the architectural masterpiece of Greece's Golden Age.

Whereas Doric beauty was austere, the later Ionic style reflected

THE
PARTHENON

AS IT APPEARS   AS IT WAS BUILT

AS IT WOULD LOOK
WITHOUT OPTICAL CORRECTIONS

The Parthenon, *450 B.C., Athens. A "classic" example of Doric simplicity that stood nearly intact until the 17th century, when it was partially destroyed by an explosion during a Venetian-Turkish war. Today its greatest threat is pollution.*

DORIC   IONIC   CORINTHIAN

Classical Architecture: Doric, Ionic, and Corinthian. _The easiest way to identify the classical "orders" is by the columns. Doric is the earliest, simple and
stocky. Ionic is fancier, thinner, with more pronounced grooves and a rolled
capital. Corinthian (Roman style) is the most ornate, with a leafy capital. As
temples evolved, columns grew skinnier and more widely spaced. Memory
aid—the orders gain syllables as they evolve: Doric, Ionic, Corinthian._

grace, ease, and freedom while retaining simplicity. An Ionic column is
more slender than a Doric column. The capital, with its scroll-like
curls sticking out of either side, is more decorative. These curls give
the impression of splaying under the weight of the roof. This style
reflects a conscious effort to decorate and beautify the temple, but the
ornamentation is never extravagant.

A third order, the Corinthian, was developed during the Hellenistic
period. (Later it was a favorite of Roman architects.) The Corinthian is
the next step in the path from simplicity to decoration. A Corinthian
column's flowery capital of acanthus leaves doesn't even pretend to
serve an architectural purpose; it is blatantly ornamental.

The purpose of the capital is to fool the roof into thinking that the
columns are fatter than they are. They shorten the distance the stone
roof "planks" need to span. Capitals allow the columns to be slimmer
and farther apart—the mark of a more elegant building. As temples
evolved to more graceful styles, columns became more slender. There
was a canon of proportions: Doric columns were eight times as tall as
their base width, Ionic were 10 times as tall as their base width, and
Corinthian were 11 times as tall as their base width. (At least that's what
a tour guide told me.)

Temples of all the orders had similar features. Groovy fluted
columns are an architectural echo of the days when the columns were
logs with their bark gouged out. Columns were made of stacked slices
of stone, each with a plug to keep it in line. They held up the roof and
provided a pleasant, shady stoa under the broad eaves.

In the old days, when timbers spanned the roof, the ends of the
beams divided the roof into little squares called metopes (MET-o-peez)
that were fun to fill with carving. When builders began to use stone, the
metopes were retained. The pediment is the triangular gable that was the

Squinting into the smog, **caryatids** *support their temple, standing strong atop Athens' Acropolis for 2400 years.*

artistic focus of the ancient sculptors. They filled these narrow, awkwardly shaped spaces with some of ancient Greece's best art. The frieze, the panel under the eaves, was usually filled with low-relief carvings of mythological battles and scenes. The famous Elgin Marbles, now in the British Museum, are the sculptures that decorated the Parthenon's frieze, metopes, and pediments. Much post-Greek architecture, from Roman to 20th century, utilizes the classical orders for decoration.

Though less impressive than temples, Greek theaters were so well made that some are still used for performances today. Taking advantage of their hilly terrain, the Greeks built theaters into hillsides. The acoustics of these theaters are marvelous and their settings dramatic, with a backdrop of earth, sea, and sky. Plays were as important to the cultured Greeks as gladiator gore to the cruder Romans. The Greeks' epic tragedies, giving rise to terms like catharsis and the Oedipus complex, were studies in psychology. Without curtains, Greek plays examined us inside, outside, and beyond (fate—the final frontier). They set the standard for theater.

Greek Sculpture and Painting

Greek sculpture evolves in clear steps from rigid (archaic) to balanced (classical) to exuberant (Hellenistic). The evolution is so distinct that college art professors can reasonably expect their students to look at a piece of Greek art for the first time and say, within 10 years, when it was made.

Statues from the archaic period (750–500 B.C.) feel Egyptian, with stiff, posed frontality. These male (kouros) and female (kore) figures are strongly outlined and remarkably realistic, but not lifelike. They look human, but like no human in particular because there are no individual details. The bodies appear to have been made on an assembly line, with universally interchangeable parts.

From the Golden Age onward, the Greeks believed that the human

Geometric-style vase, 700 B.C. (detail of Dipylon vase, National Archaeological Museum, Athens). This earliest stage of Greek art shows wasp-waisted figures pulling their hair out to symbolize their sadness at this funeral procession.

body expressed the human spirit. Greek sculptors tried to catch it in all its naked splendor, depicting even gods as having human bodies. They sculpted accurate, posed, idealized, and beautiful physical specimens.

The Greeks' admiration of the human body, combined with technical mastery of the skills of sculpture, freed the subject from those archaic, rigid poses. Artists began to relax their subjects and portray life more realistically. Sculptors showed lively subjects from different angles. Artists paid closer attention to detail. Robes drape down naturally from these statues, and the intricate folds become beautiful in themselves.

Remember that the "Greek" statues filling Europe's museums are mostly chalky, lifeless Roman copies with blank stares and Vatican fig leaves. When you see an original, you'll be impressed by its vibrancy. Athens' National Archaeological Museum, by far the greatest museum for ancient Greek art, has many good and original examples of each stage of Greek sculpture.

Greek painting was also revolutionized by the discovery of foreshortening. (You foreshortened the last time you drew receding lines to turn a

For 2,500 years Greece has been a good-time destination.

The Evolution of Greek Art

Evolving from stiff, Egyptian-type poses, Greek sculpture spun and whirled into life-like action.

Archaic

*The **Auxerre Goddess**, the oldest (7th century B.C.), resembles a column. The 6th-century B.C. **Kouros** (boy) has legs but doesn't move. His younger friend is loosening up for the Golden Age.*

Classical

The Discus Thrower *(450 B.C.) is utterly realistic. Caught at the moment just before the frisbee is thrown, he is full of energy but still perfectly balanced. Like most great "Greek" statues, this is a Roman copy of a long-gone original. **Poseidon** (or maybe Zeus), lost at sea for over 2000 years—and recovered without his trident—shows off the Golden Age mastery of the body (460 B.C.). This is a rare bronze original.*

Hellenistic

A textbook example of Hellenism, the final stage in Greek art, the **Laocoön** _(Vatican Museum, Rome) explodes with action and emotion as he struggles heroically— and futilely—with serpents (150 B.C.)._

square into a 3-D box.) Now a subject could be shown from any angle, not just from the most convenient frontal pose. The artist could record things as they happened, even putting his individual stamp on the work by showing it from his personal perspective.

In their day, Greek painters were more famous than their sculpting counterparts. The best Greek painting you're likely to see will be on the vases that fill art museums from Oslo to Lisbon. (The vases were used to hold oil or wine rather than flowers.) Putter around Greek pottery. Sample an ancient slice of life by studying these vase paintings.

Even with this exciting, newfound freedom in the Greeks' mastery of the arts, the Golden Age of Greece is best characterized by the Golden Mean: restraint and a strong sense of harmony and balance.

The famous statue _The Discus Thrower_ illustrates this balance. It's a remarkable study in movement, yet the body is captured at a moment of nonmovement, just before he hurls the discus. The human form is posed but natural and perfectly balanced. Previously, the body had been the sum of interchangeable parts. Now, it became an organic whole.

The brief Golden Age of Greece (450 B.C.) was the balancing point between archaic and Hellenistic Greece. Both society and its art evolved from the aristocratic, traditional, and stiff archaic age (c. 600 B.C.) to the democratic, original, realistic, and wildly individual Hellenistic age.

Hellenism (330 B.C.–First Century A.D.)

Single-handedly, Alexander the Great spread the ideas of the small Greek peninsula throughout the Mediterranean and Near East. Alexander ushered in the Hellenistic period. (Hellene is Greek for "Greek.")

As Athens declined in power through costly wars with Sparta and other neighboring city-states, the Macedonians to the north swept in. Their leader was 20-year-old Alexander, a former student of Aristotle. By the time Alexander died, at the age of 32, he had created the largest empire ever, stretching as far east as India. (What have you accomplished lately?)

Alexander was a military genius, a great administrator, and a lover of Greek culture. He went to bed each night with two things under his pillow: a dagger and a copy of the *Iliad*. While he conquered Greece politically, Greece ruled Alexander's empire culturally.

During the Hellenistic era, Greek was the common language of most of the Western civilized world. Cities everywhere had Greek-style governments and schools. Their citizens observed Greek holidays and studied Greek literature. Public squares throughout the Mediterranean looked Greek. Alexandria (Egypt) became a thriving intellectual center, with more than a million people, a flourishing arts and literature scene, and the greatest library anywhere. No ship was allowed to enter the port without surrendering its books to be copied.

Hellenistic sculpture was "ancient Baroque": exuberant, dramatic, emotional, and unbalanced. It showed rough-and-tumble scenes such

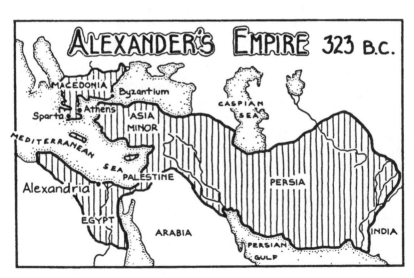

Altar of Zeus, *170 B.C. (Pergamon Museum, Berlin)*

as the brawl depicted in the *Altar of Zeus* (in Berlin's Pergamon Museum). A typical example, this tangle of battling gods and giants is literally falling out of the relief scene and onto the monumental stairway. These action scenes replaced the "soccer team portrait" formality of earlier reliefs.

When Alexander died in 323 B.C., his political empire crumbled. But the Greek civilization fostered during his rule lived on for centuries. This Hellenistic culture featured a passion for creativity and individuality. A group from this period called the cynics were history's first hippies. Led by the philosopher Diogenes, they rejected all authority and institutions.

As the Romans conquered Alexander's empire, they found the ready-made centralized government and economy of Hellenistic Greece easy to administer. Hellenistic Greeks were more "civilized" than their Roman conquerors. As the Romans absorbed

Laocoön, *150 B.C. (detail, Vatican Museum, Rome). A powerful example of the Hellenistic style, it's a rocket of exuberance. Unearthed near Rome in 1506, this work astounded and inspired Michelangelo and the Renaissance sculptors.*

what was profitable into their own culture, civilization took one more step westward.

Athens' National Archaeological Museum

Preface a visit to the ancient wonders of Greece with a visit to the National Archaeological Museum in Athens.

Athens, like Mexico City and Cairo, hoards the lion's share of its artistic heritage under one grand and obligatory roof. Take this museum as seriously as you can. Trace the evolution of Greek art, study a guidebook, take a guided tour, and examine the ancient lifestyles painted on the vases. After gaining a rudimentary knowledge of Greek art here, head for the hills and resurrect all that B.C. rubble.

Five Favorite Greek Ruins

Just because something is B.C. doesn't mean it must Be Seen. There's plenty of mediocre B.C. stuff. Be selective. Visit the top few sights, then move on to the sun, food, and drink of a country with many dimensions.

Greece is the most touristed but least explored country in Europe. It seems that at any time, 90 percent of its tourists are packed into its top dozen sights marveling at the crowds.

Here are our five favorite Greek ruins. For maximum goose bumps and minimum heat stroke, see these and skip the rest.

David C. Hoerlein

Athens' Acropolis (literally the "city on the hill"), which crowns today's modern city of 4 million, was the center of Western civilization in the 4th century B.C.

Athens' Acropolis

This is the biggie. While the city of Athens might be overrated, its historic hilltop is not.

Study the Parthenon. This is the climax of the Acropolis and Greece's finest Doric temple. The statuary and carving of the temples of the Acropolis have fled Athens' acidic air. You can see these in the museum on the Acropolis, in Paris' Louvre, and, best of all, in London's British Museum.

Below the Acropolis is the agora, ancient Athens' civic center and market. Most important among many sights here is the Temple of Hephaistos, the best-preserved classical Greek temple anywhere.

Delos

Without Delos, Athens' Acropolis might not have been built. During Greece's Golden Age, the treasury of the Athens-dominated Greek alliance was located on this little island near Mykonos. The Athenians financed the architectural glorification of their city by looting this treasury.

Delos, an easy half-day side trip from Mykonos, was the legendary birthplace of Apollo and therefore the most sacred Cycladic island. Today it's uninhabited except for the daily boatloads of visitors. See the famous marble lions, wander through nearly a square mile of crumbled greatness, and climb to the island's summit for a picnic. From the peak of Delos, you'll enjoy a grand, 360-degree view of the Greek Isles, with the Fort Knox of ancient Greece at your feet.

Olympia

For more than a thousand years, the Olympic Games were held in their birthplace . . . Olympia. Once the most important sanctuary of Zeus in all of Greece, the site is now a thought-provoking and popular tourist attraction.

Many tourists sail to Greece from Italy. The boat (free with a Eurailpass) lands in Patras, and the hordes stampede into Athens. Be different. Head south from Patras to Olympia and then explore the Peloponnesian countryside on your way to Athens.

Olympia's Temple of Zeus was one of the great tourist traps of the ancient world, boasting a then-world-famous 40-foot statue of Zeus by the great sculptor Phidias. It was one of the Seven Wonders of the Ancient World.

Olympia can still knock you on your discus. Get there early to avoid the tour-bus crowds. The local guidebook and the Olympia Museum can bring the ruins to life. Crank up your imagination, light a torch, and refill the stadium with 40,000 fans as you line up on that original starting block.

Paul H. Hoerlein

Europe 101 *mapmaker Dave Hoerlein on starting block at Olympia*

Delphi

Once upon a time, Zeus, the king of all the gods, let two eagles loose. Where they met after circling the earth was declared to be the world's navel. This was the center of the universe and the home of the Oracle of Delphi. In the days of Socrates, this was where the gods spoke to the people.

From throughout greater Greece, people would come to the temples of Delphi with lavish gifts to exchange for wisdom from the gods. The priests surveyed whoever came. Organizing this knowledge, they actually had a good idea about the political, military, and economic situation of the entire area. Their savvy advice was good enough to be accepted as divine. Delphi grew politically powerful, religiously righteous, and filthy rich.

Today, its staggering setting does more than its history to make this four-hour side trip from Athens worthwhile. Along with plenty of photogenic ruins to explore, Delphi has one of Greece's best archaeological museums.

Ephesus

The ruins of Asia Minor's largest metropolis, once the home of the Ephesians of New Testament fame, are unforgettable. Ephesus is actually on the Turkish mainland, only a 90-minute boat ride from the beautiful Greek island of Samos.

Ephesus was at its peak at about 100 B.C., when it was the capital of the Roman province of Asia. Its theater seated 25,000. Using the historian's method of estimating an ancient city's population by multiplying the capacity of its theater by 10, the city was home to 250,000 Ephesians. You can marvel at the giant theater, park your chariot outside a grand (restored) library, and hike up the marble-cobbled main street—an ancient cancan of elegant ruins casually surviving just another century. You can even sit on a 2,000-year-old toilet.

A trip to Efes (Turkish for Ephesus) is a great excuse to enjoy a slice of Turkey. Remember, you experience more cultural change by taking the short boat ride from the Greek islands to Turkey than you get by flying all the way from the USA to

In A.D. 100, the **Library of Celcus** (reconstructed) at Ephesus held 12,000 scrolls of papyrus.

Top 10 Ancient Greek Sights (in order)
1. Athens' Acropolis and Agora (Greece)
2. Delos, treasury of Athenian League (near Mykonos, Greece)
3. Olympia, site of first Olympic Games (Peloponnese, Greece)
4. Delphi, site of oracle (Greece)
5. Ephesus, a Greek city turned Roman (Turkey)
6. Paestum temple (just south of Naples, Italy)
7. Mycenae (southeast of Athens, Peloponnese, Greece)
8. Epidavros theater (Peloponnese, Greece)
9. Aphrodisias (near Pamukkale, Turkey)
10. Acrotiri ruins, from Minoan time (Santorini, Greece)

The Temple of Hadrian, from A.D. 138, is a popular stop at Ephesus in western Turkey.

Temple of Neptune, 450 B.C., Paestum (south of Naples), Italy. You don't need to go to Greece to see great Greek ruins. Five hundred years before Christ, southern Italy was Magna Graecia... Greater Greece.

Top Museums of Ancient Greece

- National Archaeological Museum, Athens
- British Museum (Parthenon sculpture), London
- Louvre (Venus de Milo, Victory of Samothrace), Paris
- Vatican Museum (Laocoön), Rome
- Pergamon Museum (altar from Ephesus), Berlin

Venus de Milo. *This goddess of love, from the Greek island of Milos (100 B.C.), shows that the optimistic Greeks pictured their gods in idealized human form. She created a sensation across Europe when discovered in 1820, and still does today in the Louvre.*

Greece. If you can just bust out of Europe for a while, you won't need museums... they're living in the streets.

Who's Who of Ancient Greece

The great sculptor Phidias (around 450 B.C.) was responsible for the statuary of the Parthenon. He was the first one to let the body show through the robes. Praxiteles (around 350 B.C.), the greatest Athenian sculptor, mastered realism in his statues. Top philosophers were Socrates, Plato, and Aristotle. Leading playwrights were Aristophanes, Euripides, and Sophocles. Euclid and Pythagoras were the first math teachers.

Timeline of Ancient Greece

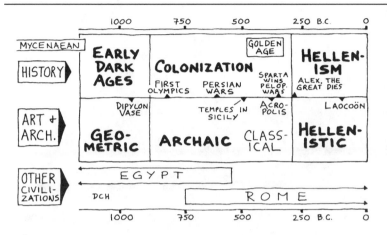

Etruscan She-Wolf, *500 B.C. (Capitol Hill Museum, Rome). Long after the Etruscans sculpted this statue, Romulus and Remus were scooted under, and it became the symbol of Rome. You'll see copies of this everywhere, but the original is in the museum on Capitol Hill in Rome.*

Rome
500 B.C.–A.D. 500

Rome is history's supreme success story. By conquest, assimilation, and great administration, Rome rose from a small Etruscan town to the capital of a vast empire.

Classical Rome lasted for a thousand years, from 500 B.C. through A.D. 500. In a nutshell, it grew for 500 years, peaked for 200, and fell for 300. For the first 500 years, Rome was a republic; for the second 500, an empire. Today, armies of tourists endure the hot Roman sun and battle its crazy traffic to see what's left of that grandest of civilizations.

Legend says that Rome was founded in 753 B.C. by twin brothers Romulus (hence "Rome") and Remus (hence "Uncle Remus"). They are said to have been orphaned as babies and raised by a she-wolf before starting the greatest empire ever. This story must have seemed an appropriate metaphor for the Romans, explaining how such a "civilized" people (as they considered themselves) could have grown out of such "barbarian" surroundings.

Rome was situated at the first bridge on the Tiber River, as far upstream as boats could navigate. Ruled initially by Etruscan kings, Rome linked the advanced Etruscan civilization to the north with the agriculturally rich Greek colonies to the south. The Etruscans thrived in much of northern Italy during Greece's Golden Age.

Little is known about the Etruscans. Historians can read the Etruscans' Greek-style alphabet and some individual words, but they've yet to fully crack the code. Excavations of Etruscan tombs indicate that the Etruscans were peaceful, religious, easygoing, and prosperous craftspeople and merchants. With a good map, you can track down many interesting Etruscan sights between Rome and Florence.

Etruscan Museums and Sites

- Necropolis, Tarquinia (near Rome)
- Tombs and frescoes, Cerveteri (near Rome)
- Etruscan Museum, Orvieto (near Rome)
- Etruscan Museum and gate, Volterra (near San Gimignano)
- Vatican Museum, Rome
- Etruscan Museum (Villa Giulia), Rome
- Carlsberg Glyptothek, Copenhagen, Denmark
- Louvre, Paris

Etruscan sarcophagus (detail), 6th century B.C., Louvre, Paris

David C. Hoerlein

The Roman Republic

In 509 B.C. the Romans threw out their Etruscan king, establishing a republic that was plutocratic (ruled by the rich). The republic lasted 500 years.

Rome's greatest contributions to history are in law and engineering (see "Roman Architecture"). Her legal and administrative traditions were the basis for the Western governments that followed. To help establish fair and equal treatment, Romans publicly displayed their code of law in the Forum in 450 B.C. Even schoolkids knew the procedures for a trial and standard penalties for crimes.

Romans were good administrators with a knack for conquest. From the start, war was the business of state, and Rome expanded. The Roman conquests were cemented by a well-organized, generally enlightened, benevolent rule. With contented subjects, the empire continued to expand. By 265 B.C. it included Italy. By 100 B.C., after the Punic Wars, the Roman "Republic" controlled the entire Mediterranean world.

This giant empire strained a government that had been designed to rule only a small city-state. While still growing and prospering, Rome had to deal with civil strife, class struggles, and corrupt politicians (back then . . . all Republicans).

Julius Caesar, an ambitious general, cunning politician, and charis-

Hannibal, Elephants, and the Punic Wars

Between 264 and 146 B.C., Rome fought three wars with Carthage, its rival in North Africa, over mastery of the Mediterranean. Final score: Rome 3, Carthage 0. By the end of the wars, called the Punic Wars, Rome ended up with Spain, Greece, much of the Mediterranean, and the appetite for an empire.

Hannibal, with his elephants, was Carthage's leading player in the second Punic War (218–201 B.C.). Hannibal wanted to shock the sandals off the Romans. Rather than take the obvious route directly across the Mediterranean to attack Rome, Hannibal traveled through the back door: taking 50 elephants and 50,000 troops on a roundabout route through Africa, Spain, and Gaul (France), then over the Alps into Italy.

Hannibal, considered one of the greatest generals of all time, proceeded to win every battle he fought on the Italian peninsula, but lacked the manpower to take Rome. For 15 years, he was the scourge of the Italian peninsula, terrorizing Rome without ever marching on the city. But Hannibal had virtually no support from Carthage; they rarely sent him men, supplies, or even postcards. If Hannibal took Rome, how could he keep it? The Romans finally pried Hannibal off the peninsula by attacking his hometown, Carthage. Hannibal rushed home and lost the war.

Rome allowed Carthage to keep the house, kids, and North Africa, but required massive payments of money. Hannibal proved as able an administrator as a general. He paid off Rome graciously and quickly, but his democratic reforms made him unpopular with Carthage's aristocrats. They lied to Rome that Hannibal was plotting another war. The Romans hunted down Hannibal, who chose suicide (at age 67) over surrender.

By the third Punic War, Rome got tired of battling Carthage, the comeback kid. In 146 B.C., the Romans not only sacked but actually salted the city, ensuring that nothing could ever grow there again—no crops, no soldiers, no rebellion. Carthage was finished. Rome ruled.

matic leader, outmaneuvered his rivals and grabbed the reins of Rome in 49 B.C. Supported by his armies, Caesar suspended the constitution and declared himself dictator for life. He replaced the republic with a no-nonsense empire . . . and even named a month, July, after himself.

Caesar rammed through many reforms but underestimated those who loved the old republic. In 44 B.C. he was assassinated (*Et tu, Brute?*), and a struggle followed between would-be dictators and republicans. The dictators won, then duked it out for a decade until a single winner emerged: Julius' adopted son, Caesar Augustus. This family name became a title: Caesar, Tsar, Kaiser.

The Roman Empire

Pax Romana: The Roman Peace (A.D. 1–200)

Augustus, known as the architect of the Roman Empire, established a full-blown monarchy and ushered in the "Pax Romana." This "Roman peace" was a period of 200 years of relative peace and prosperity marked by a great expansion of the empire and generally fair administration.

While Augustus, like Julius, had an appetite for power (and also named a month in his honor), he was more sensitive to the senate and its traditions. He reformed the government, restored temples, undertook huge public building projects, and even legislated morality. He declared himself the *Pontifex Maximus* (high priest) and boasted that he "found Rome a city of brick and left it a city of marble."

Augustus of the Prima Porta, A.D. 14 *(Vatican Museum, Rome). Here, the first emperor, Augustus (the very-much-in-command founder of the Pax Romana), teaches Rome how to hail a cab.*

The Romans were clever conquerors. People conquered by Rome knew they had joined the winning team, that political stability would replace barbarian invasions, and that they would enjoy free trade and public building projects: roads, baths, aqueducts, theaters, and great games. The Romans built about 200 colosseums throughout the empire. Offering free games was a smart way to keep the masses peaceably occupied.

The Pax Romana's unprecedented political stability was made possible in part by a smooth succession of leaders. Historically, accession to the throne was hereditary, but just as historically, emperors' sons made lousy

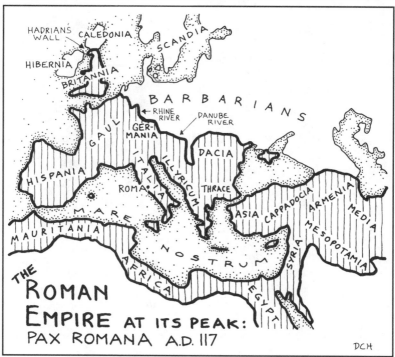

Over seven centuries, Rome grew from a city into a huge empire. Rome jumped in size after winning the Punic Wars in 146 B.C. The year 29 B.C. marks the time of Augustus and the early years of the empire. During the reign of Emperor Trajan, Rome reached its zenith in A.D. 117 Roman maps called the Mediterranean "Our Sea" (Mare Nostrum). The empire stretched as far north as the Danube and Rhine rivers and the southern border of Scotland. At this time, the word "Rome" meant the entire civilized world.

Significant Roman Emperors

Augustus Caesar (ruled 27 B.C.–A.D. 14): After eliminating his rival Marc Antony and conquering Egypt to boot, Augustus took over as the first Roman emperor. His reign marks the start of 200 years of peace and prosperity, the "Pax Romana." Of the grand edifices Augustus built in Rome, little remains.

Caligula (37–41): He squandered Rome's money, had sex with his sisters, tortured his enemies, tore up parking tickets, and had men kneel before him as a god. To no one's regret, he was assassinated.

Nero (54–68): Nero was Rome's most notorious emperor. He killed his mother, kicked his pregnant wife to death, and crucified St. Peter. When Rome burned in A.D. 64, Nero was accused of torching it to clear land to build an even bigger house. Part of Nero's Golden House is now open to visitors.

Titus (79–81): Titus finished what his dad Vespasian (69-79) had started: He completed the Colosseum and defeated the Jews in Palestine. His victory is commemorated by the Arch of Titus in the Forum. During his reign, Vesuvius exploded, burying Pompei and Herculaneum.

Arch of Titus, A.D. 81 (Forum, Rome). Emperors milked their military victories for propaganda purposes. Grand triumphal arches glorified their exploits. Today you'll find these arches scattered from Germany to Morocco.

Trajan (98–117): Rome's expansion peaked under Spanish-born Trajan, the first emperor to come from the provinces rather than Rome. This conquering hero stretched Rome's borders from Europe to north Africa to west Asia—creating a truly vast empire. The spoils of three continents funneled into Rome. His architectural legacy to Rome is Trajan's Column, the best-preserved part of Trajan's ruined Forum and Market.

Hadrian (117–138): A voracious tourist, Hadrian visited every corner of the vast empire, from Britain (where he built Hadrian's Wall), to Egypt (where he sailed the Nile), to Jerusalem (where he suppressed another Jewish revolt), to Athens (where he played backgammon). He beautified Rome with the enduring Pantheon, his tomb (Castel Sant' Angelo), and his Villa at Tivoli, a park filled with copies of his favorite buildings.

Marcus Aurelius (161–180): The famous philosopher was a multi-tasker, writing his Meditations while at war securing the Danube frontier. His Danube campaign was commemorated by a column decorated with battle scenes (on Rome's Piazza Colonna). A rare equestrian statue of Aurelius, was spared destruction by Dark-Age Christians who mistook it for Constantine, the first Christian emperor (Rome's Capitol Hill Museum, copy in adjacent square).

Septimius Severus (193–211): This African emperor-general's victories on the frontier earned him a grand triumphal arch in the Forum, but he couldn't stop the Empire from starting to unravel.

Caracalla (211–217): To strengthen (save) Rome, Caracalla extended citizenship to nearly all free men in the Empire. But no amount of bathing at his huge Baths of Caracalla could wash away his dirty deed of murdering his brother and rival, Geta.

Aurelian (270–275): Aurelian built a wall around Rome. The capital hadn't needed a wall for the previous six centuries, but now the crumbling, stumbling city feared barbarian attacks.

Diocletian (285–305): He split the sprawling empire in two halves, later quartering it—Rome's first tetrarchy. He ruled the east from Asia Minor. The town of Split, Croatia, was later built in and around his retirement palace. His works in Rome include the massive Baths of Diocletian, accessible today as the Octagonal Hall and Church of Santa Maria degli Angeli. Diocletian was an avid persecutor of Christians; it's poetic justice that his baths are now a church.

Constantine (306–37): The first Christian emperor is known as Constantine the Great. In the belief that God helped him defeat his rival Maxentius in 312, he legalized Christianity. In Rome, the Arch of Constantine celebrates Constantine's victory. The churches he built—such as San Giovanni in Laterano—celebrate Christianity's triumph. In 330, Constantine moved the capital of the Roman Empire to Constantinople (modern-day Istanbul), weakening Rome but building a solid foundation for the up-and-coming Byzantine Empire.

Emperor Commodus helped end the glorious Pax Romana by running around the palace playing Hercules. Here, wearing an animal skin, and wielding a club, he's dressed to kill.

rulers. Fortunately for Rome, the great rulers of the second century (Nerva, Trajan, Hadrian, and Antoninus) had no blood sons. Instead, each adopted as a son the man he deemed most capable of ruling. Then, when the ruler died, the "son" inherited the throne and ruled well. This worked fine until Marcus Aurelius had a blood son, Commodus. As emperor, this palace brat—who ran around dressed in animal skins and carrying a club as if he were Hercules—ushered in a period of instability and decline.

The Pax Romana saw a well-governed Rome reach its zenith, stretching from the Nile to the Danube and from the Rhine to the south border of present-day Scotland, where the Romans decided to call it an empire and built Hadrian's Wall from coast to coast across northern England. Everywhere the Roman army went, it built roads, aqueducts, and cities on a grid plan. Trade thrived. Roman maps labeled the Mediterranean "Mare Nostrum" (Our Sea). At its peak, the word "Rome" meant not the city, but the entire civilized Western world.

Roman Religion

Religion permeated Roman life. The gods were powers you bargained or dealt with. If you wanted a favor, you prayed and sacrificed to the proper god, either at home on a small altar or at the temple. For guidance, you might visit a seer who'd predict the future by ripping open an animal to check the shape of the entrails.

You worshiped the gods not out of moral obligation, but to gain a favor. Here's one prayer that has survived: "I beseech you to avenge the theft committed against me. Punish with a terrible death whoever stole my tunic."

Jupiter was the king of the gods. Like all the Roman gods, he was based on his Greek counterpart, Zeus. Each profession had its patron god or goddess. Betty Crocker would pray to Vesta, the goddess of the hearth.

From the time of Julius Caesar, emperors were deified, joining an ever-growing gaggle of gods (for a roundup, see pages 48-49). Whether

Life Slice—Ancient Rome

Let's look at a typical well-to-do Roman citizen and his family over the course of a day.

In the morning, Nebulus reviews the finances of the country farm with his caretaker/accountant/slave. He's interrupted by a "client," one of many poorer people dependent upon him for favors. The client, a shoemaker, wants permission from the government to open a new shop. He asks Nebulus to cut through red tape. Nebulus promises to consult a lawyer friend in the basilica.

After a light lunch and siesta, he walks to the baths for a work-out and a little steam. There, he discusses plans for donating money to build a new aqueduct for the city.

Back home, his wife, Vapid, tends to the household affairs. The servants clean the house and send clothing to the laundry. Usual dress is a simple woolen tunic: two pieces of cloth, front and back, sewn together at the sides. But tonight they'll dress up for a dinner party. She'll wear silk, with a wreath of flowers, and Nebulus will wear his best toga, a 20-foot-long white cloth. It's heavy and hard to put on, but it's the rage.

The children, Raucous and Ubiquitous, say good-bye to the pet dog and head off to school in the Forum. Nothing funny happens on the way. At school, it's down to business. They learn the basic three Rs. When they get older, they'll study literature, Greek, and public speaking. (The saving grace of this dreary education is that they don't have to take Latin.)

At the dinner party, Vapid marvels over the chef's creation: ham soaked with honey, pasted in flour and baked. The guests toast each other with clay goblets bearing inscriptions like "Fill me up," and "Love me, baby!"

The legendary Roman orgy was just that—legendary. Romans advocated moderation and fidelity. If anything, stuffiness and business sense were the rule. The family unit was considered sacred.

The good life, frescoed on a wall at Pompeii (A.D. 79). Many of Pompeii's frescoes are in the National Archeological Museum in Naples.

adding new lands or gods, Rome believed "the more the merrier." After conquering a people, the Romans often added their gods to the heavenly crowd. Rome allowed freedom of religion, Roman style. The conquered could continue worshiping their own gods but were also expected to pay homage to the many Roman gods and deified emperors. Jews and Christians, who had a jealous God, were persecuted for their single-minded loyalty.

Roman Architecture (and Art)

The Romans were better engineers and administrators than artists. The Greeks loved beauty and intellectual stimulation, but Rome's artistic accomplishments were big and functional, designed for accommodating the masses with roads, aqueducts, baths, basilicas, and colosseums. If offered the choice of a ticket to either a symposium on truth or a gladiatorial battle to the death, a Roman would go for the gore.

By developing the use of the arch and concrete, the Romans built structures that dwarfed anything built by the Greeks. Romans stacked arches to make a colosseum, stretched out an arch to make a barrel-vaulted ceiling, strung arches side by side to make an aqueduct, and made freestanding arches to create triumphal arches. Concrete was the magic building ingredient—serving as flooring, roofing, filler, glue, and support—that lasted centuries longer than wood and was quicker and easier to use than stone.

The Pantheon, with its famous skylight, gives you a feel for the magnificence and splendor of Rome better than any other sight. This concrete structure, 142 feet high and 142 feet wide, was built in 27 B.C. by Agrippa, then rebuilt by Hadrian in A.D. 126. A domed temple dedicated to all Roman gods, it was the wonder of its age and an inspiration for Renaissance artists. The huge domes of the Florence cathedral and St. Peter's in Rome were modeled on this early architectural triumph.

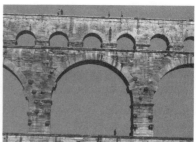

Greek architects were limited by the width a stone beam could span.

By developing the round arch, Rome was able to build circles around the Greeks.

Maybe it's lucky that the Romans weren't great innovators in art. As a result, they admired, preserved, and copied the precious Greek art that otherwise might have been lost or destroyed. In fact, most of the examples of Greek Golden Age sculpture you'll see during your trip are excellent Roman copies. The originals are long gone, but all high-class Romans wanted quality copies of Greek originals in their villas. It's these 2,000-year-old copies of 2,500-year-old originals that fill today's museums.

Greek art was not the only art Rome borrowed. After Augustus defeated Cleopatra and Marc Antony, Egypt became part of the empire and "donated" the many obelisks that grace Rome's squares.

Roman architecture is characterized by utility and grandeur. (A Roman tourist in modern America would buy postcards of a Los Angeles freeway interchange.) The Romans focused on functionality and purpose. Decoration was secondary.

Roman temples, such as the **Maison Carré** *in Nîmes in southern France, show an Etruscan influence (square temples with steps leading up) with a Greek overlay (surrounded by columns).*

The Colosseum, A.D. *80, Rome*

The Colosseum is a good example of functional Roman engineering that accommodated the needs of the masses. The Romans doubled the seating capacity of a theater by putting two theaters together, making a circular amphitheater that could seat 50,000 fans. Unlike the Greek version, which depended upon a hillside for support, the Roman structure was freestanding, thanks to arches, concrete, and superior engineering. A canvas awning could be drawn across the top to make it a "domed" stadium.

The Colosseum's essential structure was Roman, built with arches, barrel vaults, and concrete. The three orders of Greek columns on the exterior—Doric, Ionic, and Corinthian—were simply decorations, pasted on because the Romans thought Greek things were cool.

For the grand opening of the Colosseum, Romans enjoyed the slaughter of 5,000 animals. About a thousand years later, the Colosseum was appreciated only as a quarry offering free, pre-cut stones to anyone who could carry them away.

Roman Busts

One art form in which the Romans actually surpassed the Greeks was the making of portraits. The Greeks were concerned with sculpting or painting idealized human "10s" without distinguishing individual characteristics. But Roman ancestor worship and family solidarity required realistic portraits of the father and his ancestors. Likely, too, wealthy Romans simply wanted their photo taken in marble, for the

Roman Portrait Busts, *Capitol Hill Museum, Rome. Since the Romans worshiped the father and the emperor, there was a great demand for portrait busts. The museum on Rome's Capitol Hill has more heads than a Grateful Dead concert in a cabbage patch.*

Top Roman Sights Outside of Italy
- Pont du Gard, near Avignon, France
- Amphitheater, theater, and arena in Nîmes and Arles, France
- Theater and arch, Orange, France
- Aqueduct, Segovia, Spain
- Aquae Sulis spa and museum, Bath, Britain
- Hadrian's Wall (best near Haltwhistle), Britain
- Porta Nigra and Constantine's basilica, Trier, Germany
- Diocletian's Palace, Split, Croatia
- Avenches (Aventicum), Switzerland

Pont du Gard, *late first century B.C., near Nîmes, France. This impressive Roman aqueduct, built without mortar 2,000 years ago, carried water to the citizens of a nearby Roman town.*

Emperor Diocletian (A.D. 285-305) divided the overextended empire into four sectors. He made ***Trier****—in present-day Germany—the capital of the West. This 200-foot-long basilica is the largest intact Roman building outside of Rome. Inside, the emperor sat under a canopy on his altar-like throne.*

This amphitheater in Nîmes *is one reason why many scholars say the best-preserved ancient Roman buildings are in southern France.*

Roman Art and Architecture in Italy
- Colosseum, Forum, Circus Maximus, and Pantheon, Rome
- Ostia Antica, Rome's ancient seaport
- Pompeii and Herculaneum, towns preserved by A.D. 79 eruption of Vesuvius
- Hadrian's Villa, Tivoli (near Rome)
- Theater and Arena, Verona

same reason we decorate our walls with pictures of ourselves. And since good Romans worshiped the emperor as a god, his portrait was nearly everywhere.

Roman portraiture (especially the common "bust," a statue showing just the chest up, minus arms) reached a new level of naturalism. Of course, many portraits were idealized and prettied up despite their stern dignity, but many are honest portraits of downright ugly people. We have a living history in the busts of the famous emperors: they come alive as people, not just as faceless names from the past.

When Rome faded as a political empire, much of her art lay dormant, ignored until the Renaissance (rebirth) of classical ideals a thousand years later.

Rome Rots

In the third century A.D., known as the "Age of Iron and Rust," the great empire started to unravel. Taxation rose to oppressive levels, inflation skyrocketed (to 1,000 percent during a 20-year period), and people abandoned the cities. Rome found it impossible to maintain a 10,000-mile frontier as barbarians closed in on the borders. Politically, the government was more like a banana republic than a great empire. During one 50-year period, 18 Roman emperors were assassinated. The army was no longer a provider or protector; it was an expensive problem.

As any tour guide will tell you, Rome consumed everything and produced nothing. Like most ancient civilizations, Rome had a false economy based on slavery (cheap labor) and booty (cheap resources). When Rome stopped expanding, the flow of booty and slaves that had fueled the empire for so long dried up. When a society reaches this point, it must do one of three things: begin living within its means, rot out at the core, or build up a big deficit. Hmmm.

Rome's tumble inspired emperors to try drastic solutions. Two strong emperors, Diocletian and Constantine, made fundamental changes in how the empire was ruled. Diocletian (ruled 285–305), recognizing that the empire was overextended, split it in half and later into quarters (each with its own ruler). He established strict economic and political order after a century of chaos. Later, Constantine (ruled 306–337) moved the capital eastward to present-day Istanbul (named Constantinople in his honor). He ruled the eastern half of the empire, while Rome was left holding the crumbling west.

Christian Rome

Constantine (who witnessed the torture of many martyrs as a boy) made Christianity not only legal but also the official religion of Rome. He supported the Church with money and privileges. For its last 150 years, Rome was officially Christian.

Constantine claims he had a Christian vision that helped him defeat his rival and co-emperor Maxentius in battle in A.D. 312. (The huge Arch of Constantine next to the Colosseum marks his victory.) But some historians suspect that Constantine sanctioned the religion

A Roman relief of Jesus as the good shepherd.

Catacombs

The catacombs are burial places for (mostly) Christians who died in ancient Roman times. By law, no one was allowed to be buried within the walls of Rome. While pagan Romans were into cremation, Christians preferred to be buried. But land was expensive and most Christians were poor. A few wealthy landowning Christians allowed their land to be used as burial places.

The 40 or so known catacombs circle Rome about three miles from the center. From the first through the fifth centuries, Christians dug an estimated 360 miles of tomb-lined tunnels with networks of galleries as many as five layers deep. The Christians burrowed deep for two reasons: to get more mileage out of the donated land and to be near martyrs and saints already buried there. The tufa—soft and easy to cut but becoming very hard when exposed to air—is perfect for the job. Bodies were wrapped in linen (like Christ). Since they figured the Second Coming was imminent, there was no interest in embalming the body.

After Emperor Constantine legalized Christianity, Christians had a new, interesting problem. There would be no more persecuted martyrs to bind them and inspire them. Thus the early martyrs and popes assumed more importance, and Christians began making pilgrimages to their burial places in the catacombs.

In the 800s, when barbarian invaders started ransacking the tombs, Christians moved the relics of saints and martyrs to the

in a pragmatic move to gain the support of a growing, prosperous, and potentially law-abiding minority.

Regardless of Constantine's motives for turning to Christianity, he was following in his mother's kneeprints. His mother Helena was famous within the church for her fervent search for the true cross and other relics of Jesus. She brought back the "Holy Stairs" that Jesus climbed on the day he was sentenced to death. (Pilgrims now climb these stairs on their knees at Rome's San Giovanni in Laterano.)

A later emperor made Christianity Rome's only legal religion. In the year 300 you could be killed for being a Christian, and in 400 you could be killed for not being a Christian. Church enrollment boomed.

Pagans blamed Christianity for Rome's decline. They believed the Roman gods, angry at being neglected, let the empire crumble. Whatever the reason, Rome's downfall was inevitable. In 476, the last emperor was

safety of churches in the city center. For a thousand years the catacombs were forgotten. Around 1850 they were excavated and
became part of the romantic Grand Tour of Europe.

Finding abandoned plates and utensils from ritual meals in the
candlelit galleries led romantics to guess that persecuted Christians
hid out and lived in these catacombs. This romantic legend grew.
But catacombs were not used for hiding out. They are simply early
Christian burial grounds. With a million people in Rome, the easiest way for the 10,000 or so early Christians to hide out was not to
camp in the catacombs (which everyone, including the government, knew about), but to melt into the city.

The underground tunnels, while empty of bones, are rich in
early Christian symbolism which functioned as a secret language.
A dove symbolizes the soul. You'll see it quenching its thirst (worshiping), with an olive branch (at rest), or happily perched (in
paradise). Peacocks, known for their "incorruptible flesh," symbolized immortality. The shepherd with a lamb on his shoulders is the
"good shepherd," the first portrayal of Christ. The fish was used
because the first letters of these words in Greek—"Jesus Christ,
Son of God, Savior"—spelled fish. And the anchor is a cross in
disguise.

For more information, dig this: the catacombs have a Web site
(www.catacombe.roma.it).

tossed out by invading barbarians, and the Roman Empire's long termi-
nal illness was over.

Rome's ghost lives on. Its legal system provided the foundation for
western law. Its architecture spawned everything from cathedral
domes and neoclassical temples to today's stadiums and concrete
patios. Its pantheon of gods and myths have enriched literature, and
its bad emperors have given us bad movies. Greco-Roman art inspired
the Renaissance—the rebirth of classical beauty.

Rome influenced the Dark Ages as well. After Rome's fall, her urban
nobility fled from the cities, establishing themselves as the feudal lords of
medieval Europe's countryside. Latin, the Roman language, was the language of the educated and ruling classes throughout the Middle Ages.
The Roman Catholic Church inherited the empire's administrative finesse
and has been ruled by a _Pontifex Maximus_ ever since.

Top Museums of Ancient Rome

- Vatican Museum, Rome
- National Museum at Palazzo Massimo, Rome
- Capitol Hill Museum, Rome
- EUR Museum (scale model of ancient Rome), Rome
- National Museum, Naples
- Louvre, Paris
- Romisch-Germanisches Museum, Köln, Germany

Summary of Ancient Western Civilization

You've just absorbed 3,500 years of history and art, from Egypt through Rome. That wasn't so bad, was it? Before you shake off the ancient dust and plunge into the Dark Ages, let's review what we've covered.

Each of the ancient cultures influenced the following one. The early Mesopotamian cities came first, followed by the stable agricultural civilization of Egypt. The Minoans from Crete influenced the mainland Mycenaeans, who slowly progressed economically and politically into the Golden Age of Greek culture. Alexander the Great spread this culture by conquest throughout the Hellenistic world, where it was later adopted by the growing Roman Empire. The sacking of Rome marks the end of ancient Europe.

While culture moved progressively westward from Mesopotamia to Rome, Central and Northern Europe remained populated by barbarian tribes wallowing in the Stone Age.

Grauballe Man, A.D. *300 (Forhistorisk Museum Moesgard, Arhus, Denmark) Wallowing in the Stone Age*

Timeline of Ancient Rome

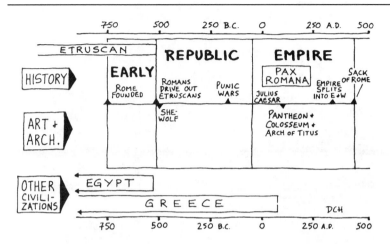

Timeline of Ancient Europe

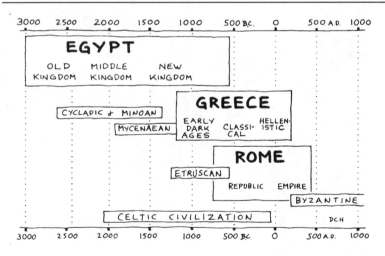

Long flight? Color this. (Flight attendants have crayons.)

The Middle Ages
A.D. 500–1500

A thousand years separate ancient and modern Europe. These "Middle Ages" lasted from about A.D. 500 to 1500. The first half of the Middle Ages were the Dark Ages (500–1000) and the second half were the High Middle Ages (1000–1500).

Most of the castles and cathedrals that fill tourists' scrapbooks are the great physical accomplishments of medieval Europe. Nearly all of these came from the High Middle Ages. It's enlightening to imagine the religious fervor that built these cathedrals and the fear that built the castles.

But first let's wallow in the darkness for about 500 years.

The Dark Ages (A.D. 500–1000)

By A.D. 500, Rome had collapsed. The fall of Rome was like a great stone column crashing across the Continent, burying Europe and scattering civilization like so much dust. It was 500 years before dazed Europeans began to pick themselves up from the rubble and build a new world. In the meantime, they lived lives of hardship, fear, and ignorance.

Whatever civilization the Romans had brought to Europe died. Roads and cities crumbled, pillaged as quarries by peasants. Rome shrunk to a ramshackle town of less than 50,000 people. There were few large towns and little trade; the economy was based on subsistence farming clustered around small villages. A bad harvest was a sentence for famine and death to a community isolated from outside help.

People lived with animals in huts, wearing the same homespun clothing all year and rarely flossing. Wild beasts and outlaws flourished throughout the countryside. Forests reclaimed cultivated land.

Skeletons unearthed by archaeologists show a people chronically undernourished, partly because of ineffective farming techniques.

Infant and child mortality rates soared. Wise elders of a village might have been only in their thirties.

The Dark Ages, A.D. 500–1000

Life was clouded by the fear of invasions. Vikings from Scandinavia, Magyars from Hungary, Huns from Central Asia, and Moslems from Spain all threatened Europe. In the days before hard and firm political boundaries, the demographic map of Eurasia was in constant flux. Tribes everywhere were migrating away from danger and resettling in more hospitable lands. It wasn't until centuries later that the invaders were defeated or absorbed, and Europeans stopped finishing off their prayers with "and deliver us from the Norsemen, amen."

Feudalism

Dark Age Europe had no effective government. "King" was more an honorary title than a position of power. Government was in the hands of local nobles, barons, dukes, knights, petty lords, and the NRA.

Might made right. Basic protection was essential and expensive. Some estimate that 75 percent of Europe's total income was spent paying soldiers for protection. A king achieved autonomy only if he could organize protectors and keep them satisfactorily paid.

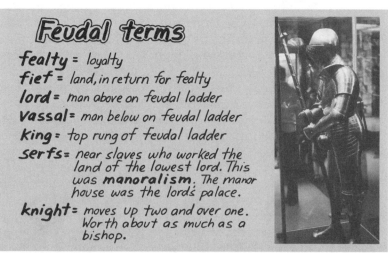

Feudal terms

fealty = loyalty
fief = land, in return for fealty
lord = man above on feudal ladder
vassal = man below on feudal ladder
king = top rung of feudal ladder
serfs = near slaves who worked the land of the lowest lord. This was **manoralism**. The manor house was the lord's palace.
knight = moves up two and over one. Worth about as much as a bishop.

Medieval Justice

Justice was meted out in "trials by ordeal." The accused might have been forced to grab a red-hot iron or to pull a stone from a cauldron of boiling water. If he was unharmed or the wound healed miraculously in a few days, he was innocent. If not, he was really punished. A woman accused of being a witch might have been bound and thrown into a lake. If she drowned, she was believed to be innocent. If she floated, she was believed to be guilty and burnt accordingly. These ordeals were usually held in or near the church, with a priest in attendance. Rothenburg, Germany, has a museum devoted to the many creative ways "criminals" suffered during medieval times.

Europeans also had to contend with demons, devils, spirits of the woods and rocks, mischievous saints, and a jealous God. Magic and local folklore were woven into Christianity. A sword could be put on trial for falling off the wall, as if a spirit had inhabited it. The hideous gargoyles that adorn Romanesque churches come straight out of the imagination of these super-stitious and frightened people.

Trial by Ordeal. *The ancient "trial by ordeal" survived well into the Middle Ages. Here, two bishops lead a queen barefoot over a red-hot grate to determine whether she has been true to her husband (left). Notice the hand of God overseeing things.*

Medieval crime and punishment museum poster, Rothenburg, Germany

A strict social and economic system called "feudalism" evolved to give this chaotic world some order and security. Feudalism carefully defined the duties of each class. Like chessmen, each group could move only a certain way. Bound by a code of honor, each class was dependent on the other for its livelihood.

The currency of feudalism was loyalty and land. The peasants pledged part of their crop to a nobleman, who in turn gave them land to work and the promise of protection and a system of justice. The nobleman (vassal) promised loyalty (fealty) to a higher-up (lord) in return for use of the land (a fief). One man's vassal was another man's lord. Each noble was in the service of a more powerful noble and so on up to the king, the pinnacle of the feudal hierarchy.

The feudal nobility played war for kicks. On sunny afternoons the knights suited up, trampled their peasants' crops, and raided the neighboring nobles' domains in an attempt to kidnap the lord. Most of medieval Europe toiled to survive while sons of the rich spent their leisure hours playing chivalrous games. The pawns in this feudal chess game were, of course, the peasants.

Nobles hardly lived lives of luxury, though. Their castles were crude structures: cold, damp, and dark, with little privacy or warmth. Scorning educated people, nobles were illiterate and proud of it. Their lives revolved around war, training for war, hunting, and feasting. Their feasts often became week-long bouts of drinking and rowdiness. Younger sons of nobles (who received no inheritance) were forced to become clergy.

Candles in the Wind: Dark Age Bright Spots

The whole world wasn't in a Dark Age. In Central America, the Mayans and Toltecs were building great cities and doing complex astronomical work. In China, the T'ang dynasty was flourishing. China provided many of the technological inventions that spurred Europe's recovery from the Dark Ages: paper, clockwork, looms, windmills, Top Ramen, spinning wheels, and gunpowder.

Even in Europe, the flame of civilization flickered throughout the Dark Ages. The church and Byzantine Empire preserved the learning of the classical world until later economic prosperity allowed it to blaze again in society at large. The ruler Charlemagne, who briefly united the core of Europe, orchestrated a mini-Renaissance.

The Church

The church bridged the ancient and modern worlds by carrying Rome's classical learning and administration through the Middle Ages and passing it along to the rising secular world during the Renaissance.

The church dominated every aspect of medieval life. A sin was a crime and vice versa. Religious authorities (often called prince-bishops) were the civil authorities. Tithes were taxes. God brought prosperity and He brought plagues. The Bible was the final word on all matters scientific, economic, social, and political. This began 700 years during which theology was the leading science. Thoughts of an afterlife concerned people more than secular growth. Money, trade, and progress had little to do with the "Dark" Ages (as we, with such an opposite outlook, still call those times).

Intellectual life survived the Dark Ages in monasteries. Copying and translating Greek and Roman writings were common tasks for monks.

After Rome fell, monks fled barbarian Europe, carrying civilization to the western fringe of the known world. Ireland was the northern intellectual capital. When St. Patrick, a fifth-century Christian monk from Romanized England, established his faith in Ireland, he found excellent schools run by the native Celtic tribes that taught classical subjects. Patrick and his successors kept these schools open, mixing Christianity into the curriculum. Latin learning was re-infused into England and the Continent (as far inland as Switzerland) by Irish missionaries. Sights such as the evocative ruins of the church at Cashel, near Tipperary, remind us of Ireland's importance to Christianity.

A loose chain of monasteries served as the center of Christianity until the popes got the church organized into a central system after the fall of Rome. The year 529 was pivotal: Christian thought triumphed over secular thinking as the Emperor Justinian closed the Platonic Academy in Athens and the first monastic order, the Benedictines, was founded. From this point on, Europe's best minds struggled with the interpretation of God's word. Every sentence needed to be understood, debated, and applied. Since contemplation

Whirlwinds, Hunger, and Plagues, Oh My!

Look at a ninth-century history book and you can see that the Dark Ages were a mix of magic, fear, fantasy, harshness, and ignorance. The years are boiled down to a few terrible and miraculous events, all told matter-of-factly. Some excerpts:

Account of the year A.D. 837: A gigantic whirlwind broke out and a comet appeared, emitting streams of light three cubits long before the amazed spectators. The pagans devastated Walicrum and abducted many women there, taking also huge sums of money.

The year 852: The steel of the pagans grew white-hot; an excessive heat of the sun; famine followed; there was no fodder for the beasts, but the feeding of pigs flourished.

The year 853: Great hunger in Saxony, with the result that many ate horses.

The year 857: A great plague with swelling of the bladder raged among the people and destroyed them with horrible festering, so that their limbs dropped off and fell away before death.

The church was the refuge from this awful and fearful world. God was a god of power, like an earthly noble, to fight the forces of evil. God's weapons were prayer, the Mass, and other rituals which, in the minds of the peasants, had magical power. Romanesque churches stood like mighty fortresses in the war against Satan. To peasants, the church was a hint of the glories that awaited them in heaven. If ever religion was "the opiate of the masses," it was in medieval Europe.

was considered the "highest service to God," the best and the brightest European minds were Christian . . . and remained silent.

After the Roman grapevine withered, fewer and fewer people learned to read and write. Priests and monks alone were literate or capable of writing and doing simple arithmetic at a time when letters and numbers were believed by the unlearned to have magical powers. (Our modern word "clerk," someone who works with words or numbers, comes from "cleric," which means a member of the clergy.)

Monasteries preserved classical literature and the Latin language. Monks were supposed to read and study, but books were scarce. When

*Detail from **Book of Kells**, ninth century A.D.(Trinity College, Dublin). The illuminated manuscript was Dark Age Europe's greatest pictorial art form. The lettering is lovingly decorative. Here we see characters pulling each others' beards and stretching their hamstrings. Other fine illuminated manuscripts are exhibited at London's British Library and cathedral treasuries throughout Europe.*

Benedict set up what later became the most influential monastic order of the Middle Ages, he scheduled a daily program of monks' duties, combining manual labor with intellectual tasks such as translating and copying ancient texts, including works that were purely secular and even heretical. Monks copied books to add to their library's collection.

Copying texts was a tedious task. To vent their creative spirits, monks would decorate title pages or chapter headings. Illuminated manuscripts became the top art form of Dark Age Europe. The *Book of Kells* (Trinity College, Dublin) and the Lindisfarne Gospels (British Library) are the best examples of this monastic flowering from 500 to 900. Both are illuminated gospels showing classical, Celtic, and even Byzantine influences.

Monks were also the keepers of technological knowledge—of clocks, waterwheels,

*A page from the **Lindisfarne Gospels** (eighth century A.D.) To own and read such a monk-u-script, you needed lots of money and a knowledge of Latin.*

Viking Sights

Britain
• Jorvik Exhibit, York
Norway
• Ships at Bygdøy, Oslo
Denmark
• National Museum,
  Copenhagen
• Viking Ship
  Museum,
  Roskilde

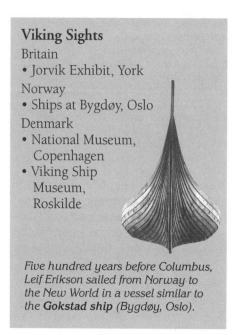

*Five hundred years before Columbus, Leif Erikson sailed from Norway to the New World in a vessel similar to the **Gokstad ship** (Bygdøy, Oslo).*

accounting, wine making, foundries, gristmills, textiles, and agricultural techniques. Cistercian monasteries were leaders of the medieval Industrial Revolution of the later Middle Ages.

While the Roman Empire was Christian from the time of the Roman Emperor Constantine, Christianity was slow to penetrate the northern countries. The Viking and Hungarian invasions in the eighth and ninth centuries slowed its spread. Not until A.D. 1000 could Europe be considered thoroughly Christian.

Much of the folk religion survived the coming of Christianity. Old folk gods got new names. Christian churches were built on holy pagan sites. The good spirits of folklore became the saints of the church, but remained the powers to be bargained with for earthly favors. The church calendar, which established holy days—hence the word "holiday"—patterned itself after old pagan feast days. (Even today, we celebrate Christmas much as the Druids of Britain celebrated the winter solstice, with trees and mistletoe.)

As the church became more organized, it followed the administrative hierarchy used by Rome's government. Roman governors became Roman Catholic bishops, senators became cardinals, scholars became priests, and the pope adopted the title originally held by the emperor—*Pontifex Maximus*.

The Christian church preserved some of Rome's sheer grandness. As you stand in the shade of the huge ruined arches of the Basilica Maxentius in the Roman Forum, remember that houses of justice such as this one served as the architectural model for almost all Christian churches to follow. The church's great wealth, amassed from tithes and vast landholdings, was invested in huge church buildings, decorated as ornately as anything Rome had ever seen. Visit Rome's lavish Christian basilicas such as Santa Maria Maggiore. The pomp and pageantry of the church rituals are reminiscent of the glorious days of Caesar.

The Byzantine Empire

The eastern Roman Empire—which became the Byzantine Empire—was another great preserver of Roman culture. In a desperate attempt to invigorate his failing empire, Constantine moved his capital from Rome to the new city of Constantinople (modern-day Istanbul) in A.D. 330.

In a sense, this was the real end of Rome. The center of the civilized West packed up and moved eastward, where it remained for a thousand years while Europe

***Byzantine Mosaic,** A.D. 550, Ravenna. The top Byzantine art was mosaics made from patterns of small stones and glass. Mosaics in Ravenna, Venice, and Istanbul (once Constantinople) still glitter with the glory of Byzantium.*

struggled to establish itself. The emperor and his court—scholars, artists, and all—moved to the East, leaving the self-proclaimed emperors in Rome with no real power outside Italy.

The political vacuum left by the fall of Rome was eventually filled by three realms: the Byzantine Empire (formerly the Eastern Roman Empire), the Holy Roman Empire (dating from the domain of Charlemagne), and Islam (which spread rapidly from Mecca).

Byzantine Sights

- Churches and mosaics, Ravenna, Italy
- St. Mark's, Venice
- Hagia Sophia Museum and Chora Church, Istanbul, Turkey
- Mystra, near Sparta on the Peloponnesian Peninsula, Greece
- Meteora pinnacle monasteries, Greece
- Mt. Athos monasteries (for men only), Greece
- Charlemagne's Chapel, Aachen, Germany
- Sacré-Coeur (neo-Byzantine church), Paris

St. Mark's Basilica in Venice is covered with intricate Byzantine-style mosaics. Imagine paving a football field with contact lenses.

After Rome fell to barbarians, Italy still kept in touch with the classical world. Always linked by trade with the enlightened Byzantines, Italy was even united briefly with the Eastern Empire under the Emperor Justinian (A.D. 550). The magnificent churches of Ravenna (south of Venice) from this period rival Istanbul's.

We think of the Eastern Empire as Byzantine rather than Roman because it quickly took on an Eastern flavor. Its language, literature, and art were Greek. The church followed "Eastern Orthodox" ways, eventually splitting with the pope's Latin church.

Nevertheless, the Byzantine Empire had a powerful influence on the West. Throughout the Dark Ages, the emperor in Constantinople was considered by Christians and barbarians all over Europe to be the civilized world's supreme ruler. Constantinople was the Christian world's leading city for centuries.

After the Crusaders lubricated communication (while looting cities) between the East and West, the long-forgotten classical Roman and Greek knowledge returned to Europe. When Constantinople was finally overrun by the Moslem Turks in 1453, scholars and artists fled to the West, where their knowledge spurred the growing spirit of the Renaissance.

Constantinople, today's Istanbul, is an exciting brew of ancient past and cosmopolitan present, Moslem East and Christian West.

Charlemagne

Throughout the Middle Ages, popes and kings struggled to establish their power. While the popes were undisputed spiritual leaders, they needed a military alliance with a king to effectively wield power. And being crowned by the pope wouldn't look bad on a king's résumé either. The alliance was born as the pope crowned Charles the Great, emperor of a "Holy Roman Empire," on Christmas Day in the year 800.

The reign of Charlemagne (SHAR-luh-mayn)—Charles the Great, King of the Franks—was a bright light in the Dark Ages. He united most of the Western Christian world, from Germany to Sicily, and established what we call the Carolingian Empire, the largest since Rome. He was the protector of Christendom.

This was a mini-Renaissance. Drowsy Europe quivered and drooled with excitement at this "Roman revival." Charlemagne's capital city of Aix-la-Chapelle (present-day Aachen, Germany; well worth a visit) became the first capital of Dark Age Europe. Trade and communication increased, and the court became a cultural center where artists and scholars worked to revive Roman ideals. Academia flourished, and classical works were studied and copied. It's said that Charlemagne could read a little (a rarity at the time) and went to bed each night with a slate to practice his writing.

Charlemagne personally set about to improve the lot of his people. He instituted trial by judge, replacing the barbaric trial by ordeal; revised the monetary system; built schools and churches; and advanced the Christian faith. Perhaps most important, his foot became *the* foot, a standard form of measurement (according to tour guides).

Despite the "Carolingian Renaissance," these were still the Dark Ages. Charlemagne was an enlightened but ruthless leader, responsible for the conversion of the pagan German tribes to Christianity. His chosen instrument of persuasion was the same used by later Crusaders— the sword. He invaded Germany, conquered it tribe by tribe, and gave the leaders a choice: convert or die. The Franks built churches that were really military outposts in the conquered lands. Resistance died hard, and the resisters died even harder. It's said that Charlemagne once ordered the decapitation of 4,500 pagans in one day.

Charlemagne was the top-dog ruler, but the Franks who succeeded him were wieners. When he died, his empire was divided among his three heirs into realms that became Germany, France, and the smaller countries in between. His successors returned to their quarreling ways, and, as they bickered, darkness fell once again.

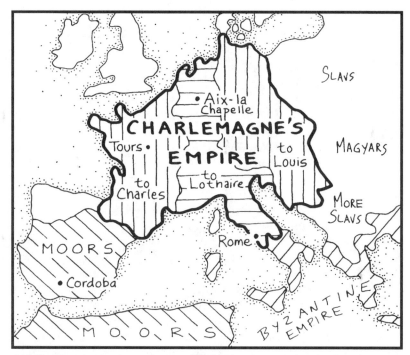

In 842, Charlemagne's empire was divided by treaty among his heirs into what became France, Germany, and the smaller states in between. Since the treaty was written in French and German rather than Latin, some historians consider 842 the year Europe was born.

Later kings in Germany and Austria claimed to rule a revived "Holy Roman Empire" like Charlemagne's; but their kingdoms, as Voltaire pointed out, were neither holy, nor Roman, nor an empire. It was to be a long time before Europe enjoyed being ruled by another leader of Charlemagne's stature and shoe size.

Charlemagne's reign was a turning point. Before his time, it seemed that darkness might dominate Europe forever. Afterward, hope for the restoration of learning and civilization was rekindled.

During much of the Dark Ages, Europe was a scattered and chaotic compost pile of barbarian tribes from which modern nations would sprout. Quietly the seeds of modern Europe were planted. There was no nation of France or England, but there were barbarian tribes of Franks and Angles. By the end of the Dark Ages, "nations" had emerged, no longer dominated by Roman culture. The Franks were becoming France, and Angleland was to become England.

End of the Millennium

Much of Europe figured life would come to an end in Y1K. After all, the Biblical book of Revelation says an angel came down and bound the devil for 1000 years "after which he must be loosed a little season." In the 990s, business stopped and people focused only on salvation. The streets were filled with people whipping themselves in remorse.

The year 1000 came and went. So did 1001. Europe breathed a sigh of relief and set about preparing for the best millennium ever. With a burst of energy, a 300-year-long boom time began.

The High Middle Ages (1000–1500)

At the turn of the first millennium, Europe began waking up. It made some basic economic, political, and ideological changes that culminated a few centuries later in the Renaissance. For the previous 500 years, progress could have been graphed as a straight, horizontal line. During the High Middle Ages, that line soared upward, carrying Europe into the modern age.

Now that barbarian invasions were no longer a great threat, Europeans built and planned for the future. Natural power sources were harnessed by the windmill and waterwheel. Agricultural advances such as improved plows, harnesses, and crop rotation increased productivity. Fewer farmers were needed to feed the society. Towns grew up, offering peasants an exciting alternative to life under their feudal masters. Job opportunities maximized earning, and the formation of universities encouraged learning. Urbanization increased trade and improved communication. Europeans were no longer hopelessly isolated in a dark feudal struggle for subsistence. Europe perked up, experiencing the same enthusiasm that marked the United States' westward movement. Land was cleared and roads and bridges were built as Europe flexed its muscles.

Dark Age thought was anchored in Augustine's City of God notion that there is one truth for both heaven and earth. New thinkers were accepting Aristotelian reason and rising above Dark Age mysticism. After 700 years of "theology rules," scholars were now fascinated by the natural world. The City of Man became as worthy of study as the City of God.

Romanesque Architecture (1000–1200)

Europe's churches are huge, free, usually open, and right on the main square. Have a look inside and out. With a little background, they become more interesting.

*Around 1100, Romanesque churches such as **Vezelay's** (France) were Europe's biggest buildings featuring round arches, heavy walls, small windows, and dim interiors.*

Medieval communities revolved around their church. Typically the only stone structure in town and a landmark for miles around, the church was the political, religious, and even recreational center of the town.

The Romanesque style is the first real "European" art form, named for its Roman features—columns and rounded arches—which create an overall effect of massiveness and strength. Romanesque churches are like dark fortresses with thick walls, squat towers, big blocks of stone, few windows, dark interiors, and a minimum of decoration.

Medieval churches were based on the ancient Roman "basilica" floor plan. The pagan temples of Rome were designed to house only the image of the god, not crowds of worshipers. But Christians worship together

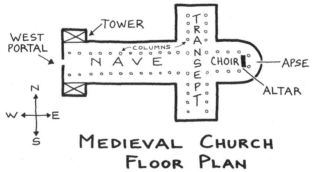

MEDIEVAL CHURCH FLOOR PLAN

European churches have basilica-style main halls with transepts added to give the rectangular basilicas the shape of a Latin cross. Note: A "cathedral" is not a type of church architecture. It's simply a church that's a governing center for a local bishop.

Basilica Aemilia, *179 B.C. (Forum, Rome). The floor plan of pre-Christian law courts became the model for churches throughout the Middle Ages. Notice the central nave (where the tourists are walking) flanked by narrower side aisles.*

and the Mass requires a large meeting hall. So when Christianity became Rome's adopted religion, new churches were modeled not after her temples, but after the largest Roman secular structures: Roman law courts, or basilicas. The same basilica floor plans that you'll see in the Roman Forum (Basilicas Aemilia, Julia, and Maxentius) were used in nearly every medieval church.

A basilica has a long central hall (nave) with narrower halls on either side, and at the far end, a semicircular area (apse) around the altar. An aisle that forms a cross with the main hall, called a transept, was added so that the building looked more Christian, but the basic pre-Christian basilica plan remained.

This floor plan was ideal for accommodating large congregations, especially the massive processions of pilgrims who came to worship Christian relics (such as a piece of Jesus' cross or the bone of a saint). Pilgrims would amble up one side aisle, around the altar, and out the other aisle, worshiping at each chapel along the way. Columns separated the walkways (ambulatories) from the long central nave where the congregation stood (sitting in church hadn't been invented yet).

Medieval churches are like a compass, pointing east, toward Jerusalem. The entry (portal) is therefore the west portal, the transepts point north and south, and the altar faces east.

Medieval Religious Art

Although the floor plan of churches was essentially Roman, the Romanesque decorations were strictly Christian. Theologians wondered, "What is art's place in the church?" The Bible stated explicitly that no "graven images" should be made for worshiping. Did that include paintings? Craftings of nature? Illustrated Bible stories? The debate lasted for centuries. By the year 600, it was generally agreed that art had great

Medieval art generally decorated churches and told Bible stories. Here, next to the front door of the Notre Dame in Paris, a seductive snake tempts Adam and Eve with an apple.

value in worship as a way of educating and inspiring the masses of illiterate Christians. Remember, in medieval times most Europeans couldn't read, write, or speak Latin, the language used in church services. They went to church to "read" the stories of their religion as told in sculpture, stained glass, tapestries, and paintings.

***Tympanum** (the semicircular area above the door) of a Romanesque church. Here you'll find a Romanesque church's most interesting sculpture. Notice how cluttered these narrative reliefs look—a far cry from the bold, freestanding statues of ancient Rome and the coming Renaissance.*

Hell, *13th century (San Giovanni baptistery, Florence)*

The images carved into the walls and doors of churches were every bit as effective as the priest's sermon. Typically, devout peasants could look at scenes of lost souls, naked and chained, being dragged off to Hell. On Jesus' right would be the blessed faces looking to heaven, hands obediently folded, content with the promise of a happy afterlife. Escapist theology was as attractive to feudal peasants (and their overlords) in medieval Europe as it is to modern-day peasants (and their overlords) in Central America.

Church architecture, the designing of God's house, was the most respected medieval art form. Arts such as sculpture and stained glass were okay because they embellished the house of God. Statues were tucked into niches carved in the church wall. Stories were told in low relief, protruding only slightly from the wall or surrounding material (as opposed to freestanding statues).

A church's most interesting and creative sculpture is often found in the tympanum (the arched area above the door) or hiding in the capitals of the columns along the nave. Sculptors were allowed a little craziness here, and it's fun to see their grotesque fantasies peeking through the capital's leaves, filling nooks, and sticking out of crannies.

Because medieval art is mostly Christian art, realism and classical beauty took a back seat to getting the message across. Artists concentrated on inspiring and uplifting the peasants by boiling their subjects

Top Romanesque Art and Architecture
- Cathedral, Durham, Britain
- Aix-la-Chapelle (Charlemagne's church and relics), Aachen, Germany
- Cathedrals, Worms and Speyer, Germany
- Bayeux Tapestry, Bayeux, France
- Cathedral, Vezelay, France
- Basilique St. Sernin and Augustins Museum, Toulouse, France
- Carcassonne (medieval walled town), France
- Sarlat (medieval town), France
- Many small village churches in Burgundy, France
- Santiago de Compostela (cathedral), Santiago, Spain
- Cathedral, Leaning Tower, and Baptistery, Pisa, Italy

down to the essential details—just what was necessary to convey the point of the story. Pictures became symbols that stood for ideas and actions rather than representations of real things. A lion was meant to be a symbol of the resurrection, not a lesson in zoology.

Classical techniques that made art realistic had been forgotten. Medieval art was stiff, unreal, and two-dimensional. Figures looked as if they'd been cut out of paper and pasted into random groups. Background, shading, depth, and proportion didn't matter. Scenes were often overcrowded.

When considered in its context and for its narrative function, there's plenty of very good and creative Romanesque art. The artist wanted to teach and inspire the viewer, and being freed from the constraints of realism enabled the medieval artist to experiment with new (and often bizarre) color schemes, compositions, and proportions, sometimes exaggerating them to enhance the spiritual effect. The final product, although far from "classical," is impressive, inspirational, and beautiful on its own terms.

Medieval art, like Chinese, Byzantine, and Egyptian art, had no need to be original. A donor would commission an artist to create a replica of an existing piece of art, possibly with finer materials but with no demand for particular originality. The artist would have no problem with copying someone else's work. It's like our notion of music. For your wedding you hire an organist and a singer, not to come up with new music but to redo nicely something you already know you like.

While most medieval art was religious, plenty of secular art decorated castles. Unfortunately, little survives. While churches and church art were respected, protected, and saved, secular work was destroyed, abandoned, or built over.

Crusades (1100–1300)

With the new millennium, Europe was feeling its oats. This new progressive spirit showed itself in the aggressive "holiness" called the Crusades.

The Crusades were a series of military expeditions promoted by various popes and kings to recapture or protect the holy city of Jerusalem from Moslem "invaders" (who also considered it holy). Although Crusades began as religious missions, nearly anyone could find a self-serving reason to join these holy wars of prophets and profits.

The East enjoyed luxuries dreamed about by many Europeans. As merchants hoped, the Crusades reopened lucrative trade routes from Europe to the East. Nobles enjoyed this opportunity to conquer new land for fiefs, while their knights sought adventure, glory, and spoils. Christians chased salvation by converting—or slaughtering—"heathens" and protecting Jerusalem. Initially the pope's prestige and authority soared with each Moslem killed.

Canaletto, _Doge's Palace in Venice (Uffizi, Florence)_

Crusades: Mission Impossible

Christianity was more literal during the Middle Ages. Relics were divine, the streets Jesus walked on were divine. The papacy believed that owning this sacred land, even if it meant killing infidels, was unquestionably fulfilling God's will. European Christians believed their pope.

When the Moslems denied Christians access to Jerusalem, the pope declared the first Crusade in 1095. As the crusaders set off to kill infidels, anyone would do. Crossing Germany, they slaughtered Jews. (Some historians call this the First Holocaust.) By the time the crusaders reached Jerusalem, the Moslems had already reopened the doors to Christians. But since the crusaders had come all that way... they massacred 70,000 residents of Jerusalem, prayed, and returned home proud.

This was one of the main reasons the Crusades failed—the crusaders went home. Soldiers move on rather than move in. It's hard to keep land without settlers.

Life wasn't a bed of rosaries for crusaders. They had to put up money to fund their journey, forage (pillage) for food along the way, and carry their own gear if their horses died. They were away from home for a couple years—unless they died in battle. They traveled a long, weary way to a parched land filled with understandably hostile fighters intent on protecting their own Holy Land.

The Moslems had the great advantage of fighting on their own turf, with lots of ready supplies and men united by a single aim—driving out these bloodthirsty Christian invaders. The crusaders-given their varied motives, languages, and national rivalries—didn't function as a team. Some Crusades didn't even make it to the Holy Land.

The most dismal example was the Fourth Crusade (1202–1204), resulting in the sacking of Constantinople, a fellow

Although the Crusades were a failure, they did have a great effect on Europe, giving it a broader, more cosmopolitan outlook. They opened a floodgate of new ideas and building techniques from the East and brought back many classical ideas that the West had lost during the Dark Ages. And the majestic flavor of sacred Byzantine art showed up clearly in Western art.

Christian city and capitol of the Byzantine Empire. The pope, so certain of the necessity of this Crusade, even gave husbands permission to go without asking their wives. Despite a tax imposed on churchgoers, the crusaders couldn't raise enough money to pay Venice for the needed ships. Venice struck a deal: if the crusaders would conquer Zara, a Christian port but a rival of Venice, they'd supply the ships. The crusaders zapped Zara. Meanwhile, the

Religion was just one of many reasons for the Crusades.

son of a deposed Byzantine king promised the crusaders huge sums of money and men if they'd restore his father Isaac II to the throne in Constantinople. The crusaders re-crowned the king, but the people of Constantinople refused to pay what the king's son had promised. In retaliation, the crusaders sacked this grand city.

The eight Crusades hardened a mutual distrust between Christians and Moslems that still exists. The papacy—which had promoted the Crusades, throwing away lives and money—lost authority. A chagrined Europe realized it couldn't push the Moslems around.

But the Crusades did stimulate trade, propelling Venice to superpower status and enriching Europe with new goods and ideas. Crusaders brought back relics and stone-working techniques, enabling them to build and furnish cathedrals back home. European Christians learned they needed to create their own Holy Land.

Venice emerged from the Crusades the big winner. Europe's appetite had been whetted by the East's luxury goods, and sea-trading Venice established itself as the dominant middleman. The Venetians prospered, expanding to control the entire Adriatic area politically and to become Europe's economic powerhouse until new trade routes to the East were developed several hundred years later by Vasco da Gama and others. Today Venice's past glory decays elegantly and her lavish architecture reflects her former lucrative position at the crossroads of East and West.

Castles and Sieges

Like a tortoise fighting a stone—that was medieval warfare when impregnable castles dotted Europe's landscape. War was a drawn-out, costly struggle as one side laid siege to the other. The only good thing to be said was that casualties were few and far between. Boredom was the common enemy of attacker and attacked.

Early castles evolved from primitive ditch and stockade fortifications. Sites offering natural fortification, like a hilltop surrounded by a river, were preferred. Later, when ditches became moats and stockades became stone walls, castles took the form we recognize today.

The medieval castle was a simple stone structure consisting of a central "keep," or main building, surrounded by a wall. The keep was usually built on a hill, cliff, or mound of earth. The wall enclosed the castle yard where the people lived. This mound and yard (or "motte and bailey") pattern was the basis of all medieval castles.

Later castles were much bigger, with more rings of walls as much as 20 feet thick. The crusaders had been impressed by the massive castles and walled cities of the Byzantines and applied many of their techniques to their castle-building back home.

Outside the wall was the moat, a ditch filled with water (they put alligators in them only in fairy tales). The main gate was made of oak, plated with iron, and often protected by a portcullis, or iron grill. Above the gate were twin towers, often four

Moats and drawbridges were just two of the innovations which gave the defense the edge in medieval warfare. The chateau of Langeais (Loire Valley, France) brings out the kid in many tourists.

Carcassonne, Europe's greatest medieval fortress city

stories high, with small windows for shooting at the enemy. The keep was the headquarters and home of the lord, and was used as a dining hall, ballroom, and as a last bastion when the outer walls fell in an attack.

Against such a formidable structure as a castle, an attacker's main weapon was hunger. The enemy camped around the castle and waited for supplies to run out. This often took years, and given the poor communication and supply lines of the period, the attacker might well run out of supplies first.

Carcassonne is Europe's greatest walled fortress city, located in southern France. The city once ran desperately low on food during a siege and was about to surrender. The attackers (who happened to be the army of Charlemagne), after waiting for years, were getting really

Rheinfels castle *(artist reconstruction), b. 1245, Germany*

Castles

For the greatest concentration of castles per kilometer, tour the Rhine in Germany or Wales in Britain.

On the Rhine

Ever since Roman times, when this was the Empire's northern boundary, the Rhine has been one of the world's busiest shipping rivers. You'll see a steady flow of barges with 1,000- to 2,000-ton loads. While today tourist-packed buses, hot train tracks, and highways line both banks, in medieval times the safe way to travel was on the river.

Many of the castles were "robber-baron" castles, put there by petty rulers (there were 300 independent little countries in medieval Germany) to levy tolls on passing river traffic. A robber baron would put his castle on, or even in, the river. Then, often with the help of chains and a tower on the opposite bank, he'd stop each ship and get his toll. There were 10 customs stops between Mainz and Koblenz alone.

Most Rhine castles date from the 11th, 12th, and 13th centuries. Some were built to control and protect settlements, and others were the residences of kings. As times changed, so did the lifestyles of the rich and feudal. Many castles were abandoned for more comfortable mansions in the towns.

After being destroyed by the revolutionary French army around 1800, the castles were rebuilt in neo-Gothic style in the Romantic Age (the late 1800s) and are enjoyed today as restaurants, hotels, hostels, and museums.

In Wales

You'll find more great castles per square mile in Wales than just about anywhere else in Europe. There's a reason. In the 13th century, the Welsh, under two great princes named Llywelyn, created a united and independent Wales. The English King Edward I fought hard to end this Welsh sovereignty. In 1282 Llywelyn was

restless. According to legend, a clever townswoman fed the last of the food to the last pig and threw the pig over the wall. Splat. When the invaders saw how well fed the pig was, they figured the people inside had plenty of food, so they packed up and headed home. The town was saved.

Caerphilly Castle survives in South Wales reminding travelers that Wales was not easily subdued.

killed (and went to where everyone speaks Welsh). King Edward spent the next 20 years building or rebuilding 17 great castles to consolidate his English foothold in troublesome North Wales.

The greatest of these (such as Conwy Castle) were masterpieces of medieval engineering with round towers (tough to undermine by tunneling), a castle-within-a-castle defense (giving defenders a place to retreat and wreak havoc on the advancing enemy... or just wait for reinforcements), and sea access (safe to stock from England). These were English islands in the middle of angry Wales. Most were built with a fortified grid-plan town attached and were filled with English settlers. (With this blatant abuse of Wales, you have to wonder, where was Greenpeace 700 years ago?)

Castle lovers will want to tour each of Edward's five greatest castles. With a car and two days this makes one of Europe's best castle tours. I'd rate them in this order: Caernarfon is most entertaining and best presented. Conwy is attached to the cutest medieval town and the best public transport. Harlech is the most dramatic. Beaumaris, surrounded by a swan-filled moat, was the last, largest, and most romantic. Criccieth, built in 1230 by Llywelyn, is also dramatic and remote.

But the patience of military men wears thin, and, later on, castles were stormed with a number of ingenious weapons. Catapults, powered by tension or counterweights, were used to fling huge boulders or red-hot irons over the walls. Under cover of archers armed with crossbows and six-foot longbows, armies would approach the castle

The Siege: *Medieval castles gave defenders the edge. Any decent castle was a pain to attack. Some castles were simply avoided, written off as unconquerable. The "starve 'em out siege" approach was the most common. Some sieges lasted years, until hunger or boredom won out. The advent of gunpowder ended the days when the best offense was a good castle.*

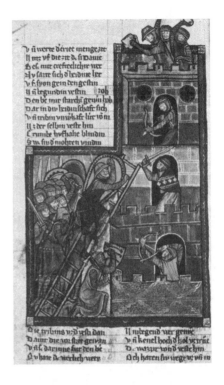

and fill the moat with dirt. Then they would wheel up the "storming towers," built of wood and covered with fire-resistant wet hides, and climb over the walls. They hammered at weak points in the wall and gate with a wood-and-iron battering ram. They even tried undermining—digging out the foundations in hopes the walls would crumble.

The defenders poured boiling water and burning pitch onto the invaders. From the turrets, archers fired arrows, flung missiles, and hurled insults. Others were stationed along the walls to overturn ladders and storming towers. Once the attackers got inside the castle, battle was fierce hand-to-hand combat. More likely, though, the defenders simply retreated behind the next inner wall to start the process over again.

Warfare changed dramatically with the coming of gunpowder. When the Turks besieged Constantinople in 1453, they had a new weapon: a 19-ton cannon that fired 1,500-pound rocks more than a mile in the air. Within a century of the arrival of gunpowder, the siege style of warfare that had gone on almost unchanged for 2,000 years was a thing of the past.

Many of the castles you'll see in Europe today never had a strategic military function. After 1500, lords built castle-forts for protection and castle-palaces for domestic life. In the romantic era of the 1800s, many castles, like those of Bavaria's Mad King Ludwig, had no practical purpose and were merely fantasy abodes.

Top Medieval Castles

- Burg Eltz and Cochem Castle on the Mosel River, Germany
- Many castles along the Rhine (Rheinfels and Marksburg are best) from Mainz to Koblenz, Germany
- Reifenstein Castle, Vipiteno, Italy
- Tower of London, London
- Warwick Castle, Warwick, Britain
- Caernarfon, Caerphilly, Conwy, Harlech, Beaumaris, and Criccieth, all in Wales, Britain
- Château Chillon, Lake Geneva, Switzerland
- Langeais and Chinon, Loire Valley, France
- Beynac, Dordogne, France
- Carcassonne, Languedoc, France

Burg Eltz, *on Germany's Mosel River*

Knights, Ladies, Love, and War

King Arthur and the Knights of the Round Table—Lancelot, Galahad, Percival, and company—are the ideal of medieval life, where men are always chivalrous and women are always kidnapped by dragons. Even though Arthur and the knights are fiction based on a minor historical figure, the myth played a big role in medieval thinking.

Knights of the Middle Ages followed an unwritten code of honor and chivalry that demanded valor in battle and service to their king, God, and ladylove. Originally intended for knights alone, it was quickly accepted by all nobility in Europe, whose lives revolved around war, religion, loyalty, and (occasionally) love.

Knights were warriors who pledged their fighting skills to some powerful lord in return for land, a title, or money. Knights on horseback were much more important than the average mercenary foot soldier. With the invention of stirrups, the rider could dig in and put force behind the lance he carried. A single knight could charge and break the ranks of

dozens of foot sol-
diers. Dressed in a
heavily armored
suit (so heavy that
if he fell off he
was as helpless as
a belly-up turtle),
a mounted knight
was like a tank
among infantry.

Later descen-
dants carried the
title of "knight"
earned by their
warrior forefathers, even when they themselves took no part in war.
Paul McCartney—who actually sang, "I'm a lover, not a fighter"—was
even knighted. The code of chivalry still applied to these gentlemen of
high society. In fact, the word for "gentleman" in several languages
(French, chevalier; Spanish, caballero; Italian, cavaliere), like the word
chivalry itself, comes from the Latin word for "horseman."

When there were no real wars in which they could demonstrate their
courage and skill, knights held tournaments, fighting each other indi-
vidually or in teams. The most common event, the joust, sent two
knights charging at each other on horseback, each determined to unseat
the other by using his lance. Sure enough, many knights died in these
"sporting" contests. In later tournaments, an attempt was made to try
to minimize injury by using blunted or wooden weapons, saving the
sport but diminishing the danger (like modern fencing). Still, as late as
1559, France lost a king (Henry II) when a wooden splinter pierced his
visor during a joust.

Medieval pageantry and contests such as jousting are reenacted
energetically in many of Europe's colorful festivals. Try to work a few
of these festivals into your itinerary (such as the Saracen's Joust in
Arezzo, Italy, on the second Sunday in September, or the medieval
Children's Fest in Dinkelsbühl, Germany, in mid-July).

The heroic deeds of knighthood were proclaimed in story and song
by troubadours, wandering poet-singer-storytellers of the Middle Ages.
These men were not journalists by any means; they didn't tell of real
men performing real deeds. Instead, they created an ideal world of
loving knights and lovely ladies. Their stories set the pattern of behav-
ior for medieval lords and ladies.

Camelot: Henry, Eleanor, and Courtly Love

The closest Europe ever came to a real "Camelot" was the court of King Henry II and Queen Eleanor of Aquitaine, rulers of a united England and France during the short-lived Angevin Empire (1150–1200). Henry was the perfect Arthur—strong and intelligent, with a dominating personality. Eleanor was the refined, strong-willed, and beautiful Guinevere with a healthy dose of political savvy thrown in. Their son Richard the Lionhearted had, by contemporary accounts, the attributes of all the Knights of the Round Table rolled into one.

Their court was Europe's center for troubadours and young knights, for days spent in jousting and nights under the stars listening to stories and songs.

It was here that a new element was added to the old warrior's code of chivalry and love. The knight of this period had to be not only valiant in war but gentle in love as well. The new code was known as "courtly love."

Love was a radical notion in a society where marriages were arranged by parents, primarily for monetary and political gain. It was the brainchild of highly educated ladies of the court tired of being treated as bargaining chips in the marriage game. They insisted that both parties, the man and the woman, had to consent for a marriage to be valid.

Queen Eleanor had strong personal reasons for supporting romantic love and opposing arranged marriages. She and Henry had become estranged when Henry took a mistress (no big deal) and insisted on being seen with her in public (big deal). She was also aware of the fate of a young kinswoman, Alais, who had been given to young Richard for a bride. Because Richard was away on a Crusade, Henry thought nothing of taking Alais for his own, keeping her a prisoner for 25 years. At his death, she was freed only to be married off to a lesser courtier.

The new code of chivalry demanded that the knight serve his lady first; next in importance came service to God and king. In

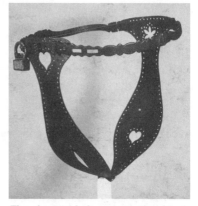

The chastity belt was another kind of fortification commonly used during the Crusades. With men away for so long these came in handy— not so much for jealous men as for frightened women.

tournaments and battles, it was customary for the knight to wear a token from the lady, perhaps a handkerchief or a flower.

The main theme of the troubadours' songs of *love* (*chansons d'amour*) was unconsummated love. The knight is head over heels for the lady but, alas, she is married or somehow beyond his reach. Nevertheless, the knight accepts this hopeless situation, pining for his true love and doing all in his power to please her, while knowing she can never be his. The songs alternate between the ecstasy of love and the bitterness of longing.

In the court of Queen Eleanor, "rules" of love were drawn up to "educate" the young men about how they should act toward the ladies. Knights had to give up their baser passions, thinking always of what would please their beloveds. Here are some of the court's "Twelve Rules of Love" (from a 12th-century book, *The Art of Courtly Love*):

- Marrying for money should be avoided like a deadly pestilence.
- Thou shalt keep thyself chaste for the sake of thy beloved. (A radical idea for the time.)
- In practicing the solaces of love thou shalt not exceed the desires of thy lover.
- Thou shalt not be a revealer of love affairs.
- Thou shalt be in all things polite and courteous.
- Thou shalt be obedient in all things to the command of ladies, and strive in the service of Love.

Historical fact shatters any illusions that Henry and Eleanor created a real-life Camelot. But the ideals of chivalry lived on long after knighthood lost its warring function. The 17th-century English gentleman and the *gentilhomme* of France owed much to the medieval code. The duel replaced the tournament as a test of courage.

Chivalry was dealt a satiric blow in literature by Cervantes, creator of the tragicomic fictional figure of Don Quixote (written in 1610). Ridiculed by his contemporaries, Don Quixote held fast to the old ideals, jousting with windmills when there were no other true knights left to fight.

Birth of Nation-States

During the High Middle Ages, feudalism gave way to urbanism. Cities broke the rural feudal mold. Merchants were natural allies of a national government, which offered political stability, uniform laws, coinage and measurements, freer trade, and independence from the whims of feudal lords.

An hour's cruise down the Rhine River, lined with castles (each a

The Battle of Hastings

The most memorable date of the Middle Ages is 1066 because of this pivotal battle. England's King Edward was about to die without an heir, and the question was who would succeed him: Harold, an English noble, or William, the Duke of Normandy?

Harold, the most logical candidate to be the next king, was captured during a battle in Normandy. To gain his freedom, he promised William that, when the ailing King Edward died, he would allow William to ascend the throne. Shortly after that oath was taken, Harold was back in England, Edward died, and Harold grabbed the throne. William, known as William the Bastard, was furious. He invaded England to claim the throne he figured was rightfully his.

Harold met him in southern England at the town of Hastings, where their forces fought a fierce 14-hour battle. Harold was killed and his Saxon forces routed. William—now "the Conqueror"—marched on London to claim his throne, becoming King of England as well as Duke of Normandy. (The advent of a Norman king of England muddied the political waters, setting in motion 400 years of conflict between England and France not to be resolved until the end of the Hundred Years' War in 1453.)

The Norman Conquest of England brought England into the European mainstream. The Normans established a strong central English government. They brought with them the Romanesque style of architecture (e.g., the Tower of London and Durham Cathedral) that the English call "Norman." Historians speculate that, had William not succeeded, England would have remained on the fringe of Europe (like Scandinavia), and French culture (and language) would have prevailed in the New World.

Bayeux Tapestry *(detail), about 1080 (Tapestry Museum, Bayeux, France). This 900-year-old embroidery tells the story of the Battle of Hastings. Typical of Romanesque art, realism takes a back seat to narration. Bayeux, a pleasant town, is only 2 hours by train from Paris.*

separate "kingdom" in its day), tells the story. In earlier times, a trading ship might have crossed 35 "national" boundaries and paid 35
customs duties just to take a load downstream. The urbanites welcomed a king who could keep the peace between the feuding feudal
nobles, creating a larger political unit more conducive to efficient business and trade. The time was ripe for the emergence of Europe's large
states.

Austria, ruled by the Hapsburg family (1298–1918), slowly bal-
looned into the vast Austro-Hungary empire, finally popped by World
War I. The Holy Roman Empire, loosely ruled for 10 centuries by
Germanic kings (800–1806), helped give a form and identity to what
later became Germany.

France, one of the earliest nation-states, pummeled England into
shape. When William the Bastard (of Normandy, France) crossed the
English Channel in 1066 and became William the Conqueror, he set
up a strong central government and forced a greater unification of
England's feudal lords.

England became part of the Angevin Empire, which, by the time of
Henry II and Queen Eleanor of Aquitaine, stretched from Scotland
south through western France to the Pyrenees. However, when Henry
and Eleanor's son Richard the Lionhearted died, England returned to
fragmented rule by local nobles. An assembly of English nobles
cemented their newly recovered autonomy by forcing the new King
John to sign the Magna Carta (1215), which constitutionally guaranteed that the king was not above the law.

The democratic victory of the Magna Carta set the stage in Europe
for hundreds of years of power struggles between strong kings and
strong nobles—who would later form the Parliaments in the new
nation-states.

Ultimately the demands of war required bigger states. For a power
to survive, it needed a big enough population and a strong enough
government to raise a viable army.

Church versus State

Throughout the Middle Ages, kings and popes played tug-of-war with
temporal power. After the year 1000, on the crest of a spiritual revival,
a series of energetic popes reformed the church, the monasteries, and
communications networks, establishing the papacy as a political
power to rival the kings.

In many ways, the medieval church operated like a nation without borders. It was Europe's greatest landowner, taxing through tithes,

Popes and the French Connection

From 1309 to 1377, popes ruled from Avignon instead of Rome—this was called the Babylonian Captivity. Then, from 1378 to 1417, two popes ruled simultaneously—one based in Avignon and the other in Rome. This was called the Great Western Schism.

The Babylonian Captivity was caused by the French King Philip IV. Unhappy with a Roman pope who threatened to excommunicate him, he engineered the election of a Frenchman as pope. The French pope ruled from Avignon, as did the six popes who succeeded him. In 1376, Catherine of Siena (later sainted) pressured Pope Gregory XI to return to Rome. He did in 1377, but the French Connection was far from over.

Pope Gregory XI died soon after returning the papacy to Rome. Cardinals were pressured to elect an Italian pope. After an Italian got the job, French cardinals met at Avignon and declared the election invalid, promptly electing a new pope who was— you'll never guess—a Frenchman.

During the Great Western Schism (1378–1417), Italian and French popes ruled concurrently. Kings and commoners chose their pope based on politics. In 1409, an ecumenical council elected a third pope, creating an unwanted Holy Trinity when the other popes didn't resign. Finally, one pope was deposed, another resigned, and the third was dismissed, clearing the way for a single pope in 1417.

These scandals torpedoed the papacy, but didn't sink it. The papal ship sailed along, badly in need of repair, en route to the Reformation 100 years hence.

influencing political decisions on all levels, and attracting Europe's most talented men to work in its service. Local kings and princes saw this rich and powerful spiritual organization as a meddler in their material realm.

This pope-king thing came to a head in the debate over who had the right to appoint bishops. The pivotal battle of wills was between Pope Gregory VII and "Holy Roman Emperor" Henry IV of Germany. The powerful German king appointed a bishop in his domain against the pope's will and was excommunicated. Despite his military might, Henry learned that his people supported him only if he was in good with the

Papal Palace
in Avignon

pope. Fighting for his political life, he "went to Canossa" (Italy, 1077) to beg forgiveness of the pope. The famous image of the Holy Roman Emperor kneeling for hours in the snow outside Gregory's window reminded later leaders that the pope was supreme.

The Vatican endorsed the Holy Roman Empire in return for its protection of papal interests around Europe. In the 14th century, the balance of power tipped away from both the emperor and the pope. The pope moved to Avignon and "ruled" as a puppet of the French king. Worse, the papacy was later split between two popes. The papacy never recovered from this humiliation. The power of the Holy Roman Empire also declined as powerful nation-states emerged.

The Inquisition

The church wielded a powerful weapon—the Inquisition. Started by Pope Gregory IX in 1231 to combat the "enemies of the Church," this network of church courts tried and punished heretics and sinners, ranging from witches, devil worshipers, and adulterers to Jews, Moslems, and unorthodox Christians. A later pope legalized the use of torture to "encourage" confessions. Among the church's enemies were the Cathars and the Hussites.

The Cathars were a heretical group of Christians based in Languedoc (southern France) from the 11th through the 13th centuries. They saw life as a battle between good (the spiritual) and bad (the material). They considered material things evil and of the devil. While others called them "Cathars" (from the Greek word for "pure") or "Albigenses" (for their main city, Albi), they called themselves simply "friends of God."

Cathars focused on the teachings of St. John and recognized only baptism as a sacrament. Because they believed in reincarnation, they were vegetarians.

Travelers encounter the Cathars in their Languedoc sightseeing because of impressive castles built during the Albigensian Crusades (1209–1240s). The king of France wanted to consolidate his grip on southern France. The pope needed to make a strong point that the only acceptable Christianity was Roman style. Both found self-serving reasons to wage a genocidal war against these people—who never amounted to more than 10 percent of the local population and who coexisted happily with their non-Cathar neighbors. After a terrible generation of torture and mass burnings, the Cathars were wiped out. The last Cathar was burnt in 1321. Today tourists find haunting castle ruins (once Cathar strongholds) high in the Pyrenees, and eat the hearty _salade Cathar_.

The Hussites were led by Jan Hus, a Czech preacher who got in trouble with the Vatican a hundred years before Martin Luther. Like Luther, Hus preached in the people's language rather than Latin. To add insult to injury, he complained about church corruption. Tried for heresy and burned in 1415, Hus roused nationalist as well as religious feelings and became a symbol of Czech martyrdom. A huge statue of Hus is the centerpiece of Prague's main square.

Monasteries

While the church played power politics and grew rich and corrupt, monasteries worked to keep the focus on religion, simplicity, and poverty. Two strong orders, the Dominicans and the Franciscans, emerged in the 12th and 13th centuries.

The Dominicans, founded by St. Dominic in 1215, were a mobile army of priests whose mission was to preach church doctrine wherever the pope felt they were needed. Their unswerving faith landed them unsavory tasks. St. Dominic and his troops tried to convert the Albigensians in southern France. They also managed the Inquisition. Today Dominicans focus on contemplation, study, and preaching. The many Dominican churches you'll see throughout Europe are easy to recognize by their simplicity.

In 1200, St. Francis caused a stir by challenging the decadence of church government and society in general. A powerful image from the movie _Brother Sun, Sister Moon_ shows a Christlike St. Francis walking down the Vatican aisle to ask an Oz-like pope to consider the possibility that the Church had lost its way.

Francis, whose father was a wealthy merchant, traded a life of power

***St. Francis receiving the Stigmata**—five marks simulating the wounds of Christ. These appear spontaneously on people of extraordinary faith after they meditate fervently on the sufferings of Jesus. (Giotto fresco, Basilica of St. Francis, Assisi)*

and riches for one of obedience, chastity, and poverty. This simple friar, like Jesus, taught by example. He advocated non-materialism, simplicity, and a "slow down and smell God's roses" lifestyle.

The huge Franciscan monastic order grew out of his teachings. Franciscan friars, known as the "Jugglers of God," became a joyful part of the community. The order was gradually embraced (some would say co-opted) by the church.

In an Italy torn by fighting between towns and families, Francis promoted peace and the restoration of order. He set an example by reconstructing a crumbled chapel. While the Church waged bloody Crusades, Francis pushed ecumenism and understanding. In 1939, Italy made Francis its patron saint.

But even determined Franciscans and Dominicans dressed in sackcloth couldn't resist the rich mortals of Europe throwing their wealth at them in hopes of a better chance at salvation. Monasticism peaked in the 13th century.

Gothic Art (1150–1400)

The combination of church wealth, political stability, and a reawakened spiritual fervor brought Europe a new artistic style—Gothic. Centered in rich, stable northern France, this style replaced the gloomy, heavy Romanesque with an exciting lightness and grace.

From the first page of the Bible, it's clear that light is divine. Abbot Suger, who "invented" the Gothic style in 1144 at St. Denis (just outside Paris, rebuilt and not worth visiting), wanted to create a cathedral of light. Europe also saw the light, and built churches with roofs held up by skeletons of support, freeing the walls to become window holders. Now when Christians went to church, they were bathed in the light of heaven.

The basic arches of medieval architecture

Gothic architecture began with technical improvements over Romanesque by lightening the massive "tunnel" vaults into graceful ribbed vaults. In a Romanesque church, the heavy stone roof arches over the supporting pillars like a bridge. These pillars had to be fortified into massive walls to support the weight, leaving only tiny windows and a dark place of worship.

Gothic architects, masters at playing architectural forces against each other, knew that while round arches send the weight of the roof straight down, pointed arches would send it outward. With pointed arches, churches could be built higher than ever while buttresses—rather than thick, fat walls—did the supporting. By using pointed arches in a crisscross pattern, spanning diagonally from column to column, the architects increased the strength still more.

To counteract the outward pressure, Gothic architects reinforced the walls with buttresses. "Flying" buttresses project away from the

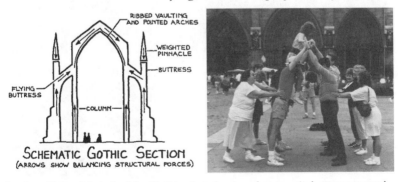

It takes 13 tourists to build a Gothic church: six columns, six buttresses, and one steeple.

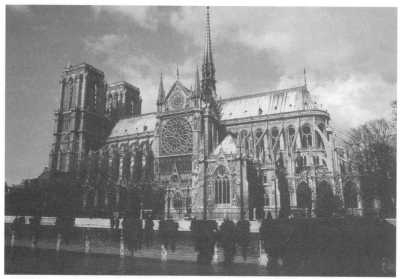

Notre Dame (b. 1163–1345), Paris, France

Duomo (b. 1386–1809), Milan, Italy

Dom (b. 1248–1880), Köln, Germany

Favorite Gothic Cathedrals

- Sainte-Chapelle (best pure Gothic and glass), Paris
- Notre-Dame (fine carving, view from top, gargoyles), Paris
- Reims (medieval and Chagall stained glass), France
- Chartres (fine glass and carvings, great tours by Malcolm Miller or his associate), France
- Mont St. Michel (worthwhile evening sound-and-light show), France
- Köln (best in Germany, great early art, worth a tour)
- King's College Chapel (best glass in Britain; bright, boxy perpendicular style; Rubens masterpiece), Cambridge
- Salisbury (fine setting, copy of Magna Carta), Britain
- York Minster, York (Britain's best)
- Toledo (best in Spain, sacristy has one of Europe's top collections of paintings, especially El Greco), Spain
- Orvieto (ornate facade, great Signorelli paintings), Italy
- Milan (a forest of Sequoia pillars and a fantasy rooftop open to the public), Italy

King's College Chapel, (b. 1446–1515), Cambridge, England. The Gothic style evolved into a very ornate "flamboyant" (flamelike) stage known as "perpendicular" in England. Here nearly all the wall space is devoted to brilliant stained glass. The essential ribbing on the ceiling is decorated with extra tracery, or purely ornamental riblets. This is aptly called "fan vaulting."

church several meters, offering even greater support while taking up even less wall space. In the end, the church was supported by a skeleton of columns, ribs, pointed arches, and buttresses. The roof became taller than ever and walls of glorious stained-glass windows lit the place of worship. Stained glass became a booming new medium for artists, providing an excellent opportunity for glorifying God in Technicolor enhanced by natural light.

The Gothic style evolved from a simple start to an elaborate finale. The basic supportive ribs of the kitty-corner arches (vaulting) were surrounded by a web of purely decorative arches called "tracery." Over time, this tracery became fantastically elaborate and complex and was often covered with gold. The last, most overripe stage in Gothic is called "flamboyant" (flamelike). You'll see the English version of flamboyant Gothic, called "perpendicular" Gothic, in the Henry VII Chapel of London's Westminster Abbey or King's College Chapel in Cambridge.

Sainte-Chapelle, b. 1246, Paris.
Supine view.

The Gothic style was very competitive. With architects, sculptors, and painters traveling all over Europe to compare and study new churches, Gothic church design was remarkably consistent.

Italy tempered the tense verticality inherent in Gothic architecture (pointy spires) to make it more compatible with the horizontal stability (temples) that came with her classic roots. This is particularly evident in the great Italian Gothic cathedrals of Florence (capped by Renaissance domes), Siena, and Orvieto—not so tall, no flying buttresses, and more likely to please a Caesar. These

Sainte-Chapelle *was built to house the Crown of Thorns. Relics were an important focus of worship in the medieval church. The king of France paid more for this crown than he paid for the Sainte-Chapelle, which was built to house the relic. Many great altarpieces are ornate relic-holders.*

This Gothic work shows the beheaded martyr, St. Denis, patron saint of Paris. Gothic sculpture protrudes from the wall and shows a sense of calm, orderly composure. In contrast, Romanesque sculpture is "low relief" (embedded deep in church walls and niches), cluttered, and tells a story. Still, Gothic carvings are symbolic rather than realistic, and sculpture remains supportive of the architecture, far from the bold freestanding works of the Renaissance.

churches make up for their stubbiness by sporting more colorfully decorated facades.

But there was more to Gothic than church architecture. There was a delight in things of beauty. Abbot Suger's favorite saying, "Man may rise to an understanding of the divine through the senses," is the intellectual basis of the Gothic love of things beautiful. Church sacristies and museums are filled with finely carved and inlaid works of Gothic art.

Throughout Europe, these largest economic enterprises of the Middle Ages represented an unprecedented technical accomplishment and tremendous spiritual dedication. The building of a Gothic church dominated the rich and poor alike of an entire area for generations. Paris' Notre-Dame took 200 years to complete.

Sculpture took a giant leap forward in Gothic times. No longer just pillars with faces, as Romanesque statues tended to be, Gothic sculpture was more natural and freestanding. Many classical techniques were used, especially in making clothing appear to drape naturally over the body. Sculpted faces reflected personality and emotions. But art was still considered to be a religious tool, and, like Gothic stained glass, every piece of sculpture had a symbolic message.

A Gothic church was carefully designed to be, and usually still is, a place of worship, not a museum. If you think of it as just a dead building to wander through and photograph, you'll see the nave but miss the boat. To best experience a Gothic church, see it in action. Attend a service.

Gothic cathedrals are especially exciting when filled with music. Attend a concert or enjoy an "evensong" service. Meditate, cup your hands behind your ears, and catch every echo as the music rinses the medieval magic into your head. Follow with your eyes the praying hands of the arches; the fingers point upward to heaven. Be dazzled by the warm light of the sun shining through the glistening treasure chest that was melted down and painted onto the timeless windows. A Gothic church can be as alive as you are.

Pre-Renaissance Troubles: The Black Death

"When was such a disaster ever seen? Even heard of? Houses were emptied, cities abandoned, countrysides untilled, fields heaped with corpses, and a vast, dreadful silence settled over all the world."
—Petrarch, 14th-century Italian writer

The medieval equivalent of a nuclear holocaust, the bubonic plague— or "Black Death"—killed as many as one-third of Europe's people in three long years (1347–1350). The disease spread quickly, killed horribly, and then moved on, leaving whole cities devastated in its wake. The economic, physical, and emotional shock is unsurpassed in European history. Most saw the plague as not just a disease but a heavenly curse "sent down upon mankind for our correction by the just wrath of God." Whatever the cause, it killed with such power and swiftness that "the living could scarcely bury the dead."

The Danse Macabre.
Fourteenth-century Europeans believed everything was going to Hell—which was an eternity of people dancing the chicken.

The Bubonic Plague: Origin and Symptoms

The plague came out of Central Asia to Europe in 1347. The Mongols, who were sieging a Genoese trading town on the Black Sea, had the plague. The clever commander catapulted diseased corpses into town and it spread. One Genoese ship escaped, bringing its terrible cargo to Sicily. By 1348, this plague had spread through Italy, France, and all of Europe. An estimated 30 million Europeans died.

The disease is caused by a bacteria carried by fleas (which travel on rats). Humans get it when bitten by the fleas, and then spread it by coughing. The unsanitary conditions in medieval Europe allowed the disease to move rapidly northward. London, Vienna, Florence, and Avignon (the papal city at the time) were particularly hard hit. In Florence alone, 100,000 died within four months. In some cities, 90 percent of the population was wiped out.

The symptoms were quick and harsh. The first sign was sneezing (hence, "bless you"), followed by the appearance of lumps or "buboes" (hence, "bubonic") in the groin or armpits, fever, constant vomiting (often blood), diarrhea, pneumonia, and, almost inevitably, death within three days.

So many died so quickly that there was no place to bury them. The survivors resorted to mass graves. After the churchyards were full, they made vast trenches where bodies were heaped. The disease was so infectious that it seemed impossible to avoid. The most frightening part was that nothing could be done to help the afflicted, and they were abandoned by the healthy to avoid contagion.

Europe was struck by a series of plagues. Convinced they were a punishment from God, certain fanatics thought worldwide repentance was necessary. The "Brotherhood of the Flatulence" tried to take the sins of Europe upon themselves. They marched through the cities, calling on the citizens to join them as they scourged themselves with whips. They became more popular in some areas than the priests, whose rituals had been powerless before the plague.

Europe Recovers: The Black Plague's Silver Lining

The plague eventually became just a lingering memory in Europe's collective subconscious. Petrarch, who witnessed the horror of the plague years, correctly prophesied: "Posterity, will you believe what we who lived through it can hardly accept? . . . Oh how happy will be future times, unacquainted with such miseries, perhaps counting our testimony as a mere fable!"

Strange as it may sound, some good came out of all the loss of life, creating the economy that would support the Renaissance more than a century later. With fewer people, labor was scarce, and the common worker could demand a better wage. Technology itself had not been affected by the plague, and there were now fewer people to divide the fruits of that technology.

The survivors went on a materialistic and hedonistic buying spree, trying to forget the horrors they'd seen. Luxury goods—fancy clothes, good food and drink, lavish houses, entertainment—were in high demand. For the first time, the lower classes enjoyed such "luxury items" as chairs, dishes, and fireplaces.

The Hundred Years' War

England and France fought each other on and off from 1337 through 1453. The war had more than enough causes. At the start, England controlled southwest France. The French tried to take that area back. Fueling the fire, the French supported the Scots in their fight with England. The French even tried to control the English wool trade in Flanders. English and French fishermen bickered over rights in the English Channel. Finally, in 1337, when King Edward III of England claimed the French throne (because his mother was the sister of three French kings), war broke out. Peasant rebellions, pillaging by unemployed soldiers, and an outbreak of the Black Plague all made this period even more of a mess.

Enter Joan of Arc, a 16-year-old peasant girl driven by religious voices. France's national heroine left home to support the dauphin Charles VII. (This boy prince was a "dauphin," heir to the throne but too young to rule.) Joan rallied and inspired the French. In 1430, Joan was captured by the Burgundians, who sold her to the English, who convicted her of heresy and burned her at the stake in Rouen.

France lost most of its battles with England, but since it was three times as rich and populous, it managed to win the war. England lost all its holdings in France—except the port of Calais, which it lost a hundred years later.

The war boosted the formation of a strong French state—hastening the decline of feudalism—and established England as a sea power.

More Pre-Renaissance Troubles

Europe suffered other labor pains in the century before the Renaissance. In addition to the deadly plague and bloody Hundred Years' War, Germany ripped itself to shreds in a lengthy civil war.

The monopoly of the papacy led to corruption and extravagance within the church. Its giant bureaucracy had become flabby and self-perpetuating, and the popes lived in a grander style than any king. When there were two popes (one in Avignon and one in Rome), they excommunicated each other. No one knew whose ring to kiss. Reform was badly needed.

It was a strange and troubled time, and social neurosis swept across Europe. People figured it had to be the wrath of God. The popularity of witchcraft soared; devil appeasement and death cults had much of Europe doing the *danse macabre*. Some figured, "What the heck, the end is near" and dove headlong into one last hedonistic fling.

The wars, like the plague earlier, thinned out and vitalized society. The dead were mostly Europe's poor. For the first time, demand for laborers exceeded the supply. The European ship of state had to treat its bilge rats with a little more respect. A lean Europe was primed and ready to ride the waves of the future. Serfs up.

Relax...

You've just covered 1,000 medieval years. Before you leave the Dark Ages and enter the bright glow of the Renaissance, let your eyes adjust and take a break.

The Middle Ages—the bridge between the ancient and modern worlds—are often misunderstood. Review the timeline. Overlay your travel dreams on the map of medieval Europe.

Timeline of Medieval Europe

After the fall of Rome, civilization stumbled through the Dark Ages, buoyed by the church, Byzantine Empire, and Charlemagne.

Then, in the pivotal year 1000, great changes began. Increased agricultural production, industry, and trade brought new prosperity. The Crusades were a dismal failure but did spark cultural exchange between East and West.

Looking at the timeline, we see the fruits of these High Middle Ages in the rise in building and art. The Crusaders brought back Eastern knowledge of castle building, and soon every feudal lord had his own stone home. The religious fervor embodied by the Crusades came to fruition in building churches, first in the Romanesque and, later, Gothic style. France, then Italy, England, and Germany, each developed its own type of Gothic, becoming increasingly more decorative.

As the European economy became more productive, centered in towns and relying more on trade and industry than on subsistence farming, feudalism was replaced by larger economic units such as city-states and quasi nations. With two (or three) popes, the Catholic Church lost its political power. The Black Plague and costly wars further destroyed the old order. But all that blood and chaos fertilized the fallow soils of European civilization. Modern Europe was about to blossom.

Europe in 1200

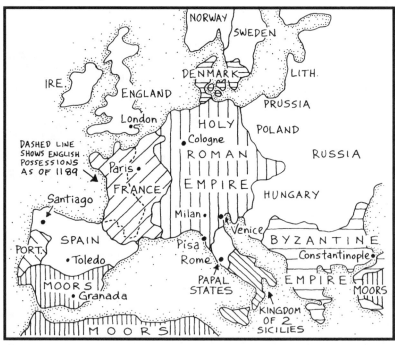

Timeline of the Middle Ages

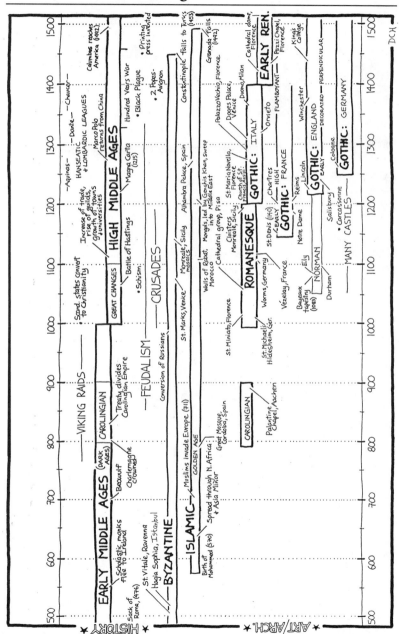

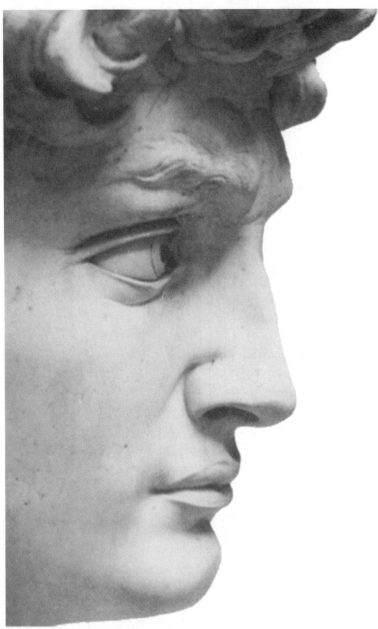

*Michelangelo, **David**, 1504 (Accademia, Florence). The face of the Renaissance. Man was the shaper of his destiny, no longer merely a plaything of the supernatural.*

The Renaissance
A.D. 1400–1600

"Renaissance" means rebirth. The Renaissance was the rebirth of the classical values of ancient Greece and Rome. Northern Italians, taking a fresh, new, secular view of life, considered themselves citizens of a new Rome.

The new Renaissance man was the shaper of his destiny and no longer a mere plaything of the supernatural. The belief in the importance of individualism and humanism skyrocketed, and life became much more than a preparation for the hereafter. People were optimistic and confident in their basic goodness and in their power to solve problems. This new attitude freed an avalanche of original thinking and creativity that gave our civilization its most exciting and fertile period of art since that great Greek streak 2,000 years earlier.

The Renaissance also did more for tourism than any other period in history. All over Europe, but especially in Italy, today's visitors set their touristic sights on the accomplishments of the creative geniuses of the Renaissance.

The Renaissance was a period of new birth, as well as rebirth, which laid the foundation of modern Europe. Politically, the modern nation-state was born. Economically, as capitalism replaced feudalism, the middle class was born. Intellectually, this period spawned the Protestant Reformation, humanism, modern science, and secularism.

Italy was the perfect launchpad for this cultural explosion. Italy's cities had become rich, serving as natural middlemen between the East with its luxury goods and the West with its merchants. Venice alone was bustling with 100,000 people and 3,000 ships in 1400. When the Byzantine Empire fell to the Turks in 1453, Byzantine scholars fled to Italy, bringing back her classical books, art, and ideas. Italy had never completely forgotten her heritage, and she welcomed its return.

The Renaissance followed the money: born in the trading and

banking capital of Florence, it migrated to Rome (as the pope gave the Vatican a face-lift) and then settled in Venice.

Northern Italy was the most urban corner of Europe. In 1400, 26 percent of its people were city dwellers, compared with the mere 10 percent of the English who lived in cities. Italian cities were generally independent, not having to cope with a pope or worry about a king. They did their own thing, and that required participation in government, more literacy, and better communication. This urban metabolism stimulated commerce and industry. The cities actively recruited skilled craftsmen, and the social structure became more flexible, offering the working class hope for improvement.

New ways of thinking brought prosperity. The most talented and ambitious men of the Middle Ages had served in the church. Now an active life of business and politics was considered just as meaningful and respectable as the passive, contemplative life of the monastery. Chasing money was not considered shameful, as long as the wealth was used properly. Secular schools based on Roman models became popular. Throughout Europe, educated upper-class people had a common culture based on a shared secular morality and language (Latin). Universities provided an international network besides the church to cut across borders and spread new ideas.

The Renaissance was not the repudiation of God; it was the assertion of humankind. In 1450, a Florentine author summed it up: "The world was created not for God, who had no need of it, but for man. Man is the most perfect work of God, the true marvel of His genius. Man has his end not in God, but in a knowledge of himself and his own creativity."

Renaissance Florence:
Cradle of the Modern World

There was something dynamic about the Florentines. Pope Boniface VIII said there were five elements: earth, air, fire, water... and Florentines. For 200 years, starting in the early 1300s, their city was a cultural hive.

Florence's contributions to Western culture are immense: the whole revival of the arts, humanism, and science; the seeds of democracy; the modern Italian language (which grew out of the popular Florentine dialect); the art of Botticelli, Leonardo, and Michelangelo; the writings of Machiavelli, Boccaccio, and Dante; and the explorations of Amerigo Vespucci, who gave his name to a fledgling continent. Florentines considered themselves descendants of the highly cultured people of the Roman Empire. But Florence, even in its Golden Age, was always a mixture of lustiness and refinement. The streets were filled with tough-talking, hardened, illiterate merchants who strode about singing verses from Dante's _Divine Comedy._

Florentine culture came from money, and that money came from the wool trade, silk factories, and banking. The city had a large middle class and strong guilds (labor unions for skilled craftsmen). Their success was a matter of civic pride, and Florentines showed that pride in the mountains of money they spent to rebuild and beautify the city.

Technically, Florence was a republic, ruled by elected citizens rather than a nobility. While there was a relatively large middle class and some opportunity for upward mobility, power lay in the hands of a few wealthy banking families. The most powerful was the Medici family. The Medici bank had branches in 10 sites in Europe, including London, Bruges (Belgium), and Lyon (France). The pope kept his checking account in the Rome branch. The Florentine florin was the monetary standard of the Continent.

Florence dominated Italy economically and culturally, but not militarily. The independent Italian city-states squabbled and remained scattered until the nationalist movement four centuries later. (When someone suggested to the Renaissance Florentine Niccolo Machiavelli that the Italian city-states might unite against their common enemy, France, he wrote back, "Don't make me laugh.")

Lorenzo de Medici (1449–1492), inheritor of the family's wealth and power and his grandfather Cosimo's love of art, was a central figure of the Golden Age. He was young (20 when he took power), athletic, and intelligent, in addition to being a poet, horseman, musician, and leader. He wrote love songs and humorous dirty songs to be sung loudly and badly at carnival time. His marathon drinking bouts and illicit love affairs were legendary. He learned Greek and Latin and read the classics, yet his great passion was hunting. He was the Renaissance Man—the man of knowledge and action, the scholar and man of the world, the patron of the arts, and the shrewd businessman. He was Lorenzo the Magnificent.

Lorenzo epitomized the Florentine spirit of optimism. Born on New Year's Day and raised in the lap of luxury (Donatello's _David_ stood in the family courtyard) by loving parents, he grew up feeling that there was nothing he couldn't do. Florentines saw themselves as part of a "new age," a great undertaking of discovery and progress in man's history. They boasted that within the city walls there were more "nobly gifted souls than the world has seen in the entire thousand years

Botticelli, **The Birth of Venus,** *after 1482 (Uffizi, Florence). More graceful, thinner, and more flowing than the massive figures of Masaccio and Michelangelo. Her long neck and smooth skin appear almost medieval.*

before." These people invented the term "Dark Ages" for the era that preceded theirs.

Lorenzo surrounded himself with Florence's best and brightest. They formed an informal "Platonic Academy," based on that of ancient Greece, to meet over a glass of wine under the stars at the Medici villa and discuss literature, art, music, and politics—witty conversation was considered an art in itself.

Their "neo-Platonic" philosophy stressed the goodness of man and the created world; they believed in a common truth behind all religion. The Academy was more than just an excuse to go out with the guys: the members were convinced that their discussions were changing the world and improving their souls.

Botticelli was a member of the Platonic Academy. He painted scenes from the classical myths that the group read, weaving contemporary figures and events into the ancient subjects. He gloried in the nude body, which he considered God's greatest creation.

Artists such as Botticelli thrived on the patronage of wealthy individuals, government, church groups, and guilds. Botticelli commanded as much as 100 florins for one work, enough to live for a year in high style, which he did for many years. In Botticelli's art we see the lightness, gaiety, and optimism of Lorenzo's court.

Another of Lorenzo's protégés was the young Michelangelo. Impressed with his work, Lorenzo took the poor, unlearned 14-year-old boy into the Medici household and treated him like a son.

Michelangelo's playmates were the Medici children, later to become Popes Leo X and Clement VII, who would give him important commissions. For all the encouragement, education, and contacts Michelangelo received, the most important gift from Lorenzo was simply a place at the dinner table, where Michelangelo could absorb the words of the great men of the time and their love of art for art's sake.

Savonarola: A Return to the Middle Ages

Even with all the art and philosophy of the Renaissance, violence, disease, and warfare were present in medieval proportions. For the lower classes, life was as harsh as it had always been. Many artists and scholars wore swords and daggers as part of everyday dress. This was the time of the ruthless tactics of the Borgias (known for murdering their political enemies) and of other families battling for power. Once, Lorenzo himself barely escaped assassination in the cathedral during Easter Mass; his brother died in the attack.

Fifteenth-century Florence was decaying. The Medici banks began to fold due to mismanagement and political troubles. The city's wealth had brought decadence and corruption. Even Lorenzo got caught with his hand in the till. Many longed for a "renaissance" of good, old-fashioned medieval values.

Into Florence rode a Dominican friar named Savonarola, preaching fire and brimstone and the sinfulness of wealth, worldly art, and secular humanism. He was a magnetic speaker, drawing huge crowds, whipping them into a frenzy with sharp images of the corruption of the world and the horror of hell it promised. "Down, down with all gold and decoration," he roared, "down where the body is food for the worms." He presided over huge bonfires where his believers burned "vanities" such as fancy clothes,

Savonarola

*Botticelli, **Slander**, 1495 (Uffizi, Florence). The Florentine Renaissance passed. Savonarola turned the city into a theocracy. High thinking is clubbed and dragged ingloriously past Renaissance statues that look down from their perfectly proportioned world with shock and disbelief. Ideal Venus looks up at God and seems to say, "Not the Dark Ages again!"*

cosmetics, jewelry, wigs, and dice, as well as classical books and paintings.

When Lorenzo died, the worldly Medicis were thrown out, replaced by a theocracy with Jesus Christ at its head and Savonarola ruling in His absence. The theocracy (1494–1498) was a grim part of the Renaissance. Many leading scholars and artists followed Savonarola's call and gave up their worldly pursuits. Vice squads of boys and girls roamed the streets chastising drinkers, gamblers, and overdressed women. Even so, governmental and church reforms promised by Savonarola were never accomplished.

As the atmosphere of general fanaticism faded, so did Savonarola's popularity. In April 1498, to prove his saintliness and regain public support, he offered to undergo the "ordeal by fire"—to be burned at the stake and escape unharmed. At the last minute he got cold feet, backed out, and was arrested. Then he had no choice. He was hanged and burned at the stake in the town square. (A plaque on Florence's main square marks the spot.) The Medicis returned.

Florence in 1500 was a more somber place than it had been during the heady days of Lorenzo. Under Savonarola's spell, Botticelli had given up painting his nudes and pagan scenes; his art took on a melancholy air.

The center of the Renaissance gradually shifted to Rome, but her artists were mostly Florentine. In the 15th century, the Holy City of Rome was a dirty, decaying, crime-infested place, unfit for the hordes of pilgrims that visited each year. The once-glorious Forum was a cow pasture. Then a series of popes, including Lorenzo's son and nephew, launched a building and beautification campaign. They used fat commissions (and outright orders) to lure Michelangelo, Raphael, and others to Rome. The Florentine Renaissance, far from over, moved southward.

Renaissance Art

The Renaissance accomplishments most obvious to the tourist are those in art and architecture. The art of the 15th and 16th centuries is a triumph of order, harmony, and the technical remastery of the secrets of the classical artists which had been lost during the Middle Ages. This period also saw the discovery and exploration of many new artistic techniques.

Like Greece's Golden Age, the Renaissance was a time of balance between stiff formality and wild naturalism. Later, in the Baroque period (as in Greece's Hellenistic era), the artists went overboard in their naturalism, losing the sense of order in their works.

Renaissance art has many classical characteristics: realism, glorification of the human body, nonreligious themes, and an appreciation of beauty for its own sake. As in Greece and Rome, the focus was earthly and humanist. As in classical times, balance—between emotion and calm, between motion and rest, and among the various figures in the composition—was important. Medieval art showed God's viewpoint. Space and time didn't matter. Now, perspective attached the viewer to the scene.

Acquiring beautiful art was a rich man's hobby. The new secular patronage stimulated art, giving it more pizzazz. The artist was hired to please the viewer sensually and to satisfy the patron. Youth, the good life, and wealth were sexy. Rich merchants of the Italian city-states commissioned art for their personal collections and for public display as a show of civic pride. They wanted art to reflect the power, dignity, and vitality of humankind.

The medieval church's monopoly on art was broken. Secular

Art from the Middle Ages to the Renaissance

From the Middle Ages to the Renaissance, art progressed from flat-narrative Byzantine to colorful, delicate Gothic to realistic Renaissance. Notice the two Botticelli nudes. They are both ideal "tens" in the classical style. At first it had to be labeled Biblical... "Eve." Later you could call a Venus a Venus.

Byzantine mosaic

Fra Angelico, **The Annunciation** *(detail), 1435 (Prado, Madrid). With no interest in anatomy, you're washing dishes with two left-hand rubber gloves.*

Botticelli's
Eve

Botticelli's
Venus

Tips on Sightseeing in Italy

- Churches offer some amazing art (usually free), a cool respite from heat, and a welcome seat. A modest dress code (no bare shoulders or shorts for men or women) is enforced at larger churches such as Venice's St. Mark's and the Vatican's St. Peter's. A coin box near a piece of art often illuminates the art for a coin (and a better photo). Whenever possible, let there be light.
- Advance reservations are advisible for some of the more famous museums (Florence: Uffizi) and mandatory at others (Milan: Da Vinci's Last Supper, Rome: Borghese Gallery and Nero's Golden House).
- Some sights are open throughout the evening, allowing easy viewing without crowds. For a listing of hours, use a good guidebook (I'm partial to ours) and confirm at the local tourist information office.
- Art historians and Italians refer to the great Florentine centuries by dropping a thousand years. The Trecento (300s), Quattrocento (400s), and Cinquecento (500s) were the 1300s, 1400s, and 1500s.
- In Italian museums, art is dated with A.C. (for Avanti Cristo, or B.C.) and D.C. (for Dopo Cristo, or A.D.). Got it?
- In museums, individual rooms can begin closing about 30 to 60 minutes before the museum closes. If your heart is set on one piece of art, don't save it for the finale.
- WCs at museums are usually free and clean.
- About half the visitors at Italian museums are English (not Italian) speakers. If the only English you encounter at a museum explains how to pay, politely ask if there are plans to include English descriptions of the art. Think of it as a service to those who follow.

patronage opened new realms for artists previously confined to religious subjects. Pagan themes were popular.

Many Renaissance artists were devout, however, and created works more emotional and moving than anything produced during the Middle Ages. They glorified God by glorifying humanity, His greatest creation. Religious themes were portrayed more realistically, emphasizing the human aspect.

Artists of the Renaissance deserved the respect they got. They merged art and science; their apprenticeships required mastery of the mathematical laws of perspective. They studied nature as a biologist would. They studied human anatomy as avidly as a doctor, learning not just how the body looks but also how it works, so they could catch it in motion. They were well-rounded Renaissance men.

Technical expertise, secular patronage, religious devotion, and the classical love of sheer beauty raised Europe to an unprecedented level of artistic excellence.

Renaissance Architecture

The proud people of the Renaissance looked down on the Dark Ages that separated the glorious ancient world from their own glorious time. They labeled the art "Gothic" after the barbarians who looted Rome. To them, Gothic cathedrals looked tense, strained, and unstable. The Renaissance architect turned to his ancient Roman forefathers and developed, or rediscovered, a style that was round, geometrical, stout, symmetrical, domed, and balanced.

Filippo Brunelleschi (broon-uh-LES-kee, 1377–1446) fathered Renaissance architecture, traveling to Rome to carefully measure and study the classical buildings and monuments. Back in his hometown of Florence, he conscientiously copied Roman styles, building with columns, arches, pediments, and domes.

Brunelleschi's masterpiece was the huge dome of Florence's cathedral, a triumph of beauty and science, demonstrating that Renaissance architects were the equals of the great builders of Rome. It was the model for many domes to follow. The classical order and the harmony of his design

*Brunelleschi, **Cathedral Dome,** 1420–1436, Florence. Inspired by the ancient Pantheon, this dome in turn inspired later ones, from Michelangelo's to the present.*

Top Renaissance Architecture in Italy
- San Miniato al Monte (church on a hill), Florence
- Cathedral dome, Florence
- Hospital of the Innocents (Brunelleschi), Florence
- Uffizi Gallery (the building), Florence
- Pazzi Chapel, Florence
- St. Peter's dome, Rome
- Tempietto, Rome
- Capitol Hill Square (Michelangelo), Rome
- Urbino Palace, Urbino
- Many palaces in Venice
- Palmanova, a planned town (north of Venice)

Pazzi Chapel, *Florence*

Palmanova, *1593, near Udine, northeast of Venice. In the Renaissance, every snowflake's the same.*

of his design caused great excitement, inspiring other artists to mix Roman forms with original designs.

Italian architects and artists, in demand throughout Europe, had no shortage of commissions to build secular palaces, homes, and public buildings in the Renaissance style. The pope hired Michelangelo to travel to Rome and design the dome of St. Peter's, Christendom's greatest cathedral. French kings built Renaissance châteaus on the Loire, and even the Russian tsar imported Italian expertise to remodel Moscow's Kremlin in the new style.

Renaissance church design echoed the upbeat optimism and confidence of the time by trading the medieval Latin cross floor plan

Brunelleschi's **Church of San Lorenzo** *(Florence, 1421) is typical of Renaissance architecture: balance, symmetry, arches, Corinthian columns, track lighting, circles, and squares.*

(symbolic of the Crucifixion) for the Greek cross floor plan (four equal arms symbolizing the perfection of God and the goodness of man, who was made in His image).

Early Renaissance Sculpture: Donatello

Like the ancients, Renaissance sculptors concentrated on portraying accurate, three-dimensional, natural, and ideally naked human bodies. They posed their statues classically, catching their subjects balanced between motion and rest.

Donatello (1386–1466) was the first true Renaissance sculptor, combining the skill of creating classical sculpture with the boldness of the Renaissance. Donatello helped sculpture emerge from the shadows of church architecture.

In earlier Gothic cathedrals (such as Chartres), stiff columnlike figures are embedded in the wall, entirely supportive of the architecture. To see how far Donatello had progressed from Gothic sculpture, compare his *St. George* with Nanni di Banco's *Four Saints,* done at the same time for the same church in Florence. Nanni's saints hide within a deep Gothic niche, attached to half columns, afraid to step from the safe support of the church. Donatello's confident *St. George* steps right up to the edge of his niche and looks boldly into the future. Renaissance Man is stepping out.

A few years later, Donatello sculpted *David,* the first freestanding nude statue since ancient times. *David* stood on his own in the light of day: proud, naked, and ready to do a little fencing. Donatello freed sculpture from its thousand-year subservience to architecture.

Donatello's *David* was bought by a wealthy citizen for private display.

From Gothic to Renaissance: Sculpture Breaks Free

Sculpture gradually emerged from the shadows of church architecture. At Chartres, the stiff, columnlike figures are embedded in the Gothic wall. Nanni's Four Saints has Renaissance solidity but still sits deep in a niche. Nanni sat on the cusp of the revolution. Donatello's confident St. George steps right up to the edge of his niche and looks boldly into the future. Renaissance Man is stepping out. A few years later, Donatello's *David* stood on his own in the light of day: proud, naked, and ready to do a little fencing.

Cathedral sculpture, 1140, Chartres, France. "Going up."

Di Banco, **Four Saints,** *1413 (Orsanmichele Church, Florence)*

Donatello, **St. George,** *1416 (Orsanmichele, Florence). He stands like a symbol of the Renaissance man: alert yet relaxed, strong yet refined, aggressive yet Christian. The serene beauty of medieval art was being replaced by the defiant and determined new outlook.*

Donatello, **David,** *1430 (Bargello, Florence). The first freestanding male nude sculpted since Roman times, this boy David (looking like Boy George) is blatant art for art's sake.*

Secular patronage freed the artist from medieval constraints. During the Middle Ages, *David* would have been condemned as a pagan idol. Although the subject matter comes from the Bible (the boy David killing the giant Goliath), it's just an excuse for a classical study of a male nude. The focus is on the curves of the body (no longer a "dirty" thing), not the action or the facial expression. The statue is a simple appreciation of beauty. Art for art's sake.

Early Renaissance Painting

The great Florentine painters were sculptors with brushes. They painted the same way the ancient Greeks had sculpted, making solid figures that had great weight, solemnity, and presence. Many of these artists, such as Michelangelo, were equally famous for sculpting and painting. During the Renaissance, both painting and sculpture evolved from the flat symbolism of medieval art to three-dimensionality and full realism.

Giotto (pronounced JOTT-o, 1267–1337), who preceded the Renaissance by 100 years, made the first radical break with the medieval past. He is the father of modern painting. Nothing like his astonishing paintings had been seen in a thousand years. Medieval artists painted stiff, two-dimensional figures with no sense of movement. Backgrounds didn't matter. Subjects were icons as seen from God's perspective. Painters told religious stories with symbols.

But Giotto takes us right to the scene of the action. He places his figures on a 3-D landscape, giving them depth, weight, and individuality. It's as though he has created small theater vignettes, designing the stage scenery and then peopling it with actors.

Much of Giotto's art was Gothic, with gold-leaf backgrounds, halos, unrealistic scale, and no visible light source. But Giotto was influenced by Byzantium and made great strides toward realism. The Byzantine influence (which the Byzantine East had stored in an artistic time capsule since the fall of Rome) gave Giotto the classical techniques of light, shading, and foreshortening, providing the illusion of depth. His style excited the West and stimulated a renewed interest in the classics. The largest single collection of his work is in Padua's Scrovigni Chapel, frescoed with more than 30 beautifully preserved scenes from the lives of Jesus and Mary.

Giotto was famous and in demand throughout Italy. This popularity for a painter was as revolutionary as his work. Giotto made it into all the gossip columns. Anecdotes were told about his social wit as well as his skill as a painter.

A century later, the Florentine Masaccio (ma-SAH-cho, 1401–1427)

Duccio, **Maesta,** *1285*   *Giotto,* **Ognissanti Madonna,** *1310*

In Duccio's purely Gothic painting (left), the angels are stacked up the sides, ornamenting Mary's throne. Just a generation later, Giotto's depiction (right) of the same scene shows more interest in realistic depth. Note how Giotto's angels are placed more naturally. Singlehandedly, Giotto nearly started the Renaissance a century before its time. To give depth to his painting, he used shadows and an architectural framework.

carried Giotto's techniques further by using light and shadow to depict depth and drama. Applying the mathematical laws of perspective that Brunelleschi developed, Masaccio portrayed objects receding into the distance (for example, a tree-lined road). Masaccio, who died at the age of 26, was more influential than he was famous. The anatomical realism

Giotto, **Return of Joachim to the Sheepfold,** *1305 (Arena Chapel, Padua, Italy). Working for the illusion of 3-D, he painted sculptural people in realistic settings. The background (the cliff) and foreground (the sheep) give the scene lifelike depth.*

Masaccio's **Trinity** *in Santa Maria Novella, Florence. The mathematically correct architectural backdrop of this early Renaissance fresco gives it a believable three-dimensionality. Notice also how the symmetrical pyramid of figures provides a solid composition.*

and dramatic power of his paintings (such as *The Expulsion of Adam and Eve from the Garden of Eden*, in Florence's Brancacci Chapel, see next page) inspired many masters who followed.

After Masaccio, lesser painters such as Uccello (oo-CHEL-lo, 1396–1475) grappled with the new problems of perspective. Uccello's *Battle of San Romano* looks like a crowded, colorful, two-dimensional work in the medieval style. It's only when we look closer that we see it as a study in perspective: all the fallen weapons form a three-dimensional grid superimposed on the background. The fallen soldier at left is scarcely larger than the fallen helmet at right in Uccello's awkward attempt at foreshortening. All in all, it's a fascinating but weak transition from two-dimensional Gothic to three-dimensional Renaissance realism.

Uccello, **Battle of San Romano,** *1455 (National Gallery, London). Panels from this early attempt at 3–D traveled from Lorenzo's study to the Uffizi, the Louvre, and London's National Gallery.*

Three Expulsions:
Medieval, Early Renaissance, and High Renaissance

In these three, look at the expulsion of Adam and Eve from the garden of Eden, and compare medieval, early Renaissance, and high Renaissance views of the same scene. Notice the artistic differences, as well as how man's view of himself in relation to God changes. In the medieval example, Adam and Eve are puny, bug-like creatures, ashamed of their nakedness and helpless before God. In Masaccio's painting, you feel the agony of a lifelike, suf-

fering Adam and Eve. Michelangelo shows a strong Adam with a gesture that almost says, "All right, already, we're going!" While Adam knows he and Eve will survive, Eve wonders, "Shouldn't we be wearing our money belts?"

Medieval church of St. Michael,
1015, Hildesheim, Germany

Michelangelo, **Sistine Chapel,**
1508–1512 (Vatican Museum, Rome)

Masaccio, **Brancacci**
Chapel, *1425, Florence*

And The Winner Is...

The contest to decorate the bronze doors of Florence's Baptistery encouraged artists throughout the city, including Brunelleschi and Ghiberti.

*Brunelleschi's entry and Ghiberti's entry. You be the judge. Here are the two finalists for the **Baptistery door** competition. Which do you like the best? The originals stand side by side in Florence's Bargello Museum.*

*Ghiberti, **Story of Jacob and Esau**, 1430.*
Here, the winning artist shows mastery of depth and perspective.

(Ghiberti's, on the left, won.)

Botticelli, **Allegory of Spring**, *1482 (Uffizi, Florence). Pagan innocence. Botticelli was part of a youthful band of Florentines who saw beauty as an expression of the divine.*

Perspective was mastered by relief artists of the period, such as Lorenzo Ghiberti (guh-BEAR-tee, 1378–1455). In Ghiberti's famed bronze doors of Florence's Cathedral baptistery, we see Brunelleschi's influence. The Story of Jacob and Esau (one of 10 Bible scenes on the door) includes imaginary Brunelleschian architectural forms in the background receding into the distance.

Botticelli (bot-i-CHEL-lee, 1445–1510) excelled in his mastery of color, detail, and line. Not as sculptural as Masaccio, Michelangelo, and other Renaissance artists, Botticelli's figures have a pure, elegant, yet dreamlike quality. He mixed Gothic grace and naked classicism in his popular and wonderfully restored masterpieces *La Primavera* and *The Birth of Venus* (both in Florence's Uffizi Gallery). A master diplomat, Botticelli was able to do justice to the pagan classical scenes he loved while not offending the religious powers with too much flesh.

The High Renaissance: Leonardo, Michelangelo, and Raphael

The High Renaissance was humanist. Artists explored sacred, secular, and sexy themes, glorifying human attributes. Huge projects were

Major Collections of Renaissance Painting
- Uffizi, Florence
- Pinacoteca Gallery, Vatican Museum, Rome
- Accademia, Venice
- Louvre, Paris
- National Gallery, London
- Kunsthistorisches, Vienna
- Alte Pinakothek, Munich
- Prado, Madrid

Leonardo da Vinci,
Self-Portrait

undertaken. Subjects were sometimes larger than life (Michelangelo's *David*). Leonardo, Michelangelo, and Raphael were revered as geniuses. Their presence at a party made the evening.

The art of the Early Renaissance had concentrated mainly on religious themes, with subjects more lifelike than heroic. Artists were still craftsmen, groveling like anonymous laborers for a prince's commission. During the High Renaissance, when every town and court was competing for a famous artist's work, the tables turned—the artist could almost dictate his terms and create what he wanted for whichever lucky prince landed him. Even though the artist still had a patron to keep happy, he could create more freely than ever before.

The art of Leonardo, Michelangelo, and Raphael was the culmination of the Renaissance. The tremendous output of "the big three" sprang from their personal genius, spurred by a huge demand for quality art. Never before had artists been asked to do so much and been given so much money and freedom to do it. Cities wanted monuments and public buildings. Wealthy individuals wanted palaces and decorations. Popes wanted churches. And all of them wanted to hire Leonardo, Michelangelo, or Raphael.

Leonardo da Vinci

Leonardo da Vinci (1452–1519) typified the well-rounded Renaissance man. He was a painter, sculptor, engineer, musician, and scientist. He learned from nature, not books, which made his observations often more accurate than those of contemporary scholars.

Leonardo wrote in his notebooks in code (backward and inside out as if reflected in a mirror) in case some of his thoughts could be construed as heretical. From his notes, we know he dissected corpses, investigated the growth of fetuses in the womb, formulated laws of waves and currents, studied the growth of plants, and diagrammed the flight of birds and insects. He also designed military fortifications and sketched many inventions, foreshadowing the development of the airplane and submarine. Some claim he even envisioned a crude carry-on-the-plane-sized convertible suitcase/rucksack.

Though learned and witty, Leonardo was considered something of a flake who never finished his projects. His claim to fame as a youth was his fine lute playing. In later life, he was best known for his painting and sculpting. In spite of his popularity and the demand for his work, he was temperamental and often left works undone. Leonardo insisted on working at his own pace. None of Leonardo's sculptures and only about 20 of his paintings survive.

The Last Supper demonstrates Leonardo's mastery of balance, realism, and drama. Depicting Christ and his 12 disciples, it's painted on the wall of a church, positioned so it looks like just another chapel extending off the aisle. The lines of the walls recede toward the horizon (following the laws of perspective) and come together at Christ's head. All the motion of the picture flows toward that serene center, giving the masterpiece a subconscious cohesiveness. Leonardo composed the Twelve in groups of three (groups of three symbolize the Trinity; four, the Gospels). Each group contributes a dramatic movement in a wavelike

Leonardo da Vinci, **Last Supper,** *1498 (Santa Maria delle Grazie, Milan). The lines of perspective tell us Jesus is the target ... whatever the price. The fresco, in a terrible state of repair, is a disappointment to visit.*

Leonardo da Vinci, **Virgin and Child with St. John the Baptist and St. Anne** *(National Gallery, London). Baby Jesus enjoys a pyramid of maternal security (while St. Anne whispers into Mary's ear, "It's just not fair when a kid's birthday falls on Christmas").*

effect, either moving toward or pulling away from the central figure of Jesus.

Despite this complex composition, the picture is highly emotional, not forced or sterile. The Lord has just said that one of the disciples will betray him. Leonardo paints a psychological portrait of each of them at the very moment they ask, "Lord, is it I?"

It's said that Leonardo went whole days without painting a stroke, just staring at the work. Then he'd grab a brush, rush up, flick on a dab of paint... and go back to staring.

Leonardo used a technique called *sfumato*. He blurred the outlines and mellowed the colors around the borders of his subject, making the edge blend with the background. This makes Lisa appear lifelike and her smile appear mysterious. Try as you will, you can't actually see the corners of her mouth.

When you finally see this most famous painting, you might wonder, "Why is she so famous?" Since *Mona Lisa* first went on public view, she's been a people's favorite because of her secretive smile and the sense that this ordinary-looking noblewoman of low rank is "one of us." The painting was Leonardo's personal favorite, one he never sold, keeping it in his possession until he died. (Leonardo spent his last years living in Amboise on the Loire, in the service of French King Francis I. So *Mona Lisa* wound up in the French collection.) The por-

Works of Leonardo da Vinci
- *Mona Lisa, Madonna of the Rocks, John the Baptist*, Louvre, Paris
- His home and models of inventions, Amboise, Loire, France
- *Last Supper*, Santa Maria delle Grazie, Milan, Italy
- National Leonardo da Vinci Science and Technology Museum, Milan
- *St. Jerome*, Pinacoteca Gallery, Vatican Museum, Rome
- *Annunciation* and *Adoration of the Magi*, Uffizi Gallery, Florence
- *Virgin and Child* (cartoon) and *Madonna of the Rocks*, National Gallery, London
- *Madonna and Child*, Alte Pinakothek, Munich, Germany

Leonardo's **Mona Lisa**, *1505, found in tourist shops throughout Paris (and in the Louvre—just follow the crowds).*

trait of Mona was kidnapped early in the 20th century. Her safe recovery made headlines, boosting her fame even higher. Artistically, she epitomizes the art of the Renaissance: balanced, subtle, and true.

Michelangelo

Michelangelo Buonarroti (1475–1564), perhaps the greatest painter and sculptor of all time, mastered nature and strove to master himself. Michelangelo's art reflects the inner turmoil of his emotional and spiritual life. His biography is as important as his work; the two are intertwined.

At the age of 15 Michelangelo was a prodigy, a favorite of Florence's leading citizen, Lorenzo de Medici. After serving his apprenticeship, he became dissatisfied with book knowledge and set out to study nature firsthand.

Michelangelo, **Capitol Hill Square,** *1550, Capitol Hill, Rome. Michelangelo, typical of the Renaissance genius, was expected to sculpt, paint, and be a world-class architect on command.* No problema. *He designed this square above the Roman Forum.*

He had the curiosity and quick mind of Leonardo, but he applied them to only one subject: the human body. Mastering the techniques of the ancient Greeks and Romans, he added to them by dissecting corpses to learn anatomy. Dissection, which was strictly illegal, was key to understanding the body and portraying it realistically.

Throughout his life, Michelangelo's talents were in great demand. He worked for nine popes. Even more than Leonardo, Michelangelo struggled to remain independent of his patrons' demands. And he succeeded.

Despite his great technical skill, Michelangelo thought that true creative genius came not from the rational planning of the artist, but from divine inspiration. He was one of the first "mad geniuses," working only when he felt inspired and then going at it with the intensity of a maniac. Michelangelo took Plato's words to heart: "If anyone tries to be an artist without the madness of the Muses, persuaded that skill alone will make him good, then both he and his works of sanity shall be brought to nothing."

Michelangelo's statues show us this divine genius trapped within the body, struggling to get out. The works are outwardly calm, stable, and balanced, but seem to be charged with pent-up energy. They con-

Michelangelo, **David,** _1504 (Accademia, Florence). Michelangelo's version of the giant-slayer shows the Renaissance Man in full bloom—alert, poised, cultured, ready to conquer his foe. Man has asserted himself. Donatello's boy-toy David now eats meat._

vey the inner restlessness and turmoil that marked Michelangelo's own life.

David, sculpted when Michelangelo was 26, displays this blend of vibrant energy and calm. _David's_ posture is relaxed, but his alert, intense stare reminds us of Donatello's Christian warrior, _St. George._ Michelangelo's _David_ became a symbol of the ready-for-anything confidence of the Florentine Renaissance.

When this monumental 13' 5"–tall _David_ was unveiled, it was understood that a new era in art history had begun. He was designed to stand atop one of the buttresses of the cathedral, but the city fathers elected to put him in a more visible spot outside the town hall (the Palazzo Vecchio) as a symbol of civic pride. Some interpret this location as a symbol of the republic's overthrow of the Medici autocracy. Today a _David_ copy stands in the square; the original is in the Accademia, a 15-minute walk away.

Donatello's _David_ is young and graceful, coyly gloating over the head of Goliath, almost Gothic in its elegance and smooth lines. Michelangelo's _David_ is pure Renaissance: more massive, heroic in size, and superhuman in strength and power. The tensed right hand, which grips a stone in readiness to hurl at Goliath, is much larger and more powerful than any human hand; it's symbolic of divine strength. When you look into _David's_ eyes you're looking into the eyes of Renaissance man.

At times, Michelangelo must have felt cursed by the "divine genius" within him and its accompanying responsibility to create. His _Prisoners,_ works that struggle to free themselves from the uncut stone

Michelangelo's **David** *with* **Prisoners,** *c. 1518 (Accademia, Florence)*

around them, symbolize the struggle of the divine soul to free itself from the prison of the body.

Many painters, including Leonardo, thought of themselves as almost divine creators who could take a blank canvas and make a beautiful picture. Michelangelo, the sculptor, disagreed. He thought of himself as a tool of God, gifted with an ability not to create, but to reveal what God had put into the stone.

Both Leonardo and Raphael were rich and famous, taking great pride in their high-class profession. They painted while wearing fine clothes, nibbling fresh fruit, sipping wine, and maybe even being entertained with live music. They'd wash up before dinner and enjoy a high-society ball that evening. But Michelangelo worked in a frenzy. In his sweaty work clothes, covered with marble dust, he'd often work deep into the night wearing a candle on his cap.

Despite their different styles, Michelangelo respected Leonardo. Vasari, the painter and biographer, insulted Leonardo's slow

Michelangelo, **Holy Family,** *1506 (Uffizi, Florence). Michelangelo insisted he was a sculptor, not a painter. This painting shows it with solid, statuesque people posed in sculpture groups. This is Michelangelo's only surviving easel painting.*

Michelangelo's Pietàs

"The" Pietà, sculpted by Michelangelo when he was 22 years old, shows a dead Christ held by the eternally youthful Virgin Mary. Jesus is believably human, his warm fleshiness contrasting with the coarse backdrop of Mary's robe. In the Pietà del Duomo, the "z" shape of Christ's elongated, lifeless body accentuates his dead weight. In the third, the unfinished Rondanini Pietà—which Michelangelo was working on when he died—Mary and Jesus are nearly weightless, rising like a single flame toward heaven. This nearly modern sculpture is reduced to its spiritual essence. Its elongated forms hint at the Mannerist period to follow. In these Pietàs, ranging from sweet to tragic to ethereal, Michelangelo shows the journey of his genius.

"The" **Pietà**, *1500 (St. Peter's Cathedral, Rome).*

Michelangelo, **Pietà del Duomo**, *1555 (Museum dell' Opera del Duomo, Florence)*

Rondanini Pietà, *1564 (Sforza Castle, Milan).*

Making a Fresco

Frescoes are paintings on plaster. A true fresco (called *buon fresco*) is painted on wet plaster, using water-based paints. A dry fresco (*fresco secco*) is painted on dry plaster, with glue-based paints.

The artist starts by drawing a cartoon on paper the same size as the intended work. To transfer the drawing to a wall, the artist pierces the cartoon repeatedly along the lines, places it gently against the plaster, and dusts the cartoon with powder. After the cartoon is removed, the artist connects the dots. The cartoon is usually tossed, unless it's by Leonardo or Michelangelo. Cartoons of masterpieces were copied, studied, and admired to pieces by aspiring artists.

Because frescoes couldn't be moved, artists in competition were required to submit cartoons for judging; the winner would then paint the fresco at the chosen location, often a church.

To paint a true fresco, the artist has to work fast but achieves long-lasting results. The artist can apply only as much plaster as can be painted in a day. Any large fresco consists of many small, seamless chunks of work. The lime of the plaster binds with both the paint and wall, creating a integral whole that lasts for centuries. Mentally compare Michelangelo's crisply painted Sistine Chapel with Leonardo's disintegrating Last Supper. As an experiment, Leonardo mixed his pigments with oil instead of water. Michelangelo took no chances.

Frescoes, which do best in a dry climate, never caught on in damp, moldy Northern Europe. Interestingly, bold frescoes were better suited for Italians' epic scale; delicate work in oil was perfect for capturing the Northern artists' love of detail.

working pace and bragged that he himself had done the painting in the entire Roman chancellor's palace in 100 days. Michelangelo responded, "It's obvious."

For Michelangelo, history's greatest bodybuilder, sculpture was the noblest art form. Michelangelo said that the more a painting looked like a sculpture the better it was, and the more a sculpture looked like a painting the worse it was. He considered himself a sculptor, not a painter. Fortunately for us, his patrons thought otherwise. Pope Julius II, as part of a massive effort to bring the papacy prestige and return Rome

Michelangelo, **Sistine Chapel,** *1508–1512 (Vatican Museum). The pictorial culmination of the Renaissance, Michelangelo's Sistine Ceiling tells the entire history of the Christian world, from Creation to Christ. Later he painted* **The Last Judgment,** *on the wall behind the altar. Today, this room is newly restored and sparkles like the day Michelangelo finished it.*

to its former splendor, bribed and pressured a hesitant Michelangelo into painting an enormous fresco on the ceiling of the Sistine Chapel. Michelangelo worked furiously for four years, producing a masterpiece of incredible proportion, unity, and emotional power.

The Sistine Chapel is the pictorial culmination of the Renaissance. It chronicles the Christian history of the world, from the Creation to the Coming of Christ to the Last Judgment. More than 600 figures not only tell the story, but add up to a unified, rhythmically pleasing composition. Their bodies are dramatic, expressive, and statuesque, in the tradition of Giotto and Masaccio.

The famous central scene shows the Creation of Man; Adam reaches out to receive the divine spark of life from God. We can see the tenderness between a fatherly God and His creation, but the most striking thing about the relationship is its equality. Man is not cowering before a terrible God. He is strong and confident. Michelangelo shows us the essential goodness of man who was created in the image of God, one Biblical idea that the Renaissance really liked.

Michelangelo was also a great architect. He designed the dome of St. Peter's in Rome, influenced by the Pantheon in Rome and Brunelleschi's dome in Florence.

The Sistine Ceiling shows the story of creation with a powerful God weaving in and out of each scene through that busy first week. Thirty-three-year-old Michelangelo spent four years on his back creating this High Renaissance masterpiece.

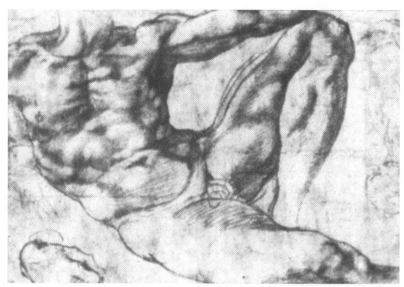

Michelangelo, **Study for Adam for the Sistine Chapel,** *1510. The Florentines were sculptors at heart. Here Michelangelo's sculptural orientation shows through. Compare this with the finished product below.*

Whether he died satisfied with his life's work, we don't know. But he lived almost 90 years and was productive until the end. As a final show of independence and artistic devotion, when he designed the great dome of St. Peter's, he refused payment for his services.

Michelangelo, **Creation of Adam,** *c. 1510 (Sistine Chapel, Vatican Museum)*

Michelangelo, **The Last Judgment**, *1534–1541 (Sistine Chapel, Vatican Museum).*

Michelangelo, **The Last Judgment** *(details, Sistine Chapel, Vatican Museum). Painted about 25 years after the original work on the ceiling, a disillusioned Michelangelo paints his own face in the flayed, wretched skin in St. Bartholomew's hand. To the right, Michelangelo portrays Christ as a powerful, wrathful, and terrifying deity posed to strike down the wicked. With the Reformation, the Vatican is on the defensive. Renaissance optimism has ended.*

Works of Michelangelo

- _Pietà_ (the famous one), St. Peter's, Vatican, Rome
- Dome of St. Peter's, Vatican
- Sistine Chapel and _The Last Judgment_, Vatican Museum
- _Moses_, St. Peter in Chains church, Rome
- _Christ Bearing Cross_, Santa Maria Sopra Minerva church, Rome
- Capitol Hill Square, Rome
- _David_ and _Prisoners_ (unfinished pieces for Pope Julius II's unfinished tomb), Accademia, Florence
- _Pietà del Duomo_, Museo dell' Opera del Duomo, Florence
- _Night_, _Day_, and others, Medici Chapel, Florence
- _Bacchus_, _Bruto_, and a minor _David_, Bargello, Florence
- _Holy Family_ easel painting, Uffizi, Florence
- Rondanini _Pietà_, Milan
- _Madonna and Child_, Bruges, Belgium
- _Slaves_, Louvre, Paris
- _Entombment_ (unfinished painting), National Gallery, London

Michelangelo's powerful **Moses** _(in the Church of St. Peter in Chains, Rome) is one of the few figures finished for the monumental tomb of the egomaniac Pope Julius II. The tomb, which the pope planned to place in the center of St. Peter's Cathedral, would have included 40 statues and taken Michelangelo several lifetimes to complete._

Michelangelo, **Apse and Dome of St. Peter's Cathedral**, _begun 1547, Rome. When asked to build the dome of St. Peter's, Michelangelo said, "I can build one bigger but not more beautiful than the dome of my hometown, Florence."_

Climb to the top, 100 winding, sweaty yards up, and judge for yourself. Matching (but not outdoing) the grandeur of ancient Rome, the builders of St. Peter's respectfully "put the dome of the Pantheon atop the Basilica Maxentius."

Raphael

Raphael (1483–1520) is the best single embodiment of the harmony and pure beauty of the Renaissance style—a synthesis of the grace of Leonardo and the power of Michelangelo. He managed to achieve what had eluded painters before him: the realistic and harmonious composition of freely moving figures.

Raphael's fresco *The School of Athens* embodies the spirit of the High Renaissance. Its subject is classical—Plato and Aristotle surrounded by other Greek philosophers (modeled by Raphael's contemporaries), all engaged in highbrow jawing. The pure Renaissance architecture of the school is actually a look at the new St. Peter's basilica, which was under construction at the time.

The composition, like Leonardo's *Last Supper,* has figures grouped rhythmically around a center of calm. The lines of sight meet at the "haloed" figures of the two "saints" of knowledge, just as they did at Leonardo's Jesus. Plato points up, reminding us that mathematics and

Raphael, **School of Athens,** *1510 (Raphael Rooms, Vatican Museum, Rome). Renaissance thought united the church and the great classical philosophers. Notice how the Renaissance architecture provides a halo for the pre-Christian saints of knowledge (and gives us a sneak preview of the unfinished St. Peter's church). As in Leonardo's* Last Supper, *the receding lines of perspective meet at the heads of the central figures, Plato and Aristotle.*

Raphael, **La Belle Jardinière,** *1507 (Louvre, Paris). A typical pyramid composition by the "Master of Grace." Most tourists burn out on the very common Madonna-and-child scene long before they get to Raphael. Save yourself for Raphael.*

pure ideas are the source of truth, while Aristotle points down, showing his preference for scientific study of the material world. The bearded figure of Plato is none other than Leonardo—Raphael's tribute to the aging master. Michelangelo is shown meditating, sitting with his head in his hand in the foreground.

The fresco shows Michelangelo's influence in the solid, sculptural bodies and the dramatic power reminiscent of the Sistine Chapel. In fact, Raphael was working on this in the Vatican Palace while Michelangelo was climbing the walls of the Sistine Chapel next door. The *School of Athens* is one of many Raphael masterpieces that adorn

Works of Raphael

- *School of Athens, Deliverance of St. Peter,* and others, Raphael Rooms, Vatican Museum
- *Transfiguration,* Pinacoteca Gallery, Vatican Museum

Most major art galleries have works of Raphael, including Florence's Uffizi, Madrid's Prado, Paris' Louvre, Munich's Alte Pinakothek, and Vienna's Kunsthistorisches.

Raphael, **The Transfiguration** *(detail), 1520 (Pinacoteca, Vatican Museum, Rome). As he was dying, Raphael set his sights on heaven and painted possibly his most beautiful work, this heavenly face of Jesus.*

the rooms through which you walk immediately before you enter the Sistine Chapel.

Raphael's fame was equal to Michelangelo's, and his influence on subsequent generations was perhaps even greater. Periodically through the centuries, artists returned to the vision of ideal beauty depicted by Raphael, the "Master of Grace." However, these imitators often ignored the realism and power of Raphael, turning out pretty pictures with little substance.

Raphael was the most beloved Renaissance painter until this century. Only in our generation have Michelangelo and Leonardo surpassed him in postcards and calendars sold. When Raphael died in 1520, the center of Renaissance painting shifted once again—this time northward, to Venice.

Renaissance Venice: Europe's Rich Middleman

In Venice, Renaissance art and architecture were financed by trade. For 500 years, Venice was known as "the Bride of the Sea" and the envy of all of Europe. The economy, glorious buildings, art, and elegant way of life all depended on sea trading. Every year the leader of Venice, after renewing a kind of wedding vow, tossed a ring into the Adriatic. This act symbolized the marriage between the sea and its bride.

Venice had been founded as a kind of refugee camp around the year 400 by Italian mainlanders. After suffering one too many barbarian rape-pillage-and-plunders, the Venetians got together and decided to move out into the lagoon, hoping the barbarians didn't like water. They built on muddy islands, pounding in literally millions of tree trunks for support. Rather than trying to build solid roads, they dredged canals for passageways.

Farming was impossible in the mud, so the Venetians quickly learned to trade fish and salt (for preserving meat) for agricultural products. Gradually, their trading took them to more and more distant lands. They were situated perfectly to link Europe with the wealthy Byzantine Empire and the treasures of the East. When the Crusades created a demand in Europe for Eastern luxury goods, Venice became the go-between.

Venice went between so well that by the year 1200, she was Europe's economic superpower. Products from as far away as Scotland and India passed through Venetian warehouses. The Rialto Bridge area became the world's busiest trading center: iron, copper, and woven textiles from Northern Europe and wine, silk, Persian rugs, leathers,

Doge's Palace, *1340, Venice. The multinational corporation known as the Venetian Empire was ruled from this palace, the home of its C.E.O., the Doge. Today, this Venetian Gothic building is packed with art masterpieces, history, and tourists.*

Doge's Palace, *today, Venice. A 1995 photograph proves that the town has changed (and sunk) little in 655 years, though the tower is clearly sliding to the right.*

precious stones, perfumes, lemons, raisins, pepper, and other spices from the East. Venetians traded by ship using a chain of ports and friendly cities in the eastern Mediterranean. Goods arrived (sometimes by camel caravan) and the Venetians shipped them westward where European land traders picked them up.

Venice, with 150,000 citizens, was the most populous city in Europe in 1500. (Paris had 100,000.) The ducat, because of its stability and high gold content, became the monetary standard for the Eastern world. (The Florentine florin was the West's.) The gross "national" product of this city was 50 percent greater than that of the entire country of France.

Her sea trading spawned other industries, including shipbuilding, warehousing, insurance, and accounting. The Arsenal, the largest single factory in Europe, employed 16,000 people at its peak and could crank out a warship a day.

Besides expanding its commercial empire, Venice hired generals to conquer many of the cities in northern Italy. And Venice profited greatly from the Crusades.

All this wealth did not go to waste. The 15th century was a time of massive building and rebuilding. The earliest structures of this century

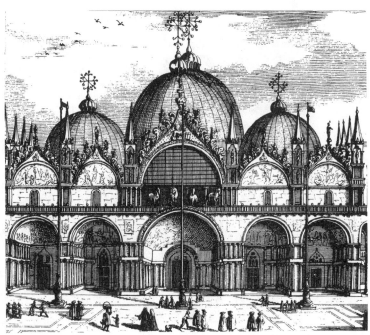

St. Mark's Cathedral, *1063–1073, Venice. Mark Twain called
St. Mark's "a great warty bug taking a meditative walk."*

show a Byzantine influence. The most distinctive, however, are "Venetian
Gothic" in style, such as the Doge's Palace. They have Gothic pointed
arches, but they're much lighter and more fanciful than the Gothic
churches of Northern Europe. Later structures are Renaissance style,
with rounded Roman arches.

St. Mark's, one of the world's most famous cathedrals, is the best
example of "Venetian Byzantine" architecture with its onion-shaped
Eastern domes, Greek-cross floor plan, and interior mosaics. But the
style might better be called "Early Ransack." The cathedral is a treasure
chest of artifacts looted from other cities during Venice's heyday.

Even the bones of Venice's patron saint, Mark, which rest under
the altar, were booty. Middle Age Europe was into relic worship. In
A.D. 829, the young but powerful city-state of Venice was really nothing on the religious map. It needed relics to give it some clout. A band
of merchants trading in Alexandria, Egypt, stole the bones of the
Evangelist (a writer of one of the New Testament Gospels) from
Alexandria's Moslem rulers, put them in their church, and, presto!

Venice became an important religious destination. St. Mark's symbol, the winged lion, replaced Theodore and his dragon as the symbol of the Venetian Republic.

With its newfound sanctity, Venice grew rapidly. The Rialto Bridge that spans the Grand Canal, originally a covered wooden drawbridge, was rebuilt as a grand stone arch. The straight, wooden planks of Venice's drawbridges had allowed horses and mules to cross. When builders installed the new arched bridges, horses were banned from the city—just as cars are today.

The Venetian empire was controlled by an oligarchy of wealthy families. This top 5 percent of the population elected a council of rulers led by a duke who served for life, known as the Doge (pronounced "dozh," not "doggie").

The rest of the population had no political rights, but they were treated well and did prosper. Until 1423 the people had final veto power over election of the Doge. The council would present him in St. Mark's Square, saying, "This is your Doge, if it please you." They invariably approved the election by cheering, until one Doge-elect, an unpopular man, feared he might not please them. From then on, the council said only, "This is your Doge." Throughout history, democracy has been a bonsai tree in the house of the powerful—it looks nice, and when it grows too big you simply cut it back.

Venetian society, while rigidly structured, was quite tolerant. It was a cosmopolitan city where traders from all over the world rubbed elbows. Some foreigners (Turks, Arabs, and others) were even allowed to settle there. (The bell at St. Mark's is rung by two statues of Moors.) There was a Jewish community, giving us our word "ghetto" to identify a neighborhood set aside for minorities. The largest foreign group was the Greek population, especially after the disastrous sack of Constantinople by the European Crusaders (in 1204) and the city's fall to the Turks (in 1453). One of the 5,000 Venetian Greeks was Domenico Theotocopoulis, who became a famous painter in Spain . . . El Greco.

The Catholic Church was often at odds with Venice, partly because of the city's close ties with the rival Greek Orthodox Christians. The proud Venetians thought of themselves as Catholics—but not Roman Catholics.

Elegant Decay: Venice's Cinquecento

Venice peaked economically in the year 1450. Then, a series of world events set in motion three centuries of slow decline. In 1453, the Moslem Turks captured and looted Constantinople. Uninterested in trading with the West, they began attacking Venice's foreign ports.

Venice not only lost its link with the East but was also forced to fight costly wars with the Turks.

The next blows came from the West, when explorers from Spain and Portugal discovered America and new sea-trade routes to the East. By 1500, Portugal was using Vasco da Gama's route around South Africa to trade with India. When Venice's Eastern monopoly was broken, her trade plummeted.

Venice's decline was a glorious one. Like so many cultures past their peak of economic expansion, Venice turned from business to the arts, from war to diplomacy, from sternness to partying, from buying gold to selling tacky souvenirs. The "Cinquecento" (pronounced "CHINK-kwa-CHEN-to"), as the Italians call the century of the 1500s, was a time for merrymaking and festivity that was legendary in Europe.

Venice's economic decline went hand in hand with political corruption and repression. Local rule grew more and more autocratic. Venice had some of Europe's most convincing torture chambers.

The renowned rogue Casanova spent time in a Venetian prison, which he described as follows: "Those subterranean prisons are precisely like tombs, but they call them 'Wells' because they contain about two feet of filthy water which penetrates from the sea. Condemned to live in these sewers, they are given every morning some thin soup and a ration of bread which they have to eat immediately or it becomes the prey of enormous rats. A villain who died while I was there had spent 37 years in the Wells."

The famous Bridge of Sighs (rebuilt in 1600 and open today to visitors) connected the lawyers' offices in the Doge's Palace with the prisons. Prisoners could be brought from the prisons, tried in closed court, and sentenced without the public knowing about it. As they passed over the bridge to their deaths, they got one last look at their beloved city—hence the name, "Bridge of Sighs."

Venice's long decline was hastened by two brutal plagues that devastated the population. By Napoleon's arrival in 1797, the city was defenseless. He ended the Republic, throwing the city into even worse chaos. It became a possession of various European powers until 1866, when it joined the newly united Italian nation.

The city today is older, crumbling, and sinking, but it looks much the same as it did during the grand days of the Renaissance. For that we can thank Venice's economic decline: the inhabitants were simply too poor to rebuild. Venice is Europe's best-preserved big city. It is the toast of the High Middle Ages and Renaissance in an elegant state of decay.

Many people actually avoid Venice because of its famously smelly canals. So that you'll know how serious this problem is, we've recreated the Venetian stench here so you can scratch 'n' sniff and decide for yourself.

Scratch 'n' sniff—Venice

Art of the Venetian Renaissance

The Cinquecento produced some of the greatest Renaissance art. Bellini, Titian, Giorgione, Tintoretto, and Veronese, whose works embellish churches, palaces, and museums throughout the city, forged a distinct Venetian style that emphasized color over outline. While Florentine painters drew massive sculptural figures with a strong outline, Venetians used gradations of color to blend figures into the background. The result was a lighter, more refined, and more graceful look understandable in an elegant city of lavish palaces and glittering canals.

The same delicate, atmospheric haze that often hangs over the city of Venice also characterizes Venetian art. It's like a picture taken with a soft-focus lens on the camera, making everything glow and blend together, bathing it in light. This is Leonardo's *sfumato* taken one step further.

Giorgione's *The Tempest*, with bright colors and a hazy quality, marks a trend new to Italian painting—the landscape. Like painters from Northern Europe, Venetians enjoyed painting pleasantly detailed scenes that show a love of the natural world. Titian the Venetian was one of the most prolific painters ever, cranking out a painting a month for almost 80 years. His canvases have a richness of color and brilliance of light burning through the night. He used color and light rather than the drawn line to balance his work and direct the viewer's eyes. (When Michelangelo met

Giorgione, **The Tempest**, 1505 (Accademia, Venice). Florentine art tended to be sculptural with strong outlines; Venice's Renaissance art, like the city, was colorful and romantically atmospheric.

Titian, **Venus and the Organ Player**, *1550 (Prado, Madrid). Rich Venetians dealt with the conflict between sacred artistic pursuits (for example, music) and worldly, sensual pursuits (for example, the naked lady). Here, the torn musician leers at Venus while keeping both hands on his organ.*

the great Titian, whose fame rivaled his own, he praised his work and then said, "But it's a pity you Venetians cannot draw.")

When Raphael died in 1520, Venice became Italy's art capital. Titian (about 1490–1576) became the most sought-after portrait artist. A famous example of Titian's prestige: once, when he dropped a brush during a sitting, his subject, Emperor Charles V of Spain, picked it up for him. Whether this actually happened is unimportant. This often-repeated anecdote represented to future generations the triumph of artistic genius.

The happy-go-lucky Venetian love of the good life can be seen in Paolo Veronese's huge, colorful scenes of Venetian high life. He once painted the Last Supper scene as if it were a typical Venetian dinner party. We see drunks, buffoons, dwarfs, a German mercenary soldier, dogs, a cat, and a parrot. The authorities were so shocked that they demanded he repaint it to reflect a more somber mood. Instead, he simply retitled it.

Venetian Art

- Accademia, Doge's Palace, Chiesa dei Frari, and Scuola San Rocco (Tintoretto), Venice
- The city of Venice herself, including many churches
- Prado, Madrid
- Kunsthistorisches Museum, Vienna
- City of Dubrovnik, Croatia

Veronese, **Feast of the House of Levi,** *1564 (Accademia, Venice). Veronese was hauled before the Inquisition for painting the Last Supper of Christ and His holy apostles looking like a Venetian orgy. Veronese didn't change a thing, except the title.*

We know the work as *Feast of the House of Levi* (see it in Venice's Accademia).

The bright colors of the Venetian style take on an almost surrealistic tint with Tintoretto (1518–1594). His works glow like black-velvet paintings. He also experimented with new techniques of composition, showing his main subjects at odd angles and in twisted poses, whipping up the excitement. Tintoretto's dramatic style went beyond serene Renaissance balance, pointing toward the next phase in art—Baroque.

The Northern Renaissance

In Northern Europe, the Renaissance was more an improvement on medieval art than a return to classical forms. Northern artists used Italian discoveries of perspective, anatomy, and knowledge of classical forms, but kept their style distinctly Northern.

In the north, late Gothic art is characterized by grace, lightness, delicate flowing lines, and an appreciation for things that are just plain beautiful. Human bodies are slender and gently curved, with smooth, unmuscled skin. Colors are bright and pleasant.

Northern artists loved detail. Like craftsmen working on a fine Swiss watch or German cuckoo clock, they thought nothing of spending hours on end slaving over, say, the hairs on a dog's head to get them just right, even when the dog was just a minor figure in a large canvas. Their appreciation of the many wonders of nature shows in their work.

Medieval paintings often look crowded. Details abound—the more,

Riemenschneider woodcarving, 1504 *(St. Jacob's Church, Rothenburg, Germany). Riemenschneider was the Michelangelo of German woodcarvers. His greatest altarpiece is in Rothenburg. Museums in Würzburg and Munich show off more of his work.*

Van Eyck, **Arnolfini Wedding,** *1434 (National Gallery, London). This early Northern Renaissance masterpiece shows the characteristic medieval attention to detail and the down-to-earth personal style typical of Belgian and Dutch art. You can even see the couple's reflection in the round mirror in the rear. "Wedding?" Women used to wear pillows to their weddings thinking that would improve their chances of becoming pregnant.*

Dürer, **Self-Portrait**, *1498 (Prado, Madrid). In this first full self-portrait by an artist, the German Dürer declares that—even in a goofy hat—artists deserve and will get respect.*

the better. Crammed with objects and minute details, Northern Renaissance works are best viewed as they were painted, slowly and carefully.

Albrecht Dürer (1471–1528), a German working at about the same time as Michelangelo, finished his apprenticeship and traveled to Venice to learn the techniques he'd heard so much about. When he returned home and achieved fame, he helped "Italianize" his world. He has been called the "Leonardo of the North."

Dürer combined the Italian painters' laws of perspective and human anatomy with the Germans' attention to detail. Although he never mastered Michelangelo's ability to make a solid, statuelike body, his paintings are astonishingly realistic. With the patience formed from his mastery of the grueling process of woodcuts and engraving, he painted with incredible detail. Dürer was Europe's first top-selling artist. His popular woodcuts and engravings were reproduced and sold in large quantities.

Dürer, **Adam and Eve** *(engraving), 1504 (Museum of Fine Arts, Boston)*

Woodcuts, a Northern Specialty

A woodcut is made by sketching black lines on a white-painted block, then chipping off the white so that only the desired lines protrude. This woodcut is then dipped into ink and used the way we use a rubber stamp today. An engraving, the opposite of a woodcut, cuts the "lines" into the plate and, when mastered, allows for even more detail than a woodcut. An etching, which is an improved version of engraving and was used by later artists such as Rembrandt, is made by coating a copperplate with wax and scratching an image into the wax, which is then burned with acid. Prints are then made from the plate in the same manner as engravings.

Dürer, **Four Horsemen of the Apocalypse,** *1498 (British Museum, London). Dürer's woodcuts were the first mass-produced art Europe had seen. His mastery of line and detail went well with this painstaking medium. Notice his famous D-inside-A monogram at the bottom.*

Dürer was impressed by the respect Italian artists enjoyed. Northern artists had always been anonymous craftsmen, laboring in guilds. Dürer helped change that. Convinced that his personal life and thoughts were as important as his handiwork, he kept journals and wrote books. His famous self-portraits (a first) portray him as an elegant, confident, even arrogant man of the world.

Matthias Grünewald (GROON-uh-vald, 1470–1528) was a great but mysterious Northern Renaissance artist. (We're not even sure that's his real name.) Like Northern Renaissance art in general, his style grew out of the Gothic stage. His anonymity is medieval, as is his gripping religious devotion. Grünewald often ignored realism (so important to Dürer

Grunewald, **Resurrection,** *part of Isenheim Altarpiece, 1515 (Colmar, France). Christ springs from the tomb.*

and the Italians) to make a religious point.

Grünewald's famous Isenheim altarpiece in Colmar, France, is one of Europe's most exciting and powerful masterpieces. In this set of scenes from Jesus' life, Grünewald uses distorted shapes and dazzling, unreal colors to grab the emotions. You feel the agony of Christ twisted stiffly and heavily on the cross, the humility of Mary, and the exuberance of the resurrected Christ springing psychedelically from the tomb as if shot out of a Roman candle.

Grünewald, **Isenheim Altarpiece,** *1515 (Colmar, France). The mysterious, late-Gothic master painted one of the most gripping crucifixions ever. Notice the weight of Christ's body bending the cross bar, his mashed feet, dislocated elbows, the grief on Mary's face (kneeling), and Jesus' stiff fingers praising God in spite of it all. Though Renaissance in technique, it includes medieval symbolism: the lamb with a cross and cup, and John the Baptist holding a book.*

Bosch, **Garden of Delights,** *1510 (Prado, Madrid). This three-paneled altarpiece takes you from the Creation to the gnashing torments of Hell via the fleeting "delights" of earthly life.*

Hieronymous Bosch (rhymes with "gosh," 1450–1516) was another interesting artist of this era. We know almost nothing about him except what we learn through his fantastic paintings. "Hieronymous the Anonymous" painted medieval fears with modern skill. His huge symbolism-packed canvases are crowded with grotesque, humorous, and all-around bizarre people.

Bosch also painted strange-looking plants and animals in many of his works. This was common among artists who painted during the years when Columbus and other explorers were bringing fascinating creatures back from the New World. Today, although much of the meaning of his art is lost, the intrigue remains.

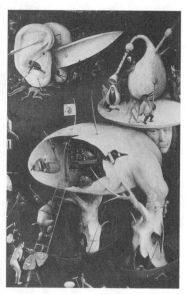

Bosch, **Garden of Delights** *(detail from Hell), 1510 (Prado, Madrid). In just a tiny bit of this monumental work we see a self-portrait of Bosch with a broken-eggshell body and tree trunk legs crashing through wooden dinghies in a frozen lake with giant birds leading naked people around the brim of his hat. Gosch.*

Northern Renaissance Art
- Kunsthistorisches Museum, Vienna
- Prado, Madrid
- Isenheim altarpiece, Unterlinden Museum, Colmar, France
- *The Last Judgment*, Hôtel Dieu, Beaune, France
- Rijksmuseum, Amsterdam
- Ancient Art Museum, Brussels
- *Adoration of the Mystic Lamb*, St. Bavo's Church, Ghent, Belgium
- Dahlem Museum, Berlin
- Alte Pinakothek, Munich

After the Renaissance: Mannerism

Looking at the ceiling of the Sistine Chapel might make you think, "How could there be anything more beautiful?" Well, that's what artists after Michelangelo thought and worried about, too. How could art advance beyond the works of the great Renaissance masters? They had explored and conquered every facet of painting and sculpture. It seemed as though the future of art would be little more than copying the forms and techniques of Michelangelo, Leonardo, Raphael, and Titian.

The Renaissance was a hard act to follow, and for a while many artists were stuck in the beautiful rut of Raphael's style. We call the style of this period (1530–1600) Mannerism because the art seemed to follow only the "manner" of the Renaissance masters, often neglecting the spirit of their work. Mannerist art typically features elongated, thinned human bodies.

Many artists made bold, occasionally ridiculous, attempts to be original, to do something new. Using Renaissance techniques of portraying nature, they experimented with more complex composition, more striking colors, the contrast of light and shadow, and a heightened display of emotions. This led to the Baroque style.

Parmigiano, **The Madonna with the Long Neck,** *1535 (Uffizi, Florence).* *"I'm melting!"*

Timeline of the Renaissance

The Renaissance spread as countries reached an economic affluence that could support the arts. It began in Florence and then took over Rome, Venice, and finally the northern countries, Flanders, France, and England.

The earliest Renaissance artists—Brunelleschi, Masaccio, Donatello, and Botticelli—lived in Florence at the time the powerful Medici banking family ruled the city. After the fall of the Medicis, the High Renaissance shifted to Rome (Michelangelo and Raphael) and then to Venice (Titian).

Meanwhile, the rest of Europe was discovering new lands and trading opportunities. Spain and Portugal broke Venice's monopoly on Eastern trade by finding new routes to the East. England, Holland, and France built large merchant fleets and banking houses to expand their trade with the rest of Europe and the New World. With the invention of the printing press, ideas were exchanged as quickly as goods.

Each of these countries was touched by its own Renaissance. Portugal flowered with the Manueline architectural style; Spain inspired the art of El Greco (he arrived via Venice); and the northern countries spawned the masterpieces of Dürer, Bosch, and Grünewald.

Europe in 1500

Timeline of the Renaissance

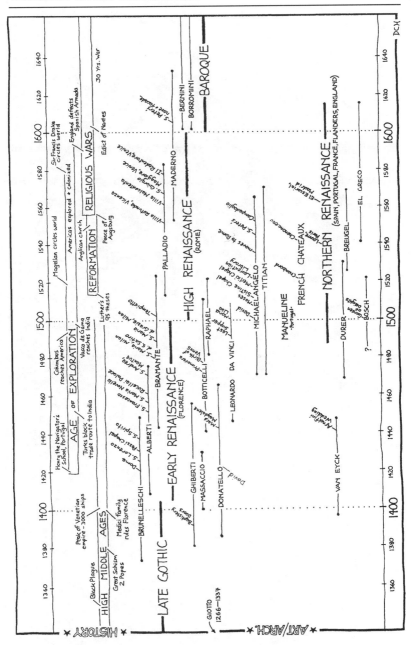

Non est potestas Super Terram quæ Comparetur ei Iob. 41. 24.

The Absolute Monarch—*ruling like a god in Heaven. The 1600s and 1700s were a time of "divine" kings and absolutism. Many a king convinced his people that he had been deputized by God to rule with complete, unquestioned power.*

Early Modern Europe
A.D. 1500–1815

In the early 1500s, Europe was entering the modern world. You could now get to Asia without a camel. You could get to heaven without a pope. You could own a book without being rich. Royal families established huge empires but milked subjects like cash cows. As the Enlightenment opened minds and nationalism stirred hearts, the Old Regime became old news. From the Reformation to the age of divine monarchs to the age of revolution, the ultimate power shifted from the pope to the king to the people.

The Reformation

Before the Renaissance, the church was Europe's richest, most powerful, and best-organized institution as well as its greatest landowner. The church collected taxes through tithes, patronized great art, and influenced political decisions. Kings and princes needed papal support to maintain their political power. Average Europeans identified themselves by their bishopric, not by citizenship in a particular country.

But as the church's rich and worldly position led to corruption, a reforming spirit grew. When political rivalries and jealousies were added, reforming changed to splitting. New churches were formed, and because religion and politics were intertwined, this caused a chaotic period of political upheaval and war. This tumultuous period is called the Reformation. Much of the Europe you see today was shaped by this period.

Church Corruption

The church certainly needed reform. Many priests were illiterate and immoral. Bishops meddled in politics, governing like petty tyrants. The church had lost touch with ordinary folk; mass was celebrated in Latin,

Tickets to heaven: the sale of indulgences. In this German woodcut, people buy letters of forgiveness in the marketplace. This peddling of pardons bothered Martin Luther.

a language spoken only by the educated. The church had lost touch with its roots, showing not a hint of the voluntary poverty of the early Christians. The clergy even sold important church offices and dispensations (exemptions from church laws) to the highest bidder.

To pay for Rome's face-lift, the pope sold indulgences. (Renaissance artists didn't come cheap.) To anyone who paid the price, the pope promised "forgiveness for all thy sins, transgressions and excesses, how enormous so ever they may be, so that when you die the gates of Hell shall be shut and the gates of Paradise shall open with delight"... a bargain at twice the price.

Church corruption and the sale of indulgences brought on the Reformation, but there were deeper, underlying causes: the decline of papal power, a new secularism, and strong, opportunistic kings.

The pope had lost prestige among both kings and commoners. During their medieval heyday, popes could make or break kings. But after the popes moved to Avignon, France (1309–1377) to enjoy the protection of the strong French kings, they were seen as French popes and their international influence suffered. When a second pope popped up back in Rome and each pope excommunicated the other, papal prestige sank to mud-wrestling depths.

Secular Forces

Europe's new secularism was bolstered by the rise of capitalism and many Renaissance ideas. The newly invented printing press quickly disseminated news of scientific discoveries. After Copernicus (in 1543) and Galileo (in 1632) disproved the church's traditional explanation of the earth-centered universe, nothing was accepted blindly. A new, more independent, scientific, and political world confronted the church. Reformers risked death to print local-language versions of one especially radical book: the Bible.

Kings jumped on the Reformation bandwagon out of political greed. They saw the church as a rival power within their borders. The church was Europe's number-one landowner. Tithes sent to Rome were taxes lost. The clergy was exempt from taxes and could ignore local laws. Many kings wanted not only to reform the church, but also to break with it for good. The political rewards were obvious. Kings and princes encouraged people to challenge church authority.

Martin Luther

At first, Martin Luther (1483–1546) was merely an ordinary German monk trying to reform church abuses from within. He never meant to create a new church. He simply believed that the word of God lay not in the doctrine of the church but in the Bible. The Bible talked of salvation solely by faith in God. Salvation was a free gift to believers, not something anyone could earn or buy. Elaborate church rituals made no sense to him. The granting of dispensations and selling of indulgences by the church cheapened, and even denied, the grace of God.

Priests had turned into indulgence salesmen. Here is a typical sales pitch used by the German archbishop Tetzel: "Listen to the voices of your dear dead relatives and friends beseeching you and saying 'Pity us, pity us. We are in dire torment from which you can redeem us for a pittance.' Remember that you are able to release them, for as soon as the coin in the coffer rings, the soul from Purgatory springs." Luther could not accept Tetzel's spiel.

Martin Luther, 1483–1546

Gutenberg and the Printing Press

A silversmith, Gutenberg was used to working with metal. In 1450, he came up with the simple, profound idea of casting letters in metal. By setting these sturdy letters tightly in trays, inking the trays, then pressing the inked type against paper, he could copy books faster than a thousand monks. Other than a few minor improvements, Gutenberg's revolutionary method for printing was used until the early 19th century.

As we're buried by junk mail, it's hard to comprehend what a difference his invention made. Imagine not being able to afford a single book. You had to take a priest's word—in Latin—for what the Bible said. Then imagine being able to afford your own Bible—or any other book in print. The printing press opened the doors of knowledge, ultimately bringing power to the common people.

With the printing press, news traveled faster—it really was news. Europe became smaller. If Martin Luther had nailed his 95 theses on the Wittenberg cathedral door a hundred years earlier, few would have found out about it. But Gutenberg's new-fangled printing press was Luther's megaphone, and all of Europe listened.

Because of how the printing press empowered people and sped the spread of information, Gutenberg is considered by many to be the most influential person of the millennium.

In 1517, Luther nailed to the door of the Wittenberg cathedral a list of 95 ideas for debate. In Thesis #82 Luther wrote: "If the pope redeems a number of souls for the sake of miserable money with which to buy a church, why doesn't he empty Purgatory for the sake of holy love?" Not interested in debating, the church called Luther a heretic and sent him a papal bull of excommunication. Not cowed, Luther burned the pope's letter—the Renaissance equivalent to burning your draft card, only much more serious.

Now a criminal as well as a heretic, Luther took refuge in the castle of a sympathetic German prince. From behind those walls he established the German church, translated the New Testament into German (giving birth to the modern German language), and led the rebellion against the pope. Printing presses churned out Luther's ideas, which spread quickly and widely to an audience weary of the Church's insatiable greed. Local kings confiscated church lands, established their own "protestant" (protesting) state churches, and geared up to face the armies of the nations loyal to the church.

Reformation and Religious Wars

And the religious wars began. Luckily for the German Protestants, the pope's strongest defenders (the southern countries that remained Catholic) were preoccupied with internal problems and with fighting the Turks who were invading Eastern Europe. The Treaty of Augsburg (1555), which allowed each German prince to choose the religion of his territory, caused a lull in the fighting, but the religious wars continued into the next century.

The Reformation spawned more than one new religion. In Switzerland, around 1550, Geneva was ruled by a theocratic government under the direction of John Calvin. Like Luther, Calvin believed in salvation by God's grace, but placed more importance on the clergy's role and on leading a holy life. Calvinism spread from Switzerland through France, the Netherlands, and beyond to Scotland.

England's break with the church had political roots. King Henry VIII wanted the pope's permission to divorce Catherine of Aragon so he could marry Anne Boleyn. The pope refused to grant a divorce and so, to break all ties with Catherine, Henry broke all ties with Rome (1534). He confiscated church lands, formed the Church of England, and married Anne. The Church of England was largely an English Catholic church without a pope. For the next hundred years, England struggled as her kings and queens tried to impose their various personal religions on the people.

The religious wars between Catholics and Protestants lasted for more than 100 years (1527–1648) and were some of the bloodiest in

Catholic and Protestant Differences

The differences between Protestant and Catholic doctrines have divided Christians for centuries. Protestants emphasize a more direct relationship between the individual and God, rejecting church rituals and the necessity of ordained clergy for salvation. Bible study and personal prayer are seen as more valuable than sacraments presided over by a priest. Some Catholic practices rejected by Protestants are: celibate priests, veneration of saints and the Virgin Mary, and holy orders of monks and nuns.

European history. Kings generally fought for purely political reasons, but the soldiers were fueled by religious fervor, convinced that God was on their side.

The grand finale was the Thirty Years' War, Europe's first "world war," with mercenary warriors from just about every country taking part. When the war ended in 1648, Europe was devastated, a third of Germany was dead, and Western civilization realized what it should have known from the start—that Catholics and Protestants would have to live together.

The Peace of Westphalia (1648) ended the wars, decreeing that the leader of each country would decide the religion of his nation. Generally, the northern countries—Scandinavia, the Low Countries, northern Germany, and England—went Protestant and the southern ones—Spain, Portugal, Italy, France, and southern Germany— remained loyal to Rome. The line dividing Protestant from Catholic Europe was (and remains) almost the same line that separated bar-barian Europe from Roman Europe way back when the Christians were still hiding out. Hmmm.

Counter-Reformation

The Vatican countered the Protestant revolution with the Counter-Reformation—an attempt to put the universal Catholic church back together by means of internal reform, missionary work, propaganda (including the effective use of art), and the Inquisition.

From 1545 to 1563, the Catholic church held the Council of Trent, a series of conferences that addressed each of the Protestant concerns, defined church doctrine, and encouraged more careful training and supervision of the clergy. The pope approved the formation of the Society of Jesus. Their members—the Jesuits—became known for their fine teaching and missionary work. At the same time the Catholic church was losing members in Europe, it was gaining recruits in the Americas.

Earlier, in medieval times, a powerful church weapon had been the Inquisition. In 1542, its Counter-Reformation reincarnation was used to haul Protestants and heretic Catholics before the courts on the slightest evidence of guilt or nonconformity.

Torture, terror, imprisonment, and confiscation of property were often used to extract confessions. It was the standard judicial practice of the day. Once the accused confessed, they were really punished. Punishments ranged from recitation of a certain number of prayers, fasting, and alms-giving to imprisonment and death.

Heretics, Protestants, Jews, and others could be punished quite thoroughly by the church.

Reformation Art

The period of the religious wars took its toll on European culture. In England, Henry VIII left the countryside littered with the ruins of Catholic abbeys. The great York Minster was spared so Henry's church would have a northern capital. In Spain, the only major building of a generation was the palace of the Inquisition, El Escorial, just outside of Madrid.

Museums throughout the north show early Bibles and books printed by Gutenberg's revolutionary printing press. With the vernacular languages established and the printing of books affordable, common people had access to ideas—a powerful mix.

Catholic art was royal, dazzling, and excessive, with a source of funding (selling of indulgences) that prompted the Reformation. Protestant communities preferred a simpler art, with a greater emphasis on music.

Absolutism and Divine Monarchs

The religious wars reshuffled Europe's political cards. The old-style baronies and dukedoms were replaced by new, more modern governments headed by strong kings. In the Middle Ages, the nation had been a weak entity. Popes, nobles, and petty kings bickered for power while the common people went about their business, ignoring the affairs of state.

Now government functions were specialized, bureaucrats ran things, and the state took over many jobs that had been carried out by the church. A strong "divine" monarch was all powerful, claiming that his right to rule came directly from God. More than ever, the government was leading its people. And after 100 years of war, most Europeans didn't mind.

Growing Economy

The growing merchant class welcomed this strong central government. Traders needed stable governments, common currency, standard measures, and fewer tariffs. Early medieval trade had been stifled by the chaos of rural, feudal kingdoms. The trend toward unification, begun in the High Middle Ages, was paying off. Centralized governments and wealthy, urban merchants were natural allies.

Overseas trade gave these new governments wealth and strength. The newly discovered Americas and routes to the Far East opened a floodgate, bringing in waves of raw materials and luxury goods. The sale of captured Africans as slaves in the New World brought unprecedented wealth. Spain, England, France, and the Netherlands maintained large merchant fleets, which required naval protection, which required more taxes to maintain, which required more efficient governments to collect and administer the taxes. The state grew.

Louis XIV: Controlling Nature, Controlling Nobles

France's Louis XIV was Europe's king of kings—the absolute example of an absolute monarch. Louis ruled for 70 years (1643–1715), making France the political and cultural heartbeat of Europe. He strengthened the military, expanded France's borders, stimulated trade, and built a large and effective government.

The France that Louis inherited was the strongest nation in Europe, with 18 million people. (England at this time had about 5 million.) The economy, directed by Minister Colbert—the first man to take a balance sheet seriously—was healthy at home and growing, thanks to a large merchant marine and trade with the luxurious East and West Indies. Louis organized an efficient bureaucracy for gathering taxes, yet he himself remained at the helm. He was no scholar—in fact, he was "extraordinarily unlearned," but as a ruler he was top-notch.

Although he was neither tall (5' 5") nor handsome, he seemed to strike people as both. He was charming, a great conversationalist, and an

Rigaud, **Louis XIV**, *1701 (Louvre, Paris). Louis XIV, the premier monarch of Europe, was every king's role model. He ruled the "Oz" and "Hollywood" of Europe for more than five decades and, even as an old man, looked good in tights.*

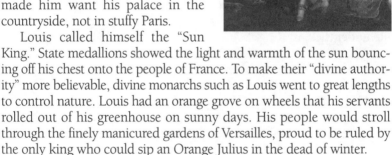

excellent horseman. He played the harpsichord and guitar (acoustic) and loved ballroom dancing. He was perhaps the most polite king ever, listening closely to his courtiers and tipping his hat to everyone on the street. Most of all he loved the outdoors, and that made him want his palace in the countryside, not in stuffy Paris.

Louis called himself the "Sun King." State medallions showed the light and warmth of the sun bouncing off his chest onto the people of France. To make their "divine authority" more believable, divine monarchs such as Louis went to great lengths to control nature. Louis had an orange grove on wheels that his servants rolled out of his greenhouse on sunny days. His people would stroll through the finely manicured gardens of Versailles, proud to be ruled by the only king who could sip an Orange Julius in the dead of winter.

Louis "domesticated" his nobles by reducing them to petty socialites more concerned with their position at court than with political issues. It worked so well that Louis had the high-and-mighty dukes and earls of France bickering over who would get to hold the candle while he slipped into his royal jammies. The tremendous expenses of court life weakened the nobility economically. Louis had them in a state of loyal servitude.

As Louis said, *"L'état, c'est moi!"* ("The state, it's me!")

Louis XIV, the Sun King. *"If Louis XIV had not existed, it would have been necessary to invent him."*
– Voltaire

Versailles: Europe's Palace of Palaces

A divine monarch needs a big house. Louis moved his court to Versailles, 12 miles outside Paris. There he built Europe's greatest palace, at the cost of six months' worth of the entire income of France. Swamps were filled in, hills were moved, and a river was rerouted to give Louis a palace fit for a divine king. He established a magnificent court (the Oz and Hollywood of Europe) that attracted the leading artists, thinkers, and nobles of the day. Though it was France's capital for only a century (1682–1789), Versailles was the social, cultural, and intellectual capital of Europe.

The enormous palace was dwarfed by endless gardens dotted with fountains, pools, and manicured shrubs. Great halls were decorated in the "Grand Style" with chandeliers, mirrored walls, tapestries, gold leaf, and silver plating. We can marvel at these today at Versailles, but they hardly give a full picture of the glory and decadence of everyday life under the Sun King, Louis XIV.

What we don't see: those thousand orange trees planted in silver tubs; the zoo with exotic animals in cages; the sedan-chair taxis shuttling nobles from château to château; the 1,500 fountains (only 300 remain); the works by Leonardo, Raphael, Titian, Rubens, and Caravaggio (now in the Louvre) that hung in halls and bedrooms; the gondolas from Venice poling along the canals at night, accompanied

Europe's Palace of Palaces, **Versailles**

The Hall of Mirrors, _Versailles. This is where France's beautiful people partied. Pass the Fromage-Whiz._

by barges with musicians; and the grand halls lit by a galaxy of candles for a ball. Most of all, we don't see the thousands of finely dressed nobles and their servants and the center of all the gaiety, Louis himself.

Louis lived his life as though it was a work of art to be admired by all. He rose late and was dressed not by servants, but by nobles and barons. Around noon he ate breakfast, and then he attended Mass. In the afternoon Louis worked, and worked hard, meeting advisers, generals, and bishops. At 5 p.m. he ate dinner, either alone or with the queen, though he wasn't ever really alone. Every action was a public ritual attended by nobles of the court.

Louis had an enormous appetite. His typical dinner might have included four different soups, two whole fowl stuffed with truffles, a huge salad, mutton, ham slices, fruit, pastry, compotes, and preserves. Nighttime was spent playing royal games, gambling, or socializing. Louis then had a late supper (near midnight) and retired.

Even Louis' life of leisure couldn't match that of the nobility, who had absolutely nothing to do day after day except play. They had no government function in France's modern bureaucracy except to attend to Louis' daily rituals. They survived on favors from the king: pensions, military and church appointments, and arranged marriages with wealthy nobles. It was essential to be liked by the king or you were lost. If Louis didn't look at you for weeks on end, you knew you had to seek an audience with him and apologize with many tears and much hugging of the royal knees. Compare the position of France's weakened nobility with that of England's nobles at the same time: the English lords in Parliament had just beheaded their king.

Versailles in its heyday had 5,000 of these domesticated nobles (with at least as many dependents) buzzing about the grounds seeking favors. Business was conducted at the billiards tables, dances, concerts, and receptions, and gambling—the most common pastime. (They usually played a version of "21.") Large gambling debts made many nobles still more dependent on Louis.

Dressing properly was part of the favor-seeking game. Men shaved their rough beards and put on stockings and silk clothes. Big, curly wigs became the rage when Louis started to go bald. A contemporary wrote, "It was possible to tell the women from the men only when it was time to go to bed."

One of the "fashions" was adultery, an accepted, almost obligatory social ritual. Louis' succession of mistresses was legendary. Still, he remained faithful to the institution of marriage itself and fulfilled his obligation to the queen, Marie-Therese of Spain, by sleeping with her every night (after a rendezvous with one of his lovers).

Versailles allowed the perfect escape from life's harsh realities. Even in his choice of art, Louis preferred grandeur and idealized beauty to simplicity and realism. He detested the naturalism of the Dutch and Flemish masters and encouraged Baroque opulence.

Still, on his deathbed, he advised his 5-year-old great-grandson Louis XV, "Don't imitate my extravagance. Alleviate the suffering of your people and do all the things I was unfortunate enough not to do." Perhaps little Louis was too young to understand, for he, too, succumbed to the lure of wealth. The Sun King's words went unheeded, and his successors in the Old Regime at Versailles continued in their gambling, fashion shows, and canoodling, oblivious to the world changing around them, right up until the French Revolution literally burst through the palace doors.

The grounds surrounding Versailles are a sculptured forest, a king's playground. Explore the backyard. Marie Antoinette's little Hamlet (*le Hameau*) gives goose bumps to any historian or romantic. This is where the queen (who eventually laid her neck under the "national razor" during the Revolution) escaped the rigors of palace life by pretending she was a peasant girl, tending her manicured garden and perfumed sheep.

Palaces of the Divine and Absolute Monarchs
- Versailles (near Paris)
- Schönbrunn, Vienna
- Hofburg (Imperial Palace), Vienna
- Royal Palace, Madrid
- La Granja, outside Madrid
- Residenz of the Prince Bishop, Würzburg, Germany
- Residenz, Munich
- Frederiksborg Slot (north of Copenhagen), Denmark
- Drottingholm, Stockholm, Sweden

"Stop yawning! This is baroque." "But Dad, after a while, broke palaces all look alike."

Other Absolute Monarchs

Louis was every king's role model. Every nation in Europe had its "Louis" and its own "Versailles." As you travel, you'll notice that most palaces, from La Granja in Spain to Peter the Great's Summer Palace outside St. Petersburg, are modeled after Versailles with sculpted gardens and Halls of Mirrors—all trying, but none succeeding, to match the splendor of the original.

In Vienna, the Hapsburg King Leopold built the impressive Schönbrunn Palace. A musician at heart, he established Vienna as the music capital of Europe. Vienna later produced Haydn, Mozart, Beethoven, and many of the classical superstars, who lived, worked, taught, and occasionally jammed together in the city.

King Frederick William of Prussia (eastern Germany) copied France's centralized government and turned his loose collection of baronies into a monolithic European power. The "goose step" and Germany's strong military tradition came from Prussia.

England also had strong monarchs, but her people insisted on constitutional limits. Henry VIII's daughter, Elizabeth I, made England the world's top naval power and enjoyed the loyalty and support of nobles and commoners alike. However, her successors, the Scottish Stuart family, alienated the English with their divine-right style. The English Parliament rebelled against King Charles (Stuart), and a civil war broke out in the mid-1600s. In the end, the king was beheaded and a member of Parliament, Oliver Cromwell, took power. When Cromwell died, the monarchy was restored, but the ruler's power came from Parliament, not from God. (You'll find much more about England's bloody and glorious history in Part II.)

Baroque Art

After 100 years of religious wars and squabbles over who would rule whom and who would worship which way, Europe chose religious toleration, stability, strong absolute monarchs, and a pro-status-quo art called Baroque. Baroque contrasts with the simplicity and balance of Renaissance art.

Baroque is propaganda art. It was meant to wow the masses into compliance with authority. Artists promoted respect for their patrons—the church and the king—by using the most complex, dazzling, and moving effects ever. Ornamentation abounds. Abundance abounds.

While Renaissance art appeals to connoisseurs with its logic, Baroque appeals to the masses with emotion. This was pop art with superdramatic interpretations. If Renaissance art was meditation, Baroque art was theater.

Church decoration became a cooperative adventure, with painters, sculptors, stucco workers, and metalworkers all teaming up to portray Heaven itself. The average person could step into a world of glittering gold, precious stones, and a ceiling painted as if it opened up to the sky, with angels, saints, babies that looked like clouds, and clouds that looked like babies—everything (in better Baroque) balanced into a unified whole.

Baroque architecture uses Renaissance symmetry decorated with lots of ornamental curlicues, stucco work, ovals, and elliptical shapes. The interiors are bright, with clear windows, whitewashed walls, colored marble, and gold leaf. Many darker medieval buildings were given an update as centuries-old frescoes were whitewashed and fine old sets of stained glass were replaced by clear windows. Subtlety was out, as straight lines were interrupted whenever possible with medallions and statues. Art showed that God is great and so is your king.

St. Peter's Basilica, _Vatican City, Rome. The Baroque movement was born here, in the grandest church in Christendom._

Bernini: Father of Baroque

Baroque was born in Rome. Its father was Lorenzo Bernini (1598–1680), its mother the wealthy Catholic church. Rome bubbles with Bernini fountains and sculpture. Bernini spent 40 years embellishing St. Peter's Cathedral and creating St. Peter's Square. Bernini was a master of all the Renaissance techniques, but wasn't chained by its classical rules of simplicity.

His art maximizes emotion in the subject as well as the viewer. His famous statue of the mystic nun, St. Theresa, is a perfect example of a

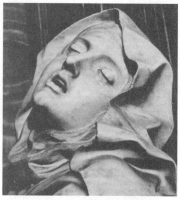

Bernini, **St. Theresa in Ecstasy** _(detail), 1652 (Santa Maria della Vittoria, Rome)_

Bernini, **Apollo and Daphne,** *1624 (Borghese Museum, Rome). Bernini, the father of the Baroque movement, captures the exciting moment when Apollo thinks he's caught the nymph Daphne. But just as he's ready to pounce, she turns into a tree—her fingers sprout leaves, her feet sprout roots, and Apollo is in for one rude surprise.*

Michelangelo's David and Bernini's David

Michelangelo's _David_ (1504) is textbook Renaissance, while Bernini's _David_ (1623) is the epitome of Baroque. Compare the two styles: Michelangelo's _David_ is a thinker—rational, cool, restrained. Bernini's is a doer—passionate, engaged, dramatic. Renaissance _David_ is simple and unadorned, carrying only a sling. Baroque Dave is "cluttered" with a braided sling, a hairy pouch, flowing cloth, and discarded armor. A model of perfection, Michelangelo's _David_ is far larger and grander than we mere mortals. We know he'll win. Bernini's _David_, with his tousled hair and set mouth, is one of us; the contest is less certain. Winding up for the pitch, Bernini's _David_ threatens to break out of the very stone. Michelangelo's _David_ will throw the rock when he's good and ready.

Michelangelo, **David,** _1504_
(Accademia, Florence)

Bernini, **David,** _1623_
(Borghese Museum, Rome)

complex but unified composition, expressive portraiture, and details suggesting movement and passion, all adding up to a theatrical and emotional work. Bernini shows her with a heart pierced by an angel's arrow. Theresa described the feeling as "a pain so great that I screamed aloud; but simultaneously I felt such infinite sweetness that I wished the pain would last forever." As we gaze at the statue, Bernini makes us feel the same ecstasy, the same "sweet pain."

Rubens' Fury of the Brush

In painting, Baroque meant big canvases of bright colors, classical subjects, optical illusions, and swirling action.

Bernini's painting counterpart was Peter Paul Rubens (1577–1640) from Catholic Flanders (Belgium). Rubens studied in Rome, where he picked up the Italian fad of painting giant compositions on huge canvases.

He could arrange a pig pile of many figures into a harmonious unit. Each painting was powered with an energy and gaiety that people called his "fury of the brush."

Rubens: A self-portrait

Rubens' work, while colorful, intricate, and lively, was always robust, strong, and solid. Like Bernini, Rubens draped clothing on his subjects in a manner that suggested rippling motion and energy—a popular trick.

A famous scholar and diplomat, Rubens was welcomed at every royal court in Catholic Europe. His Antwerp house (now a fine museum) was an art factory, designed to mass-produce masterpieces. After he laid out a painting, his apprentices painted the background and filled in the minor details. Rubens orchestrated the production from a balcony, and before a painting was carried outside his tall, narrow door, he would put on the finishing touches, whipping each figure to life with a flick of his furious brush.

In Madrid's Prado museum, Centaurs race lustily after Lapiths (R-rated Baroque action, brought to you by Rubens). Compare this Baroque vibrancy to the Renaissance composure of a Raphael **Madonna and Child** *or Leonardo's* **Mona Lisa.**

Caravaggio

Caravaggio (car-a-VAW-jee-o, 1573–1610) set out to shock people with his paintings. He depicted subjects realistically, no matter how ugly or unpleasant. He set sacred Bible scenes in the context of the seedy, seamy side of his Roman neighborhood. Caravaggio lived much of his life on the edge of society. Quick-tempered and opinionated, he killed a man over a dispute in a tennis match and spent years as an outlaw. Twelve years after he first picked up a brush, he died of a knife wound.

Caravaggio, **Entombment of Christ,** _1604 (Pinacoteca, Vatican Museum, Rome). Not only does this thrilling composition draw you into the action, the action threatens to come to you._

Caravaggio painted with a profound psychological realism that captures the inner feelings of the common people he used as subjects. It brings to mind the style of his contemporary, Shakespeare, who acquainted himself with English lowlife and incorporated it into his plays.

You'll recognize Caravaggio's works by the strong contrast between light and dark. Whole sections of canvas are in shadow, with details obscured. If light does shine on a subject, it's a harsh, unflattering,

Caravaggio, **David with the Head of Goliath,** _1605 (Kunsthistorisches Museum, Vienna). Using harsh, exaggerated light/dark contrasts, Caravaggio powers his early Baroque paintings with emotion. The severed head is his self-portrait._

Caravaggio, 1599,
Doubting Thomas
*(Sanssouci,
Potsdam,
Germany)
Caravaggio was
revolutionary in
his gritty and
vivid realism.*

"third-degree interrogation" light that pierces through anything glorified or idealized, exposing the real person underneath.

As Caravaggio's art shows, the Bible happened to real people and miracles transform the commonplace. His saints have dirty feet. Caravaggio paints Doubting Thomas as an old common laborer. Depicting the scene when Jesus said to Thomas, "Reach hither thy hand and thrust it into my side," Caravaggio paints Thomas with his grubby finger actually sticking inside Jesus' wound.

Royal Art Court Painters

You'll see plenty of royal portraits in European museums. The court painter was the official "photographer" of the day. To keep the royal egos happy, most court paintings were unrealistic, melodramatic, and flattering. One royal portraitist, Velázquez, was unusually realistic, offering a rare, real look at royal Europe.

Diego Velázquez (vel-LAHS-kes, 1599–1660), the Spanish royal

Velázquez, **Prince Balthasar Carlos on Horseback,** *1635 (Prado, Madrid). To keep his boss—the king—happy, even "realistic" Velázquez had to make the prince look really good on a horse.*

Velázquez, **The Maids of Honor**, *1656 (Prado, Madrid), shows the Spanish court and the painter himself (at left) in a realistic way, without emotion. In this unusual court portrait, the artist captures the royal couple's view as they sit for a portrait. Their reflection appears in the mirror at the back of the room. More art historians consider this the greatest single painting than any other.*

court painter, was ahead of his time. Influenced by Caravaggio's hypernaturalism, he painted without showy emotion or unnecessary ornamentation. His work appears intricately detailed, but if you look closely, you see a new technique in brushwork. Velázquez suggested details with a quick stroke of the brush, a bit like Rubens but also with a peek at a future style, Impressionism.

His *Prince Balthasar* is typical of most court portraits of the time (unnatural, grandiose, focused on royalty), but his *Maids of Honor* is a stunning departure. In the relaxed setting of his studio, the artist himself appears with the royal family, the maids are on equal footing with the royal child, and the king and queen are just a reflection in the background.

Christopher Wren

England's chance to make a radical break with the medieval past came when London burned in the Great Fire of 1666. Almost before the ashes had cooled, a young architect named Christopher Wren was in the mayor's office with exciting plans to rebuild the city. He got the job and set out to decorate the new downtown with more than fifty of his churches.

Wren, **St. Paul's Cathedral**, *1675–1708, London. Wren's tomb inside the church bears the epitaph: "If you seek a monument ... look around you. "*

Wren's style shows Baroque and Gothic influences (Gothic remained popular in England long after the Middle Ages) as well as many classical features. Although architects feel that better examples of Wren's genius can be found in his smaller churches nearby, his most famous (and my favorite) work is St. Paul's Cathedral. In studying St. Paul's, you'll notice a central Baroque cupola lined with classical columns and flanked by Gothic towers. The overall effect, however, is one not of Baroque movement, tension, or exuberance, but of classical restraint and stability.

Rococo: Uncontrolled Exuberance

The Baroque movement spread from Rome throughout Catholic Europe by way of the court of Louis XIV at Versailles. Louis' great-grandson, Louis XV, championed a new style called Rococo (ro-KO-ko).

Rococo was an early 19th-century celebration of happiness and love. Rococo is lighter and daintier, without the Renaissance-like robustness and classical balance of Baroque. Light pastel colors, ivory, gold, mirrors, and slender columns with curvy frills characterize Rococo interior decoration. This giddy style, using decoration almost to the obliteration of form, spread quickly from Paris to Germany and Austria during the 1700s. Rococo survives today only on the stage sets of TV evangelists.

Boucher:
Textbook
Rococo

Wieskirche, _1746–1754, near Oberammergau, Germany. A breathless example of Bavarian Rococo, the Wieskirche (or church of the meadow) sits peacefully in the countryside of southern Germany. Built to enshrine a wooden
crucifix (believed to have miraculously wept in 1738), this church has long
been a popular destination for pilgrims and tourists._

Baroque and Rococo Art and Architecture

- Versailles, France
- St. Peter's church (including Bernini's altar canopy, dove window, and statues), Vatican City, Rome
- Il Gesu church (its scroll-shaped facade was the model for Jesuit churches throughout Latin America), Rome
- *St. Theresa in Ecstasy*, Church of Santa Maria della Vittoria, Rome
- Piazzas of Rome, especially St. Peter's Square
- Bernini fountains, Rome
- Residenz and Chapel of the Prince Bishop, Würzburg, Germany
- Bavarian churches (Wieskirche, Oberammergau, Ettal, Asam in Munich), Germany
- Schönbrunn, Vienna
- Benedictine monastery, Melk on Danube, Austria
- Salzburg's Old Town, Austria
- St. Paul's, London
- Charles Bridge and most of old Prague, Czech Republic
- Rubens' home, Antwerp, Belgium
- Paintings by Rubens in the Prado (Madrid), Louvre (Paris), National Gallery (London), and most major museums
- Music by Bach, Vivaldi, Scarlatti

Fake dome, 1684, Church of St. Ignazio (near the Pantheon), Rome. Baroque artists (like late 20th-century Republican economists) were masters of illusion. This flat ceiling was painted to look like a dome from the pews.

Northern Protestant Art

There's not a single great Protestant building or statue. The art in Protestant Northern Europe is entirely different from the flashy art that filled the churches and palaces of the Catholic world. Protestant artists had to manage without the rich and powerful Catholic church's patronage. Depiction of elaborate ritual and anything with even a hint of idolatry was out. Religious art fell out of favor, and Protestant artists specialized in subjects that had nothing to do with the church.

During this period, many Northern European churches channeled their artistic energy into music, with orchestras and elaborate church organs. Choirmasters, composers, and organists (such as J. S. Bach, who did it all) enjoyed a new, loftier status.

While the Reformation frowned on fancy paintings, pipe organs were big in Protestant churches. This one fills an entire end of the Church of St. Bavo in Haarlem, Netherlands.

New Patronage, New Art

The wealthy merchants of the prosperous middle class became the new patrons of northern art. These city burghers were playing catch-up with the ruling class, and a great way to rise above society's small-fries was to commission a distinguished portrait of yourself.

The commissioned portrait was the artist's bread and butter.

Rembrandt, **De Staalmeesters** *(a.k.a. The Dutch Masters), 1662 (Rijksmuseum, Amsterdam). Even in his later years, Rembrandt could paint better portraits than anyone. He shows us not just faces but personalities as well. These men were members of a textile guild (clothes, but no cigars).*

Jan Steen, **Die Verkehrte Welt** *(The Topsy-turvy World) (Kunsthistorisches Museum, Vienna). Without a king or the Catholic Church to buy their art, Dutch artists painted fun, unpreachy, and affordable art for the urban middle class.*

Northern artists made portraits come alive without employing the artificial or flattering poses of Baroque portraiture. From Hans Holbein to Frans Hals to Rembrandt, portraitists got better and better at capturing the real character of their subjects in relaxed, "unposed" poses.

Sadly, many of those who paid and posed were tightfisted, more interested in value for their money than in encouraging good art. Great artists often wasted their talents on unimaginative works simply to earn a meager living from the fickle patronage of a nouveau riche whose taste was mostly in its mouth.

The only alternative for artists was to sell their work on the open market—an art-history first. Art was sold in marketplaces and fairs as well as through art dealers.

This new patronage pointed art in new directions. Along with portraits, artists painted scenes the average person would like and buy, such as landscapes, seascapes, slices of daily life, and fun looks at human folly. Paintings were generally small and affordable.

Slice-of-Life Art

Peter Brueghel (1564–1638) used Italian techniques to depict Flemish peasant life. A townsman himself, painting for fellow townspeople, he depicted peasants as peasants, simple and happy, but also as hicks worth a laugh. His crowded and brightly colored scenes of people are fun and entertaining. At the same time, we can sympathize with his characters, seeing a bit of ourselves in their actions.

Brueghel's paintings were popular and often imitated. They give travelers a great glimpse of old peasant lifestyles. (The Museum of Ancient Art in Brussels and the Kunsthistorisches Museum in Vienna have two of

Brueghel, **Peasant Wedding,** _1565 (Kunsthistorisches, Vienna). Crowded, colorful, detailed look at everyday peasant life. These scenes were popular with the urban middle class._

Rembrandt, **Self-Portrait,** _1669 (National Gallery, London)_

Vermeer, **Kitchen Maid,** _1658 (Rijksmuseum, Amsterdam). Vermeer creates a quiet little world where we can see the beauty in everyday things._

Europe's best collections of Brueghels and Brueghel-style art.)

In a more serious style, Jan Vermeer (1632–1675) perfected the art of showing the natural beauty of common people and simple, everyday objects. His tiny domestic scenes and tranquil landscapes are a far cry from the huge, colorful, fleshy, and exciting Baroque scenes of Greek gods.

Rembrandt

The plight of the creative artist at the mercy of unenlightened patrons is epitomized by the life of Dutch genius Rembrandt van Rijn (1606–1669). Young, successful, and famous as a portrait painter for wealthy merchants, he fell out of favor, probably because he had a mind of his own and refused to compromise in his portraits. If his painting's composition required it (or if he didn't like someone), he might

Rembrandt, **The Night Watch**, 1642 (detail, Rijksmuseum, Amsterdam). Rembrandt makes this much more than a group portrait. It's an action scene, capturing the can-do spirit of the Dutch Golden Age.

Van Der Helst, **Schuttersmaaltijd** (Rijksmuseum, Amsterdam). Everyone got his money's worth in this colorful group portrait—every face is flashbulb perfect. Compare it with Rembrandt's rowdy Night Watch.

Northern Art Museums

- Rijksmuseum (Dutch art, especially Rembrandt and Vermeer), Amsterdam
- Museum of Ancient Art, Brussels
- Alte Pinakothek (German art), Munich
- Kunsthistorisches Museum, Vienna

depict his patron in a shadow or even with an arm in front of his face. Few would invest in a wonderful but risky Rembrandt portrait. He spent his last years painting portraits of himself and poor street people. He died in poverty.

The silver lining to this story is that by failing to get commissions, Rembrandt was free to paint whatever he wanted. His Bible scenes are illuminating, showing the inner workings of the soul. Like Caravaggio, he used common people as his models, refusing to idealize or beautify his subjects.

Also like Caravaggio, Rembrandt can be recognized by his experimentation with contrasting light and shade. He played around with the source of light and the illumination of his figures. When he shines a light on his subject, the effect is powerful and dramatic.

The Age of Enlightenment

The scientific experimentation begun in the Middle Ages and the Renaissance finally bloomed in the 1600s. Copernicus (born 1473), Galileo (b. 1564), Kepler (b. 1571), and Newton (b. 1642) explained the solar system, disproving the church's view that the earth was the center of the universe.

The "scientific method" was seen as a way to solve all problems: if science enabled humanity to figure out the motion of the planets and explain the circulation of blood through the body, this enlightened thinking should be useful in answering moral and political questions as well.

The philosophers of the Enlightenment (1700s) thought that nature obeyed laws and that all of those laws could be understood by reason. Every institution and every established school of thought was given the "test of reason." Superstition and ignorance were attacked. The Old Regime (the era of divine monarchs, feudalism, serfdom, and so on) was picked to pieces. Thinkers and writers proposed a complete reorganization of society determined by reason, not by accident of birth.

England and France produced the social philosophies that laid the foundation of modern thought. Adam Smith established the basis for laissez-faire, the free economy of capitalism. Rousseau wrote about the "Social Contract," saying that the government is the servant of the people and that a people's revolution is justified when their government screws up. A kind of "religion of reason" was created, and for the first time, many people—respected people—said, "Christianity is stupid."

John Locke and Voltaire wrote of "natural laws" and "self-evident truths" in human relationships that make necessary a more democratic form of government. Many of Locke's phrases are used in the U.S. Declaration of Independence, a document based on the ideals of the Enlightenment. Despite owning slaves, Thomas Jefferson prided himself on being a part of this enlightened movement.

The kings of this period are called "enlightened despots." They ruled efficient, modern states and supported many ideas of the Enlightenment. But while royal parlor talk might have been enlightened, royalty still refused to share power with the lower classes. The growing urban middle class, often as wealthy and educated as the nobility, wanted more power. But the Old Regime lived on, and people were divided by birth, not by ability or wealth, into the rulers and the ruled.

In the Enlightenment, a new world was conceived. Europe was fast outgrowing its archaic shell. Enlightened thoughts turned to violent actions.

The French Revolution

In France, the decay of the Old Regime made especially fertile conditions for the seeds planted by the Enlightenment to blossom.

The Old Regime became the dying regime. While the three-part feudal order of nobility, clergy, and peasantry survived legally, it no longer fit the European reality. Two new social forces—the merchants and nationalists—would forcibly reslice Europe's political and economic pie.

Nationalism

Basic loyalties had shifted, over the centuries, from tribe to church to monarch to nation. Nationalism was the "ism" of the 19th century.

Nationalism and the democratic ideas of the Enlightenment were tested and proven practical and possible by the American Revolution. The United States was the first truly modern nation to have a constitution based on democracy, freedom of religion, and protection of individual rights. In 1776, Europe's eager revolutionaries were taking careful notes.

France, the home of the Enlightenment, was ruled by a very unenlightened government. Two percent of the country—the nobles and clergy—owned one-third of the land and paid no taxes. The ambitious middle class, or bourgeoisie, was economically strong but politically weak. France was ripe for revolt.

France's National Assembly, the First Step to Revolution

The restless middle class got its chance in 1789 when King Louis XVI (the Sun King's great-great-great-grandson) called an assembly of representatives to raise taxes.

The parliament met as three "estates," or classes: nobility, clergy (on the right), and peasants (on the left). The merchant class, newcomers to the social scene, were lumped in with the peasants as part of the

"Third Estate." Historically, the estates voted as a unit, and the nobility and the clergy always outvoted the peasantry two to one. The middle class demanded that the assembly be restructured so that the vote would be general rather than by estate. Because the peasant estate had more representatives, this would break the Old Regime's monopoly on power. After a six-week deadlock on this issue, the Third Estate declared itself the National Assembly whether the other two liked it or not, and vowed not to go home until a modern constitution had been created.

This was a revolutionary step. In an act commoners perceived as a show of loyalty to the nobles, the king called out 18,000 troops. Traditionally, the king was anti-feudal and pro-people. The masses felt betrayed. Sides were drawn and royal orders were boldly defied.

The National Assembly became a forum for all kinds of democratic ideas. The privileged classes protested feebly as the common people shouted, *"Liberté, Egalité, Fraternité."* Liberty, Equality, Brotherhood would now be fought for.

Mass Revolution

Like most revolutions, the French one started moderately and then took off. The masses had been awakened, and before they knew it the rich and liberal middle-class leaders of the Third Estate were riding out of control on a lower-class revolutionary stallion.

The masses were hungry and restless, having suffered several bad harvests. By allowing the price of bread to climb to record heights, the rulers had ignored the first rule in keeping the people docile. (Even today, authoritarian governments subsidize the price of bread to pacify the masses.) When the mad mobs of Paris demanded cheaper bread, Queen Marie Antoinette enraged them with her famous solution, "Let them eat cake." ("Cake" was the burnt crusts from the oven normally fed to the cattle.)

On July 14, 1789, angry Parisians stormed the Bastille, a prison that symbolized the Old Regime. The revolution escalated when prisoners were released. The mayor of Paris was beheaded with a dagger, and the mob paraded through the streets with his head on a pole. Bastille Day, the French "Fourth of July," is celebrated today with comparable pageantry but fewer deaths. (All that's left of the actual Bastille is a mark on the pavement.)

Angered by a lavish and well-publicized party at Versailles, mobs marched on the palace. They brought the king to Paris, where the government had come under the control of the radical city elements.

Throughout the countryside that summer, peasants went on the

"La Marseillaise"

There's a movement in France to soften the lyrics of their national anthem. Sing it now... before it's too late.

Allons enfants de la Patrie, (Let's go, children of the fatherland,)
Le jour de gloire est arrivé. (The day of glory has arrived.)
Contre nous de la tyrannie (The blood-covered
    flagpole of tyranny)
L'étendard sanglant est levé, (Is raised against us,)
L'étendard sanglant est levé. (Is raised against us.)
Entendez-vous dans nos campagnes (Do you hear
    what's happening in our countryside?)
Mugir les féroces soldats? (The ferocious soldiers are groaning)
Qui viennent jusque dans nos bras (They're coming
    nearly into our grasp)
Egorger nos fils et nos compagnes. (They're slitting the
    throats of our sons and our women.)
Aux armes citoyens, (Grab your weapons, citizens,)
Formez vos bataillons, (Form your battalions,)
Marchons, marchons, (March on, march on,)
Qu'un sang impur (So that their impure blood)
Abreuve nos sillons. (Will fill our trenches.)

Dubbed **"The Marseillaise in Stone,"** *1836, decorating
the Arc de Triomphe, Paris*

rampage, sacking châteaus, rousting the nobility, and burning the feudal documents that tied them to the land. The manorial system (serfdom) was physically destroyed. The National Assembly followed by legally abolishing serfdom, manorialism, tithes, and so on.

Feudalism was dead in France and shock waves rippled through Europe. Royalty quivered, nobility shivered, and the middle classes and peasantry drooled with delight as the French created the "Declaration of the Rights of Man and of the Citizen."

Much of France's ruling class took refuge in foreign palaces. They tried to push their European counterparts into war against France, warning them they'd be the next to go if they didn't do something quickly.

The revolutionaries running France also wanted a war, both to establish and solidify their new republic by banding against a common enemy and to spread their enlightened revolutionary gospel.

By 1793, it was France against the rest of Europe. France declared war on Britain, Spain, and the Netherlands. Then Austria, Piedmont, and Prussia joined the battle against France. A _levée en masse,_ or complete mobilization of the society, fueled by tremendous national patriotism and led by brash young risk-taking generals, powered France to victory.

Reign of Terror

On the home front, pressures of the war and economic problems drove the revolution to wild extremes. During this "Reign of Terror" (1793–1794), the king and queen were beheaded and wave after wave of people went to the guillotine. Political factions accused each other of halting the progress of the revolution. Enemies of the current ruling party were executed in public demonstrations in Paris' Place de la Concorde. People were sent to the "national razor" if they were even

The head (left) of King Louis XVI (right). Thousands of heads rolled in the early 1790s. The guillotine was set up on Paris' Place de la Concorde.

suspected of insufficient patriotism. Flags waved furiously as the blade dropped on over 17,000 necks. Even the raging fanatic liberal Robespierre was made a foot shorter at the top. Paris cooled off when it realized that the revolution was out of control and actually destroying itself. Some people even considered reinstating the monarchy.

The revolution struggled along for five years. At the same time, from his Italian refuge, the French heir to the throne was calling for revenge. To keep the revolution alive, the revolutionary leaders decided to give the army control rather than lose everything to an Old Regime king. They needed a revolutionary hero...an enlightened, charismatic, dashing general...a short guy who kept his feet on the ground, his eyes on the horizon, and a hand in his shirt. In 1799, a 30-year-old general named Napoleon took power. He promised to govern according to the principles of the revolution.

Napoleon

Although Napoleon was basically a dictator (who later proclaimed himself emperor) and suspended many civil liberties, he was true to his promise to carry out what the revolution was all about. Church lands were confiscated and sold and privileged classes were abolished.

During his rule (1799–1814), Napoleon carried the revolution by war to the rest of Europe. His arsenal was France-Europe's richest, most populous, and best-educated state. With the barriers of class and privilege smashed, he opened positions to talent. The French army had grown strong and tough during the wars of the revolution, and Napoleon had no trouble conquering Europe. A grand Napoleonic Empire covering the entire Continent was created, and many people spoke of Paris as the "New Rome."

Napoleon Bonaparte—galloping into history

Britain was one of the few countries to frustrate Napoleon. By winning the Battle of Trafalgar (off the coast of southwest Spain) in 1805, Britain successfully established control of the seas, thwarting Napoleon's hope of a French takeover. The British hero Admiral Horatio Nelson died in the Battle of Trafalgar. Today, London's main square is named after this battle. The square is decorated by a huge column with Nelson at its top, looking out in the direction of the battle that saved Britain from Napoleon.

Ingres, **Napoleon I on the Imperial Throne** _(detail), 1806 (Museum of the Army, Paris)._ "We must not leave this world without leaving traces which remind posterity of us." – Napoleon, Emperor of France

To some Europeans, Napoleon was a genius, a hero, a friend of the common people, and an enemy of oppression. (Beethoven had originally planned to dedicate his Third "Heroic" Symphony to him.) To others, he was the tyrant of his century—pompous, vain, and egotistical, suppressing a desire to be like the royalty he opposed.

Born of Italian parents on the Mediterranean isle of Corsica (the year after it became French), Napoleon was educated in French military schools. Originally an outsider, he quickly lost his accent and rose through the ranks of the army during the chaotic French Revolution.

Napoleon's personality was as complex as his place in history. He was actually of average height, with a classic, intense profile. He was well read, a good writer, and a charming conversationalist who could win friends and influence people with ease. Although he was easily flattered, he never let flattery cloud his judgment. He had few of the vices that plague world conquerors: he cared little for expensive palaces, fancy clothes, and good food and drink. He worked himself as hard as he worked others. Nevertheless, he could be cold, distant, and ruthless with his enemies.

Above all else, he was egotistical and power hungry, convinced of his inherent right to rule others. Yet when it came to military and political administration, Napoleon was a genius.

Russia, Waterloo, and a New King

Napoleon's empire didn't last long. In 1812, he led 600,000 soldiers into Russia. The vastness of the country, Russia's "scorched earth" policy (destroying everything when retreating, leaving nothing to sustain invaders), and its special ally, the horribly cold winter, spelled disaster for Napoleon's Grand Army. Only 100,000 Frenchmen returned to France. The nightmares of that ill-fated invasion haunted soldiers' minds for generations. (One of Europe's best military museum, Les Invalides, is in Paris, next to Napoleon's tomb.)

With Napoleon reeling, all of Europe called for a pig pile on France, vowing to fight until France was defeated. The French people took the hint, toppled Napoleon's government and sent him on a permanent vacation to the island of Elba, off the Italian coast.

As evidence of Napoleon's personal charisma, he soon returned from his exile-in-disgrace, bared his breast to the French people, and said, "Strike me down or follow me." They followed him into one last military fling. It was only after the crushing defeat at Waterloo in 1815 that Napoleon was finished. (The battle site is in Belgium, south of Brussels, but not worth a detour except to true Bonapartisans.) Napoleon was exiled again, this time to a tiny island in the south Atlantic.

Napoleon was the last of the enlightened despots of the Old Regime

Europe in 1815, after the Congress of Vienna

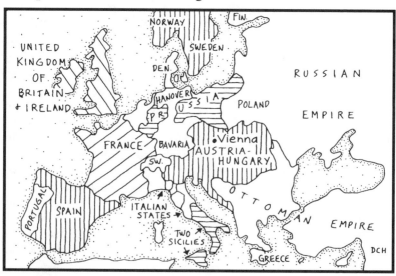

Congress of Vienna—1815

Napoleon, steamrolling through Europe, had torn up boundaries and toppled monarchies. After his defeat, the Congress of Vienna met to put together the pieces of a broken Europe. The major powers at that time—Austria, Russia, Prussia, Great Britain, and France—redrew national boundaries with the goal of creating a Europe that would stay at peace.

The Congress, at that time the biggest diplomatic summit ever, brought about a century of general peace and stability for Europe through these major decisions:

- France lost all territory Napoleon had acquired.
- Kings were restored in France (Louis XVIII) and Spain (Ferdinard VII).
- Germany was tidied up into the Confederation of the Rhine (replacing the Holy Roman Empire that Napoleon had dismantled).
- Russia ended up with Finland and control over Poland.
- Switzerland was declared neutral.
- Austria's holdings in the Netherlands were made part of the Dutch Republic, and, as compensation, Austria got Venice and a first-round draft pick.
- Britain hung onto its far-flung colonies, added a few more, and continued to rule the waves.
- Sweden got Norway, ya sure.
- Prussia got bigger. Watch out.

A milestone in European cooperation, it accomplished what it set out to do. Its weakness: Its "balance of power" favored royal families over nationalism—a problem not to be remedied until Europe's next great war. . . coming up in 99 years.

and the first of the modern popular dictators. He was a rationalist, an agnostic of the passing age of Voltaire and the Enlightenment, and the model heroic individual of the future Romantic world.

After swinging from Louis XIV to the Revolution to Napoleon, France finally settled down with another king. But French kings after Napoleon were limited by a constitution and the echo of the guillotine. Knowing they'd better keep their wigs and leotards out of sight, they went to work every day like any businessmen: wearing suits, carrying briefcases.

Neoclassicism

Baroque had been the art of the Old Regime—of divine-right monarchs, powerful clergy, and landed aristocracy. The French Revolution killed that regime and its art, replacing it with a style more in tune with the Enlightenment. This new art was "neoclassical," modeled not on the aristocratic extravagance of Versailles or the Rococo excess of the Wieskirche, but on the "democratic" simplicity of ancient Greece and Rome.

Archaeological discoveries had roused France's interest in the classical world. Pompeii, the Roman city buried by a volcano in A.D. 79, was rediscovered in 1748, giving Europe its best look ever at Roman daily life, dress, customs, art, and architecture. Books on Roman and Greek life came into vogue. Parisian women wore Pompeiian hairdos. Artists studied ancient art, trying to capture the true Greek and Roman style. Ancient became modern, and classical was in.

Throughout Europe, but especially in Paris, tourists are fooled by classical-looking buildings that are actually neoclassical—only 200 years old.

Boucher's Rococo **Madame Pompadour** *(left, from 1756) and David's Neoclassical* **Madame Hamelin** *(right, from 1800) could well have been mother and daughter. But in the age of revolution, Europe dumped its curls and ribbons for pure classical truth. Talk about a generation gap.*

French Art of the "New Rome"

In France, the official style of the Revolution and the Napoleonic era was neoclassical. The French thought of themselves as citizens of a new Rome and wanted art to match. In Paris, the Arc de Triomphe and Pantheon were built to look like grand Roman monuments. Funded by the spoils of Napoleon's conquests in Europe, Paris was rebuilt and ornamented with gas lamps and new bridges.

Napoleon had himself crowned emperor in an elaborate ceremony in the style of the Caesars. Classical backdrops masked the Gothic columns of Notre-Dame cathedral so the emperor could be crowned as "Romanly" as possible. Paris was the new Rome. Napoleon was the new Caesar.

The great painter Jacques-Louis David (dah-VEED, 1748–1825) was France's virtual dictator of fashion during this period. Marriage ceremonies, clothing styles, hairdos, and giant government propaganda spectacles were designed according to David's interpretation of neoclassicism. David's painting style was realistic, dignified, and simple, like a classical statue.

David, **The Coronation of Napoleon***, 1807 (Louvre, Paris). There's Napoleon with his wife Josephine (kneeling) and his proud mom, not actually in attendance but painted (looking on from the balcony). The pope (seated behind Napoleon) came all the way from Rome to crown him. But no ordinary mortal was good enough for that job, so Napoleon crowned himself.*

Napoleon's armies spread neoclassicism throughout Europe. (In Britain, the style is called Georgian.) Then, like the Enlightenment, neoclassicism spread to the New World. Thomas Jefferson, a child of the Age of Reason, designed his residence, Monticello (of nickel fame), in the neoclassical style. The Capitol of the United States and many state capitols have similar architecture. "Enlightened" people everywhere rejected the gaudy ornamentation of Baroque in favor of austere arches and pure columns.

New Patronage: The Academy

The French Revolution and the rise of democracy in Europe changed the economics of art just as the Reformation had changed the economics of art in the Protestant countries of the North. As art became less and less the domain of the elite class and the church, it became more the domain of the middle class. As commissions became rare, artists had less money but more freedom.

Previously, artists had studied as apprentices under a master who was employed by a wealthy patron. Now they went to "Academies" (pompously named after Plato's Academy of Philosophy in Athens) to study art history, theory, and technique. Here, artists were free to pursue and paint their own ideas of beauty, not those of whomever was paying them. Art became an expression of individuality—not merely a craft, but Art with a capital "A."

David, **Death of Socrates**, *1787 (Louvre, Paris). Classical scenes were in vogue in neoclassical Paris.*

Neoclassical Art, Architecture, and Music
- Neoclassical room (*Ingres, David*), Louvre, Paris
- Arc de Triomphe, Pantheon, and La Madeleine, Paris
- Royal Crescent and Circus, Bath, England
- Georgian mansions in Bath, England, and Edinburgh, Scotland
- Lutheran Cathedral and Senate Square, Helsinki, Finland

*Pantheon, Paris.
Built during
France's bold
experiment in
democracy and
free-thinking, this
was like a Greek
Temple of Reason.*

*"Georgian" is
English for neo-
classical. In the
1770s, **"The Circus"**
was one of several
elegant Georgian
rowhouses in the
trend-setting resort
town of Bath.*

David C. Hoerlein

*Since 1852, **Helsinki's
Lutheran Cathedral**
has been the center-
piece of one of
Europe's finest
neoclassical squares.*

Musical Vienna

While France dealt with revolution and Napoleon, Vienna enjoyed Europe's greatest age of music. Vienna was to music what ancient Athens and Renaissance Florence were to painting and sculpting. Never before or since have so many great composers and musicians worked and competed side by side. Haydn, Mozart, Beethoven, and Schubert all worked in Vienna at roughly the same time (1775–1825). Their works changed music forever, raising it from simple entertainment to High Art.

Why Vienna? A walk through the city explains part of it. The peaceful gardens, the architecture, and the surrounding countryside inspired the composers, many of whom wrote tunes in their head as they strolled through the streets. Beethoven was a familiar sight, striding quickly, his hands behind his back, staring straight ahead with a brooding look on his face. He claimed he did his best composing away from the piano.

Maria Theresa

Of the Habsburgs who ruled Austria from 1273 to 1918, Maria Theresa (ruled 1740–1765) stands out. Her reign followed the Austrian defeat of the Turks, when Europe recognized Austria as a great power. She was a strong and effective queen. (Her rival, the Prussian emperor, said, "When at last the Habsburgs get a great man, it's a woman.")

Maria Theresa was a great social reformer. During her reign she avoided wars and expanded her empire by skillfully marrying her children into the right families. With daughter Marie Antoinette's marriage into the French Bourbon family (to Louis XVI), a country that had been an enemy became an ally. (Unfortunately for Marie, she arrived in time for the Revolution, and she lost her head.)

In tune with her age and a great reformer, Maria Theresa's "Robin Hood" policies helped Austria slip through the "age of revolution" without turmoil. She taxed the church and the nobility and provided six years of obligatory education to all children and free health care to all in her realm. She also welcomed the boy genius Mozart into her court

Money Makes Music

But the true root of all musical inspiration in Vienna was (as is the case with most art) money. The aristocracy found music more interesting than politics. Concerts were the social hub of high society. Many leading families employed their own orchestras to play at their parties. Some nobles were excellent amateur musicians: Emperor Joseph II played both violin and cello; Empress Maria Theresa was a noted soprano.

Professionals were needed to perform, conduct, compose, and give lessons. Musicians from all over Europe flocked to Vienna, where their talents were rewarded with money and honor.

Before 1750, music had been considered a common craft, like shoemaking, and musicians were treated accordingly. Composers wrote music to order, expecting it to be treated like Kleenex—used once and thrown away. Beginning with Haydn, however, the new breed of composers saw music as a lasting art on par with painting and sculpture.

Composers demanded respect from their employers. Beethoven, it is said, considered himself to be superior to his employers: he was an artist; they were merely royalty. When Mozart became composer-in-residence for a Viennese prince, he was paid a princely sum and then told to eat his meals with the servants. Mozart turned on his heel and walked out, refusing from then on to accept an "official" position.

Vienna fawned over its composers but only as long as they cranked out pleasant tunes. The minute they tried something new, daring, or difficult, the public turned on them.

Mozart was adored as a cute, clever six year old who could play the harpsichord as well as anyone in Europe. He won the hearts of the nobility by declaring that he wanted to marry the Princess Marie Antoinette.

Portrait of the child prodigy,
Mozart. _It's said Wolfgang
had his cheeks kissed by
more queens than anyone
in history._

But as a grown man writing mature and difficult works, he was neglected and often maligned. When he died, broke, at 35, his body was buried in an unmarked grave. Only later was his genius fully appreciated and a statue erected to honor him. As the saying goes, "To be popular in Vienna, it helps to be dead."

Beethoven, like Michelangelo before him, played the role of the temperamental genius to the hilt. His music and personality were uncompromising. A bachelor, he lived in rented rooms all his life—69 different ones at last count. He had some bad habits that explain his migratory existence, such as playing the piano at 2:00 a.m. and pouring buckets of water on himself to cool off. His rooms were always a mess, with music, uneaten meals, and atonal chamber pots strewn about.

While America will be known for bringing together the best basketball players of the age, Vienna assembled a musical "dream team" of its own: Beethoven, Mozart, and Haydn. "Papa" Haydn (so called because of his fatherly way with younger musicians) encouraged Mozart and gave lessons to Beethoven. Beethoven also learned from Antonio Salieri, Mozart's composing rival. With so many talented people rubbing oboes, music flourished in Vienna.

Strauss Waltzes

And then there was Strauss. And then Strauss Jr. The waltz craze swept through Vienna in the early 19th century and has continued in three-quarter time to the present. The two leading composers and conductors of the waltz were father and son: Johann Strauss Sr. and Johann Strauss Jr.

The waltz was the Beatlemania of its time. Many considered it decadent because of the close contact of the partners and the passionate sound of the music. Dances lasted from dusk to dawn, night after night. Johann the Elder played the violin and simultaneously conducted with wild gestures, whipping the crowd to "bewildering heights of frenzy till they were frantic with delight and emitting groans of ecstasy," according to composer Richard Wagner.

Young Johann took the baton when his father died and raised the waltz to respectability. His "Tales from the Vienna Woods" and "Blue Danube" immortalized his beloved hometown.

Imagine the lavish balls and mirrored halls where this music was played during the Golden Age of Emperor Franz Joseph. Chandeliers, carriages, sumptuous costumes, ceremony, and white-gloved ritual were the heart and soul of the conservative aristocracy.

The Vienna of today clings to the elegance of its past and maintains much of that musical tradition. The Ministry of Culture and Education is the new patron. The State Opera, the Philharmonic Orchestra, the Vienna Boys' Choir, and the Society of Friends of Music still thrive as they did in Beethoven's time. There are statues of all the famous composers who were neglected in their day. And if you dial 1509 on a telephone in Vienna, you will hear a perfect A note (440 Hz) for tuning your instrument.

Congratulations...

You've survived the wars, despots, and revolutions of Europe's early modern age. Next come the wars, despots, and revolutions of modern Europe. But first, see if you can make some sense of this timeline.

Timeline of Early Modern Europe

The Reformation and religious wars split Europe into two camps: the Protestant North (northern Germany, the Netherlands, England, Scandinavia) and the Catholic South (Italy, France, Spain, southern Germany). The northern countries, relying on a strong middle (merchant) class, were generally democratic. The South tended toward rule by absolute (and occasionally enlightened) despots. In succeeding centuries, the democratic ideals of the Enlightenment sank in and old regimes gave way to more modern governments.

This historical journey from religious division to absolute monarchy to democracy is also apparent in art styles. The rich, swirling Baroque style, associated with the Catholic church and absolute monarchs such as France's Louis XIV, was centered in Italy and France. At the same time, the middle-class Northern Protestant countries (Holland and England) developed a more subtle, thoughtful style, exemplified by the works of Rembrandt. As both North and South moved toward democracy, a new style appeared that reflected the ideals of the ancient Rome—neoclassicism. This was the dominant style of the French Revolution and the reign of Napoleon, the emperor of the "New Rome."

Timeline of Early Modern Europe

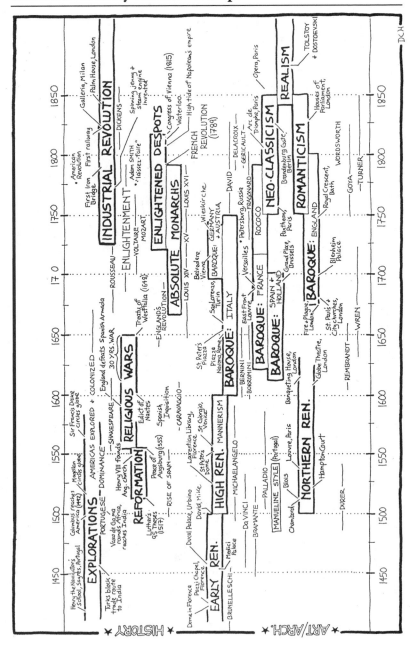

*Delacroix, **Liberty Leading the People**, 1830 (Louvre, Paris). This dramatic scene captures the spirit of patriotism. Liberty, in the form of a woman, carries a gun in one hand and a flag in the other—the winning combination for 19th-century nationalist movements.*

Modern Europe
A.D. 1815–Today

The Age of Nationalism

A brief conservative backlash followed the French Revolution and Napoleon, but, overall, the rights of individuals and nations had forever replaced the world of feudalism and the Old Regime.

Nationalism, a patriotic desire for national unity, was the dream and the political drive of the 1800s. When you travel in Europe, keep in mind that 150 years ago Germany and Italy did not exist. They were patchwork quilts of feudal baronies, dukedoms, and small kingdoms. As you tour castles, treasuries, and palaces scattered across these nations, you're seeing the White Houses and crown jewels of such "countries" as Piedmont, Saxony, and Bavaria.

In the 1800s, as democratic ideals became popular among the middle class and intellectuals, the people were no longer satisfied to be ruled by a royal family that was usually from another country. In the previous century, most of Europe had been ruled by the Bourbon (French), Hapsburg (Austrian), and Hohenzollern (German) families. The king often spoke a language different from that of his subjects.

Now people insisted on a government that reflected their language, ethnic heritage, culture, and religion. People identified themselves as citizens of a particular ethnic heritage, even if their nation was not yet a political reality. The stove setting switched from "simmer" to "high" and Europe's nationalistic stew was ready to boil over.

Unification of Italy

In the mid-1800s, the petty kingdoms and city-states of the Italian peninsula began a move toward unity. The governments were content but the people weren't, and talk of the *"Risorgimento"* (resurgence) of national pride was everywhere. As national revolts were crushed by

ITALIAN UNIFICATION

Four Italian leaders welded the Italian States into the Kingdom of Italy. Dates indicate year of annexation to the Kingdom of Sardinia (after 1861, the Kingdom of Italy).

Garibaldi

Cavour

Mazzini

Victor Emmanuel

local governments, patriotism grew. The liberals of Europe supported the Italian cause, and a local writer, Mazzini, made unification almost a holy crusade. Several shrewd patriots organized a campaign for unification, channeling nationalistic fervor into the formation of Italy.

The logical first king of Italy was the only native monarch of the region, Victor Emmanuel II, King of Sardinia. His prime minister, Cavour, a cunning, liberal, yet realistic politician, orchestrated Italy's unification. Guided by Cavour, Sardinia joined the Crimean War in order to get allies who would later support Sardinia in a war with Austria (a war Cavour needed for unification, though Sardinia couldn't win it alone). Sure enough, Cavour wrested Italian Lombardy—North Italy—from Austria. His clever statesmanship, combined with many local revolutions that were legitimized by plebiscites (local votes of popular support), brought most of northern Italy together by 1860.

Meanwhile, the powerful revolutionary general Garibaldi sailed with his motley army of a thousand "red shirts" to Sicily, where his forces were joined by local revolutionaries in annexing the Kingdom of Two Sicilies into the New Italian State in 1861.

Remember the names of these Italian patriots. Throughout Italy you'll find squares and streets named after the "Washingtons" and "Jeffersons" of the Italian resurgence—Via Cavours, Piazza Garibaldis, and monuments to Victor Emmanuel. (The most famous of these is the giant Victor Emmanuel monument near the Roman Forum.)

National pride was fueled by the romantic movement in art. Artists returned to their ethnic roots, incorporating folklore into their novels and folk music into their symphonies. In Italy, Giuseppe Verdi used the opera to champion the unification movement. In a time when flying the Italian colors was still dangerous, opera houses rang with the sound of patriots singing along with anthemlike choruses. The letters in Verdi's name were used as a nationalistic slogan: Victor Emmanuel _Roi_ (king) _di Italia_.

Unification of Germany

In 1850, Germany was 39 little countries. When it was united 20 years later, it was Europe's number-one power.

During that period of growth, German iron and coal output multiplied sixfold, surpassing that of France. Cities, industries, and trade boomed. German unification seemed inevitable. The big question was: would Germany be united under Prussia or Austria?

Otto von Bismarck, one of the greatest political geniuses of all time, knew the answer. He was the prime minister of Prussia, a militaristic German state, and the goose-stepping force behind German unity. The original master of "realpolitik," Bismarck said, "Not by speeches and majority votes are the great questions of the day decided, but by blood and iron."

Bismarck united Germany as if reading from a great political recipe book. With a logical, calculated, step-by-step approach, he created the dish nobody in Europe wanted—a united Germany.

Bismarck accomplished

Otto von Bismarck, 1815–1898. The great realistic politician of the 1800s, Bismarck created a united Germany.

Germany Before Unification

his objective by starting and winning three wars after carefully isolating each opponent. He got into a war with Denmark over the disputed territory of Schleswig-Holstein. Bismarck won easily, with Austria's unnecessary help. Dividing the spoils gave Bismarck the excuse he needed to fight Austria. His goal was only to knock her out of the lead, which he did. The last step necessary for German unification was to get the small German states between Prussia and France in his fold. The only thing these states hated more than Prussia was France. So, Bismarck got into a war with France and these states were forced to choose. The Franco-Prussian War lasted only a few weeks and the Sparta of modern Europe emerged as the leader of a united Germany.

Bismarck made alliances simply to break them, thereby creating a handy excuse to fight. After wiping out his opponent, he would make a fast and generous peace so he could work with that country in the future. He made concessions to the liberals of his parliament to win their support. He levied and collected unconstitutional taxes to build up his armies. He winked at Europe's great leaders, gained their confidence, and proceeded to make them history's fools. He leaked inflammatory comments to the press to twist public opinion into just the political pretzel he needed.

He did whatever he had to, and in the end he got exactly what he set out to get. In 1871, the fragmented Germany that Europe had enjoyed for centuries as a tromping ground became a Prussian-dominated conservative and militaristic German empire. The leaders of Europe were concerned. The balance of power had been disturbed. They hoped the unification of Germany would not lead to a large war or two.

Romanticism and Romantic Art

Nationalism and the artistic movement known as "Romanticism" went well together. Romantics and nationalists each threw rules and authority out the window to assert their right of personal expression. And just as national groups could not be suppressed by Old Regime aristocratic rulers, Romantic artists refused to conform their powerful inner feelings to society's code.

Romanticism, which has little to do with roses and chocolate hearts, was a reaction to the stern logic and reason of the neoclassical movement. While neoclassicism was a return to Europe's Greco-Roman roots, Romanticism was a return to a country's indigenous roots, folklore, and nature. Like neoclassicism (which carried on through much of the romantic period), Romanticism went beyond art—it was a way of living. It meant placing feeling over intellect and passion over restrained judgment. The rules of neoclassicism were replaced by a spirit that encouraged artists to be emotional and create not merely what the eyes saw but also what the heart felt.

Romantics made a religion of nature. They believed that taking a walk in the woods and communing with nature taught us about our true self—the primitive, "noble savage" beneath the intellectual crust. They looked back with nostalgia at the medieval age and appreciated the timelessness of the sublime. While many abandoned Christianity in the 18th century, those who did still needed to find the divine. They found it in nature.

The cultural heartbeat of this movement came not from the rich Medici palace in Florence or the elegant salons of Paris but from a humble log cabin in England's Windermere Lake District, the poet William Wordsworth's "Dove Cottage." English poets Blake, Coleridge,

Gericault, **Raft of the Medusa,** *1819 (Louvre, Paris).Gericault goes to great lengths to portray the death and despair on this raft. At the same time, a powerful pyramid of hope reaches up to flag down a distant ship.*

and Wordsworth rejected the urban, intellectual, scientific world for "simple living and high thinking." They nourished their souls in nature.

At Oxford and Cambridge, a stroll through the woods was a part of every scholar's daily academic diet. Even today, the Lake District in northern England is a popular retreat for nature lovers. Its hostels (more per square mile than any place on earth) are filled with rucksack romantics worshiping the wonders of nature-walking.

Until the Romantic era, mountains were seen only as troublesome obstacles. Now they attracted crowds of admirers drawn to their rugged power. High-class resorts, such as Interlaken in the Swiss Alps, were born. Why did people climb these mountains? Because they were there. Romanticism.

Constable, Delacroix, Gericault, and Ludwig II

Romantic artists glorified nature. Landscapes illustrated nature's power. Englishman John Constable (1776–1837) painted honest, unidealized scenes. He let nature be natural. His contemporary, J. M. W. Turner, differed by charging his landscapes with emotions, using bright supernatural colors and swirling brushwork. Peopling his paintings with clouds, Turner personified nature. He gave it the feelings and emotions of a romantic human being. (London's Tate Britain has the best collection of Turner landscapes.)

Eugene Delacroix (1798–1863) is a classic example of a Romantic painter. Solitary, moody, emotional, and endlessly imaginative, he broke all the neoclassical rules. His exotic and emotional scenes, wild color schemes, and complex, unrestrained compositions bubble with enough movement and excitement to ring any viewer's emotional bells. (See *Liberty Leading the People,* facing this chapter's title page.)

Theodore Gericault (1791–1824), in preparing to paint his gripping masterpiece *Raft of the Medusa,* visited an insane asylum and slept in a morgue so that he could better portray death and terror on the faces of his subjects. Nature was awesome, emotions were truth, and the Romantic artists were the prophets of this new religion.

The fairy-tale castle of Neuschwanstein is textbook Romanticism. King Ludwig II of Bavaria put it on a hilltop not for defensive purposes... but for the view. The king was a romantic. His architect was

Neuschwanstein Castle, *1869-1886,*   **Disneyland Paris,** *1991*
near Füssen, Germany.

The fairy-tale castle of Bavaria's "Mad King" Ludwig II is typical of the Romantic period. It was built on a hilltop in medieval style long after castles had lost their function as fortresses. Ludwig put it here for the view. The only knights in shining armor you'll find in his castle are on the wallpaper.

*London's **Houses of Parliament** look medieval but are Romantic, built around 1850 in a neo-Gothic style. In the wake of the Age of Revolution, mid-19th century Europe took a more romantic look at the previously disdained Middle Ages.*

a designer of theater sets. His best friends were artists, poets, and musicians. Scenes from Wagner's Romantic operas decorate the castle. His dreams were not of empires and big armies, but of fairy-tale castles and candlelit concerts.

Ludwig II is known as "Mad" King Ludwig because of his romantic excesses. He drowned mysteriously before Neuschwanstein castle, his dream about to come true, was completed.

Ludwig almost bankrupted Bavaria building his Disneyesque castles, but Germany is recouping its investment a hundredfold as huge crowds of tourists from all over the world pay to see Europe's most popular castle. Get there early or late, or you might spend more time in line than in the castle.

Goya

Francisco de Goya (1746–1828) was a portraitist for the Spanish royal court. A Romantic painter, he's been described as the first painter with a social conscience. His *Third of May, 1808* is a gripping combination of nationalism and Romanticism, showing a faceless government execution squad systematically gunning down patriots with all the compassion of a lawn mower.

Goya, **Third of May, 1808** *(Prado, Madrid). Romanticism expresses itself here in a powerful social statement against war and repression by faceless foreign invaders. The victims are Spaniards gunned down by Napoleon's troops for resisting French occupation.*

Artistically, Goya went through several stages. His last, after he lost his hearing and became bitter and disillusioned with life, was one of nightmarish fantasy. It's as if his innermost emotions finger painted in blood the grotesque figures that mirrored the turmoil that racked his soul. (Romantic, huh?)

The Prado Museum in Madrid has a room dedicated entirely to the bizarre visions of Goya's "Dark Stage." One of the most gripping is the painting, *Saturn Devouring His Son,* detailing in ghastly, twisted lines and vivid, garish colors how time eventually "eats" us all. "Romantic" isn't only "mushy kissy." This is Romanticism at its emotional best. No matter how cheery you are when you enter, you'll leave Goya's Dark Stage in a gloomy funk.

Goya, **Saturn Devouring His Son,** *1823 (Prado, Madrid). While this gives "child's portion" a new meaning, Goya's intended message is that "Time devours us all."*

Romantic Art Highlights

- Paintings in the Louvre's Romantic art room (Delacroix and Gericault), Paris
- Chopin's grave, Pére Lachaise Cemetery, Paris
- Tate Britain (Blake and Turner), London
- Neo-Gothic Halls of Parliament, London
- Neuschwanstein and Linderhof castles, Bavaria, Germany
- The Rhine and the Loreley poem, Germany
- The Alps, Switzerland
- Poetry by Wordsworth, Shelley, Keats, Byron, and Blake
- Music by Liszt, Chopin, Beethoven, Wagner, and Schumann

Delacroix, **Frédéric Chopin,** *1838 (Louvre, Paris). One romantic artist's tribute to another.*

Blake

William Blake of England was another master at putting inner visions on canvas. A mystic, nonconformist poet, he refused to paint posies for his supper. He made a living only through the charity of fellow artists who recognized his genius. Blake's watercolors (in London's Tate Britain), with their bizarre, unearthly subjects and composition, reveal how unschooled he was in classical technique. But his art grabs the viewer by the emotional lapel. That's what Romanticism is all about.

Blake, **Elohim Creating Adam,** *1795 (Tate Britain, London). Blake, who hobnobbed with the heavenly hosts, painted God creating Man.*

The Industrial Revolution

The Industrial Revolution, along with the rise of nationalism and democratic governments, powered Europe into the modern world. While the scientific achievements of the Enlightenment broadened human knowledge, practical inventions and applications (such as the steam engine and telegraph) didn't crank into motion until the 1800s.

This century of exciting technological advancement shifted nations from dependence on agriculture to dependence on industry. Britain's textile industry led the way as new, steam-powered factories lured people from the countryside to the cities.

The invention of the train shifted the revolution into high gear. As more products could be shipped more quickly to more people, huge new trade markets opened up. Rails laced European nations together. A person could travel across a country in a day's journey or less. From 1830 through 1860, one-sixth of all the world's track was laid (and then came the Eurailpass).

Europe's business boom stoked its colonial appetite. The world was Europe's buffet line, and it was "all you can eat." Europe divided up the underdeveloped world, harvested its raw materials, processed them, and sold the resulting products at great profits. Although every European nation grabbed a slice of the world's economic quiche, Britain's empire included nearly a quarter of the world's land and people. England boasted, "The sun never sets on the British Empire." (While others added, "Because God can't trust the English in the dark.")

The riches of England's Industrial Revolution came with its problems. This 19th-century engraving shows poor, dirty, overcrowded slums housing masses of industrial workers under roaring smokestacks.

Technological progress gave Europe a false optimism. Seeing how quickly technology changed nature and lifestyles, people figured it was the answer to the world's problems. Unfortunately, it led to many new difficulties: slums, polluted and overcrowded cities, child labor, unemployment, overwork, and the alienation of workers from the fruits of their labor. As we step out of this Industrial Age and into the Information Age, these problems persist. While we have become ace producers/consumers, quality of life is a different story.

Socialism and Communism

The Socialist movement tried to solve the social ills brought on by the Industrial Age. Socialists challenged government's lack of intervention in business affairs. Socialists and trade unions worked to restrict the power of factory owners and distribute wealth more fairly.

Karl Marx (1818–1883) and Friedrich Engels (1820–1895), both from Germany, cowrote the influential *Communist Manifesto* (1848), developing the fantasy that workers, not factory owners, should benefit most from industry. They predicted that a worker (proletarian) revolution would overthrow the capitalist (bourgeois) establishment. In the 19th century, communist and socialist organizations gained power throughout Europe. Though there was never a classic "workers' revolution," Marx's and Engels' ideas spurred reforms to benefit the working class.

*Soviet Marxism's Fab Four keep watch over a meeting of the Communist International, 1935. **Marx, Engels, Lenin, and Stalin** (left to right) were the propaganda poster-boys of communism. Their faces decorated factories throughout Eastern Europe and the USSR until the revolutions of 1989 and 1990.*

Vladimir Lenin (1870–1924), a Russian, used Marxist ideas to plan the Bolshevik Revolution and overthrow Russia's monarchy (1917), giving birth to the Soviet Union. He had to adapt industrial Marxism to a country still mired in medieval feudalism. Josef Stalin (1879–1953) succeeded Lenin as ruler of the Soviet Union, instituting the iron rule we associate with Russian totalitarianism.

One way or another, those denied their fair slice of the pie revolt to get it. The French Revolution irrevocably resliced the pie with a guillotine to accommodate the merchant class. Now the urban peasantry clamored for its economic share.

Social Realism

The USSR (and after World War II, its client states in Eastern Europe) attempted to control everyone and everything. They used whatever they could to achieve that end, including the media and art.

Soviet art was propaganda. Called "social realism," the style draws repeatedly on a few Socialist or Marxist-Leninist themes. (For example, the noble, muscular worker is depicted bashing the chains of capitalism and overcoming the evils of the bourgeois world.) With flags blowing heroically in the wind, the art portrays family ideals, Socialist morality, and undying respect for the fathers of the ideology (and, of course, the imperial power behind the ideological cloak, Russia). Russia is featured as the liberator from the Turks, from the Nazis, and from the evil Western world.

Although art as propaganda is nothing new, only in the sphere of the Soviet Union was creativity channeled so effectively into one

Soviet propaganda poster. "Social realism" art was intended to rouse nationalist and class feelings against the threat of the capitalist West. Here the workers are shown victorious through passionate dedication to their state, industry, and military. Soviet art was a broken record of worker-triumph propaganda.

purpose. Art was justified only if it promoted the system. Abstract art, which serves no purpose in inspiring the masses, was discouraged. Even artistic mediums as nebulous as music were censored for what they did not promote.

The Industrial Revolution and Art

The Industrial Revolution put new tools and materials in artists' hands. Concrete, iron, and glass opened new architectural doors. People were proud of their modernity and their ability to build like never before. More buildings were raised in the 19th century than in all previous centuries put together. It was the day after Christmas and Europe was a child with a colossal erector set.

At world's fairs and exhibitions, giant structures of iron ribs and glass walls were proudly assembled and promptly disassembled on rigid time schedules just to prove it could be done. People traveled from all over Europe to marvel at London's short-lived Crystal Palace. Paris, also feeling its industrial oats, built the Eiffel Tower to celebrate the centennial of the French Revolution. The French planned to take down the tower, which many considered ugly, but it became a symbol for Paris and so it stands today. As you travel around Europe, you'll see huge iron-and-glass train stations—more products of Europe's early industrial muscle.

But the Industrial Revolution also threatened art. New building techniques and materials made previous architectural styles obsolete, except as decoration. Like the ancient Romans who used Greek facades on buildings, architects would build modern buildings (such as the neo-Gothic British Houses of Parliament), then adorn them with fake Gothic arches or Renaissance columns.

Painters were threatened by the newly invented camera (developed around 1830), which could

Eiffel Tower, 1889, Paris. The Industrial Revolution made life one big erector set. This was built to celebrate the 100th anniversary of the French Revolution.

Industrial Revolution Sights

- Blists Hill Victorian Town (open-air museum) at Ironbridge Gorge—the birthplace of the Industrial Revolution, near the Cotswolds, Britain
- Covent Garden, London
- National Railway Museum, York, Britain
- Blackpool Tower, Blackpool, Britain
- Eiffel Tower, Paris
- Orsay Museum (originally an iron-and-glass train station), Paris
- Gallerias (grand iron-and-glass shopping arcades) in Milan and Naples, Italy
- Galleria, Brussels, Belgium

Galleria Vittorio Emanuele, 1877, Milan. In the age of iron and glass, fancy gallerias decorated European cities.

*When England learned to make iron efficiently, the Industrial Age was born. It happened at **Ironbridge Gorge**. This is the first iron bridge ever built (1779).*

make portraits faster, cheaper, and sometimes better than they could. The challenge and incentive to portray nature was gone. With the camera, the artist's traditional role as the preserver of a particular moment, person, or scene became obsolete.

Technology widened the gulf between the artist and the public. Modern people could get homes, arts, crafts, and furnishings from engineers and technicians, thanks to the affordable efficiency of mass production. Artists grew to disdain those who put a price on art the same way they priced pork, kerosene, or a day's work in the factory.

Struggling to come to terms with the modern industrial world, art left technology behind, focusing the artistic lens of the Western world on hazy frontiers of the future.

Art Nouveau

The Art Nouveau (new-VOH) style was a reaction to the mechanization and mass production of the Industrial Revolution. Longing for the beauty of the pre-industrial age, artists rebelled against mass-produced goods and T-square art. Emphasizing uniqueness, their art included the artists' personal touch.

Whereas industrial art and architecture were geometrical, with rigid squares and rectangles, Art Nouveau ("new art") used delicate, flowing lines, like the curvy stems of plants. Iron grillwork became a new art form.

Art Nouveau influenced architecture, painting, ironwork, furniture, graphic design, and even women's fashions. In America, Louis Tiffany's natural-looking "flower-petal" lamps were the rage.

Antonio Gaudí, born near Barcelona, employed the Art Nouveau style (called *"Modernista"* in Spain) in his distinctive architecture. Many architecture students make pilgrimages to Barcelona to see his famous "melted ice cream" works. He's considered a pioneer, a prophet, and a dreamer who was lucky enough to see his dreams become concrete.

Art Nouveau's intentional curviness eventually gave way to

Gustav Klimt *(1862-1917), took the decorative element of Art Nouveau to extremes. In many of his paintings, only the face and bits of body show through gilded ornamental friezes.*

Art Nouveau Sights

- Green iron grillwork at old Métro stops, Paris
- Orsay Museum (exhibits on mezzanine level), Paris
- *Jugendstil* facades throughout Vienna
- Gaudí architecture (especially Sagrada Familia cathedral), Barcelona, Spain

Gaudí, **Casa Mila** *apartment house, 1905, Barcelona, Spain. This ice-cream castle of a building does everything possible to disrupt the rigid angles of the industrial world.*

David C. Hoerlein

the straight lines and rigidity we see in modern "International Style" skyscrapers, but its influence has been seen throughout modern times.

Paris, Vienna, Barcelona, Brussels, Munich, Glasgow, Helsinki, and Alesund in Norway are all famous for their Art Nouveau, or *"Jugendstil,"* as the style is called in German.

Impressionism

Impressionism was the greatest revolution in European art since the Renaissance and the first real "modern" style of art. While the Renaissance found realism, Impressionism threw it out. The artist was interested only in the fleeting "impression" made by the light, shadows, and atmosphere of a scene.

Although its name was originally coined as an insult (like "Gothic"), Impressionism is actually one of the few appropriate art labels. Claude Monet (1840–1926), the movement's father, called the style "instantaneity." The artist, sometimes with only a few quick brush strokes, captures a candid, momentary "impression" of a subject.

The realistic and the Impressionist styles can be illustrated by com-

Monet's Garden at Giverny *(an easy side trip from Paris) inspired much of Monsieur Lily Pad's art. Impressionists cried, "Out of the studio and into nature!"*

paring what Leonardo da Vinci and Monet each see as they drive across the Nevada desert on a hot summer day. Ahead of his Ferrari, realist Leonardo sees heat rising from the asphalt, making the black road look like a bright, shimmering patch of silver. In spite of the way it appears, he knows the road is really black and so he will paint it that way, disregarding the momentary impression of silver.

Monet, an Impressionist, excitedly stops his Peugeot, sets up his easel, and captures the impression of the shimmering heat waves cutting a silver slice through the yellows and browns of the desert.

We don't actually see objects or people, but rather the light that bounces off them. The realist paints what his mind knows is there; the Impressionist paints what his eye sees.

Light and Color

Light plays endless games on the same subject and, to the Impressionist, that same subject is different with each time of day and atmospheric condition. Monet, the most famous Impressionist, often did a series of paintings of a single subject (for example, Rouen Cathedral) at different times of day.

The physical object has become just the rack upon which hangs the real subject: the light and colors. Paint is usually laid on thickly, with heavy, textured brush strokes.

Sometimes the painter, not even bothering to mix the colors on the palette, dabs bits of blue and red side by side to make a purple that shimmers in the viewer's eye. This brush technique was taken to extremes in Georges Seurat's "pointillism," a mosaic of colored dots with no lines at all. (If you look carefully at a newspaper photo, you'll see that it is a mechanical form of pointillism.)

Compare the **photo** of the **Rouen Cathedral** with the Impressionist **painting** by Monet (1893, Orsay Museum, Paris). We can see the artist's fascination with the play of light on the building. Detail fades away and we are left with a blurry, yet recognizable, impression of the cathedral.

Seurat, **Bathers at Asnieres**, 1883 (Tate Gallery, London). Here Seurat uses a technique called "pointillism," a mosaic consisting entirely of colored dots.

From Ridicule to Acceptance

Impressionism was born in the "Salon of the Rejected," the "off-off Broadway" of struggling Parisian artists. Initially, people were outraged by this rough, messy style. A newspaper reported that after seeing an early Monet painting, one visitor went mad, rushed out into the street, and started biting innocent passersby. (Although it's much safer today, caution is still advised near Parisian modern-art galleries.)

Although many Impressionist artists (Manet, Degas, Renoir, and Rodin) had first-class classical backgrounds, the stuffy board of the Louvre Museum refused to display the new art—even after the public accepted it. The nearby Jeu de Paume, a former indoor tennis court, was used to store the masterpieces of the movement. Today, Impressionism, far from radical, hangs

Rodin, **The Kiss,** *1901 (Tate Modern, London)*

Renoir, **Moulin de la Galette,** *1876 (Orsay Museum, Paris)*

in living rooms and corporate boardrooms and fills some of Europe's most popular galleries. The Jeu de Paume collection is now the major attraction in Paris' wildly popular Orsay Gallery.

Auguste Rodin (ro-DAN, 1840–1917) blended Impressionist ideas with his classical training to become the greatest sculptor since Michelangelo. He had the uncanny ability to capture the essence of a subject with his powerful yet sensitive technique. The rough "unfinished" surfaces, particularly of his bronze works, reflect light the same way the thick brushwork of an Impressionist painting does. Check out the Rodin Museum in Paris, filled with the work of this great artist.

Post-Impressionism

After Impressionism, the modern art world splintered, never again to be contained by any one style. Within 20 years, Impressionism had branched into two Postimpressionist movements. One stressed form and order (led by Cézanne, a forerunner of the Cubists) and the other demonstrated emotion and sensuousness (Gauguin and van Gogh, who inspired the Expressionists and Fauves).

Paul Cézanne (say-ZAWN, 1839–1906), a man of independent means, ignored Paris, the critics, and the buying public. Cézanne worked to capture the best of both artistic worlds: the instantaneity of Impressionism and the realistic depth and solidity of earlier styles.

Paul Gauguin (go-GAN, 1848–1903) was a stockbroker who chucked it all to become a painter. Like Cézanne, he left the artsy folk of proud Paris for inspiration in simple surroundings. He spent time with van Gogh in southern France, but, after Vincent attacked him in a fit of artistic rage, Paul sailed for Tahiti.

Gauguin's bright, bold paintings of native scenes hit Europe like a ripe

Cézanne, **Still Life.** *Cézanne painted numerous still lifes in his experiments with form and composition. He once remarked that nature reveals itself in the geometric forms of spheres, cylinders, and cones.*

Gauguin, **Arearea**, or Pleasantries *(Orsay Museum, Paris)*

mango. He used "primitive" techniques—simple outlines, sharply contrasting colors, and a flat, two-dimensional look—to create a naive and naturally expressive style that inspired many 20th-century artists.

Van Gogh

Vincent van Gogh (pronounced "van-GO," or "van-GOCK" by the Dutch and the snooty, 1853–1890) used Impressionist techniques powered with passion. Painting what he felt as well as what he saw, his art truly reflects his life.

Vincent's early life was religious, not artistic. Disillusioned with the shallow values of the modern world, he served as a lay preacher for poor coal miners. In his late twenties, he channeled that religious vision and spiritual intensity into his art.

After learning from the Impressionists in Paris, he moved to southern France to cloister himself in nature and his art. He did most of his great paintings there in the space of three years. They show the extreme loneliness, the emotional ecstasy, and the spiritual struggles he went through. Several times his work was interrupted by mental illness. Finally, believing that insanity was destroying his creative abilities, he killed himself.

Van Gogh's art is an oil-on-canvas translation of his soul, his genius, and his emotions. The subjects were simple—

Van Gogh, **Self-Portrait,** 1890, hangs in the Orsay Museum, Paris. With swirling brush-strokes, Vincent charged Impressionism with emotion. His canvases take you through the rapids of his life.

Impressionist and Post-Impressionist Sights
- Orsay Museum, Paris
- Rodin Museum, Paris
- Marmottan Museum (Monet), Paris
- Orangerie Museum (more Monet), Paris
- Monet's garden, Giverny, near Paris
- Toulouse-Lautrec Museum, Albi, France
- Arles, St. Remy, and Auvers (all in southern France; although without Vincent sights as such, these are towns that inspired van Gogh)
- Tate Modern, London
- National Gallery, London
- Van Gogh Museum, Amsterdam
- Kroller-Muller Museum (van Gogh), Arnhem, Netherlands

Van Gogh, **Sunflowers,** *1888 (National Gallery, London). Other versions exist elsewhere. Two years after painting these sunflowers, the artist killed himself. Vincent van gone.*

common people and landscapes. His style was untrained and crude. By distorting and exaggerating certain colors and details, he gave his work spirit and emotions.

Van Gogh's love of common people shines through in his painting. His subjects seem to glow with, as he put it, "that something of the eternal which the halo used to symbolize."

Perhaps the best examples of van Gogh's art are his self-portraits. Haunted and haunting, these show the man as well as his talent. We see in his burning eyes the passionate love of all things and the desire to paint them on canvas.

In his landscape *Crows in a Wheatfield,* we see a simple, peaceful scene "van Gogh-ed" into a stormy sea of turbulence and emotion. He uses the strong, thick brush strokes and bright colors of the

Van Gogh, **Crows in a Wheatfield**

Impressionists not to capture the light of the scene but to churn it up with emotion. The waves of wheat vibrate with an inner force that van Gogh believed inhabits all things.

Europe's van Gogh treasure chest is the great Van Gogh Museum in Amsterdam (next to the Rijksmuseum). His art is well displayed, in chronological order, with each of his artistic stages related to events in his personal life. It's one of Europe's most enjoyable museums.

Europe in the 20th Century

Twentieth-century Europe was just as exciting as historic Europe and shouldn't take a back seat to Old Regime palaces and ancient ruins. While most of the sights tourists chase in Europe date back a few centuries or more, an understanding of our tumultuous age is important in understanding Europe's number-one tourist attraction—its people.

The 20th century began with the sort of easy happiness and nonchalance of a summer barbecue. The average European in 1910 felt lucky to be living during those prosperous and peaceful times.

Behind the scenes, however, tension was growing. Germany's late entry onto the European economic game board caused competitive rivalries. Tension mounted as Germany grabbed for its "place in the sun." Germany understood that capitalist economies need colonial sources of raw materials and marketplaces for finished products. By the time Germany arrived, most of the underdeveloped world was already controlled by other European powers.

A united Germany was the biggest, strongest, scariest kid on the block. There was a scramble for alliances across Europe. No one wanted to be left without an ally, so most countries dove headlong into an international game of "Let's Make a Deal." Alliances were secret, often conflicting, and no one knew for sure exactly where anyone else stood.

The modern nationalities of Europe were awakening, and, particularly in the vast Hapsburg Empire, national groups were working aggressively for independence.

World War I

Beneath its placid exterior, Europe was ready to explode. The spark that set things off was the assassination of Archduke Ferdinand. The heir to the Hapsburg throne was shot by a Serbian nationalist in 1914. The Hapsburg government, which ruled Austria, jumped at the opportunity to crush the troublesome Serbs.

One by one, Europe's nations were drawn by alliance into this regional dispute. Each had a self-serving interest. Russia, slavic Serbia's big brother, aided Serbia. Germany gave Austria a curious "blank check" of support. Germany knew that Russia was about to complete a new railroad mobilization plan that would give Russia first-strike capabilities. Many speculate that Germany thought a war sooner, while Russia was still slow to mobilize, was preferable to a war later, when Russia would be better prepared.

So, when Austria attacked Serbia, the Russians mobilized, and Germany invaded . . . France! France was allied to Russia, and Germany hoped to wipe out France by surprise, rather than risk getting embroiled in a two-front war.

Well, it didn't work out quite the way Germany planned. Flank, flank, flank, from the Alps to the Atlantic, the Franco-German stalemate that became the Western Front dug in. Soldiers dug trenches to duck machine-gun bullets. France and Germany settled into a battle of attrition, in which the political and military leaders of opposing nations decided to bash their troops against each other, each knowing it would suffer horrific losses but calculating that the other would bleed white and drop first.

For four years, generals waved their swords and wave after wave of troops climbed out of their trenches and fell back into their graves. On many occasions, France lost 70,000 people in one day. That's more than the U.S. lost in the entire Vietnam War. By 1918, half of all the men in France between the ages of 15 and 30 were casualties.

Too often, military leaders are the heroes of previous wars who

EUROPE IN 1914

- NORWAY
- FINLAND
- SWEDEN
- NORTH SEA
- GREAT BRITAIN
- DENMARK
- ATLANTIC
- RUSSIA
- NETH.
- GERMAN EMPIRE
- POLAND
- BELG.
- OCEAN
- FRANCE
- AUSTRIA-
- SWITZ.
- HUNGARY
- PORTUGAL
- RUM.
- BLACK SEA
- SPAIN
- Sarajevo
- SERBIA
- BULG.
- ITALY
- ALB.
- GREECE
- TURKEY (OTTOMAN EMPIRE)
- SPANISH MOROCCO
- MEDITERRANEAN
- SEA

⊞ **ALLIES** BASIS: TRIPLE ENTENTE (1907)
☰ **CENTRAL POWERS** BASIS: TRIPLE ALLIANCE (1882)
◪ **ITALY** (LEFT CENTRAL POWERS & JOINED ALLIES 1915)
☐ **NEUTRAL**

—DCX—

underestimate the new war technology. In World War I, that technology was the machine gun, a tool so awesome that a newspaper columnist of the day called it the "peacekeeper" because it was assumed no civilized commander would send his boys into its fire.

Russia and Germany fought a mobile and bloody war with the help of trains on the Eastern Front. Meanwhile, Austria had trouble with the stubborn Serbs.

Europe dove into the "War to End All Wars" expecting a quick finish. It took four bloody years for the Allies (France, England, Russia, and, ultimately, the United States) to defeat Germany and Austria. By the 1919 signing of the Treaty of Versailles, 9 million of the war's 65 million soldiers were dead. For a sense of the loss, visit the battlefields at Verdun, France.

Verdun

Little remains in Europe today to remind us of World War I. Verdun provides a fine tribute to the million-plus lives lost in the World War I battles fought here. While the lunar landscape of World War I is now forested over, countless craters and trenches are visible in the woods as you drive through the region. One thing you won't see are the millions of undetonated bombs in vast cordoned-off areas. Drive through the eerie moguls that surround the city of Verdun, stopping at melted sugar-cube forts and plaques marking where towns once existed. With two hours and a car, or a full day and a bike, you can see the most stirring sights and appreciate the awesome scale of the battles. The town of Verdun is not your destination but a starting point for your visit to the surrounding battlefields.

The Ossuaire is the tomb of 130,000 unidentified French and German soldiers whose last homes were the muddy trenches of Verdun. It's surrounded by a sprawling field of crosses and the memories of a battle of attrition between two mighty countries which left half of all the fighting age men in France either dead or wounded.

Germany lay crushed and saddled with demoralizing war debts. Once-mighty Austria was reduced to a poor, tiny, landlocked country with a navy of three police boats on the Danube. France was finished as a superpower. Europe lay dazed and horrified at the unthinkable which had just happened.

After the war, the map of Europe was redrawn. The old ruling families of Germany, Russia, and Austria and the Ottoman rulers of present-day Turkey were finished. New, democratic nations drew borders along cultural and ethnic boundaries, defining Finland, Austria, Hungary, Czechoslovakia, Poland, Yugoslavia, Latvia, Estonia, and Lithuania. Germany handed over the provinces of Alsace and Lorraine to France.

Compared with war-ravaged Europe, the United States was a dominant, seemingly boundless superpower. In the decade after World War I, it boasted a whopping 42 percent of the entire world's industrial output.

Between the Wars: Totalitarianism

After World War I, the big question was: would Germany be democratic or Communist? Russia had wrapped up its revolution and had become the Soviet Union. According to Marxist theory, industrial-based Germany was the perfect candidate to lead the world into Communism. But the victorious Allies (the United States, Great Britain, and France) managed to install the Western-style Weimar government, and the German Communist party was literally buried in one night when the top 1,000 Communists, including leaders Rosa Luxembourg and Karl Liebknecht, were shot.

Many German people figured they could have hung on and won the war. They associated their "stab in the back" Western government with the hated Treaty of Versailles. Although the Weimar government was technically a modern constitutional democracy, behind the scenes ticked the old ruling order—the army and industrialists—scheming to reverse the war's outcome and revive Germany as Europe's foremost power. Many people view World War II as the logical continuation and conclusion of World War I, and the misguided Treaty of Versailles as only the kickoff of an intermission.

Mussolini

Meanwhile, in Italy, a violent, melodramatic nationalism and an anti-intellectual movement called Fascism were born. Benito Mussolini led the Fascist party, stressing unity and authority. Capitalizing on Italy's corrupt government, miserable economy, and high unemployment, he rose easily to power. As in Germany a few years later, the rich and the businessmen believed Fascism to be distasteful but supported it as the only alternative to Europe's rising red tide of Communism.

In 1922, Mussolini took the reins of government. Il Duce went straight to work, filling the government with Fascists, organizing the

*This **stamp from Ethiopia,** licked by Mussolini in 1935, shows the Fascist alliance of Hitler and the Italian dictator. The slogan reads: "Two peoples, one war."*

strongman *squadrisi* to "encourage" Italians to support him, and building a strong, supernationalistic, self-sufficient Fascist Italy.

Although Mussolini's government had its problems, it was Italy's only strong government in the 20th century. As a tourist, you'll drive on a system of superfreeways commissioned by Il Duce's government. Some of Rome's buildings, including the Olympic Games complex and the futuristic suburb of EUR, are Fascist in style. EUR, 10 minutes by subway from Rome's Colosseum, with its bold and powerful architecture, is worth exploring.

The Palace of the Civilization of Labor, a.k.a. Square Colosseum, is the very fascist-feeling centerpiece of Mussolini's futuristic city, EUR (Rome).

Hitler

The roots of Adolf Hitler's success took hold in Germany's anger at the Treaty of Versailles and the Weimar government. As hyperinflation ripped up Germany's moral fabric, Hitler and his party leaped into the news. When the value of the mark dropped from 4 marks = U.S.$1 to 4 trillion marks = U.S.$1 in 1923, the hardworking German middle class lost faith in society. All debts, savings, and retirement funds were wiped out. (It took a wheelbarrow full of paper marks to buy a pretzel.) People were ready to believe the promises of a charismatic madman.

Like Mussolini, Hitler expertly capitalized on society's problems; when he couldn't find a solution, he found a scapegoat. His party boomed until Germany did. When Germany entered these happy-go-lucky cabaret years in the mid-1920s, people wrote off Hitler and other political extremists as fringe lunatics.

When the Great Depression hit in 1929, Hitler rose again. With his political genius, terror tactics, scapegoating of the Jews, and the

Nazi campaign poster. This political ad tells voters they can free Germany from its chains— by voting for Hitler.

support of the rich elite of the day (who saw Fascism as the only defense against Communism), Hitler became Germany's dictator.

In 1933, he proclaimed that his "Third Reich" would last a thousand years. (The first two reichs were pre–World War I Germany, 1871–1918, and the Holy Roman Empire, usually dated from Charlemagne's reign in 800, toppled by Napoleon in 1806.) Hitler's agenda was to turn Germany into a monolithic slab of nationalistic rock. There were to be no states, no classes, no questions, and no alternative to the Nazi party. There was to be only Germany. The Nazi party was purged, the Gestapo kept the flags waving, concentration camps and unmarked graves were filled with dissenters, and Nazism became the religion of state.

In his own frothing way, Hitler was a genius. Germany prospered. The economy boomed and everyone was employed. His goal of complete self-sufficiency (necessary to wage a world war) was right around the corner.

It was clear to Germany that more "living room" was justified. Hitler said, "Space must be fought for and maintained. People who

Nazi propaganda. Translation: "Judaism is criminal." Signs like this were common in Hitler's Germany. Someone had to take the blame for Germany's problems, and the Jews were a traditional scapegoat.

Totalitarianism

Totalitarianism was big in the 1930s, gaining power in Germany, Italy, Spain, and the USSR. In *The Origins of Totalitarianism*, Hannah Arendt describes this harsh form of government:

The very ethics of totalitarianism were violent and neo-pagan. It declared that men should live dangerously, avoid the flabby weakness of too much thought, throw themselves with red-blooded vigor into a life of action. The new regimes all instituted youth movements. They appealed to a kind of juvenile idealism, in which young people believed that by joining some kind of squad, donning some kind of uniform, and getting into the fresh air, they contributed to a great moral resurgence of their country. Young men were taught to value their bodies but not their minds, to be tough and hard, to regard mass gymnastics as patriotic demonstrations, and camping trips as a preparation for the world of the future. Young women were taught to breed large families without complaint, to be content in the kitchen, and to look with awe upon their virile mates. The body-cult flourished while the mind decayed. The ideal was to turn the German people into a race of splendid animals, pink-cheeked, Nordic, and upstanding. Contrariwise, euthanasia was adopted for the insane and was proposed for the aged. Later, in World War II, when the Nazis overran Eastern Europe, they committed Jews to the gas chambers, destroying some 6 million human beings by the most scientific methods. Animals were animals; one bred the kind one wanted and killed the kind one did not.

Mussolini's fascist art and architecture in EUR (a short subway ride from downtown Rome).

are lazy have no right to the soil. Soil is for he who tills it and protects it. If a nation loses in the defense of its soil, then the individual loses. There is no higher justice that decrees that a people must starve. There is only power, and power creates justice.... Parliaments do not create all of the rights on the earth; force also creates rights. The question is whether we wish to live or die. We have more right to soil than all the other nations because we are so thickly populated. I am of the opinion that in this respect, too, the principle can be applied; God helps him who helps himself."

And the German people marched in lockstep.

World War II

The peace in Europe following the shortsighted Treaty of Versailles was unstable. It couldn't last—World War II was inevitable.

While most of Europe between the wars was pacifist and isolationist, Hitler waged a careful campaign of "gradual encroachment." Each year he ranted and raved and threatened to go wild. When he would take just a little, the world felt relieved and hoped he was satisfied.

But even the most naive pacifist couldn't ignore Germany's invasion of Poland in 1939. England and France declared war, and it was one big pigpile all over again.

For Hitler, 1940 was a good year. By April he controlled Austria, Poland, Czechoslovakia, Denmark, and Norway. In May, impatient at his "slow" progress, Hitler launched his ingenious Blitzkrieg ("lightning war"). Attacking swiftly by land and air, the Nazis conquered the Netherlands, Belgium, and France within seven weeks. By mid-1940, Hitler held most of central and northern Europe.

In April 1940, Winston Churchill took the English helm, offering "nothing but blood, toil, tears, and sweat...but a faith in ultimate victory." He successfully inspired and led England through the desperate Battle of Britain (July 1940), when German bombers doggedly pummeled London.

Frustrated by British planes and the English Channel, Hitler turned eastward and sank his iron teeth deep into vast Russia. The Soviets suffered, but a harsh winter and the Russian "scorched earth" policy thwarted the Nazis just as they had foiled Napoleon's army 130 years earlier. (Hint to would-be conquerors: Don't invade Russia.)

The war raged in Africa. And in Asia, Japan grabbed a million square miles. After Japan's unprovoked attack on Pearl Harbor in 1941, the United States joined in the melee. America's fresh forces and underestimated industrial might turned the tide.

WW II EUROPE
(1942 THE HEIGHT OF AXIS POWER)

- ▦ Axis nations
- ▥ Axis-controlled
- ▤ Allies
- ☐ Neutral nations

The Allies took North Africa and invaded Italy. They crossed the English Channel to Normandy on D-Day (June 6, 1944), gaining a vital toehold in France from which to attack Germany. And Russia made great advances in the East. In 1944, the Allies gained complete air control of German skies, bombing its cities almost at will. By May 1945, Hitler was dead and Germany lay quiet, smoldering, and exhausted.

The tourist today sees very few sights produced by the world wars—what is important is what the tourist doesn't see. You won't see the wonders of Dresden, Germany, one of the most beautiful medieval cities in Europe. You won't see the lovely original old towns of Berlin,

World War II, Fascist, and Nazi Sights

- Kaiser Wilhelm Memorial Church, Berlin
- Käthe-Kollwitz Museum, Berlin
- Hitler's Eagle's Nest, Berchtesgaden, Germany
- Haus der Kunst (exterior), Munich
- Dachau Concentration Camp, near Munich
- Buchenwald Concentration Camp, Buchenwald, Germany
- Mauthausen Concentration Camp, Mauthausen, Austria
- Cabinet War Rooms, London
- Imperial War Museum, London
- Mussolini's planned city, EUR, Rome
- D-Day landing sights, Normandy, France
- Battle of Normandy Museum, Caen, Normandy
- Bayeux WWII Memorial Museum, Normandy
- Deportation Monument (behind Notre-Dame), Paris
- Oradour sur Glane (bombed and burned memorial ghost city), near Limoges, France
- Anne Frank's House, Amsterdam
- Nazi Resistance Museum, Amsterdam
- Corrie Ten Boom's "Hiding Place," Haarlem, Netherlands
- Auschwitz Concentration Camp, Auschwitz, Poland
- Jewish Quarter museums and synagogues, Prague, Czech Republic
- Nazi-Resistance Museum, Oslo, Norway
- Nazi-Resistance Museum, Copenhagen, Denmark

Speculating on Heroic Death, *1934 (Dachau Museum). The artist predicts the coming world war.*

After much suffering, concentration camp survivors cheered their saviors. The horrifying conditions of the camps caused battle-hardened soldiers to break down and cry.

Köln, Munich, or Rotterdam. Air raids leveled these cities during World War II, and the survivors rebuilt them in a modern style.

Europe Since 1945

World War II left much of Europe in ruins. Even before the shooting stopped, it was evident that a post-war world would be bipolar, dominated by an American sphere and a Soviet sphere. Scrambling to pick up the broken pieces of earlier powers, each side did what it could to grab the technology and great minds of Germany and turn former enemies into economic and political allies.

The Soviets "liberated" the Eastern European nations from the Nazis, installing Moscow-trained governments in each capital. The "Iron Curtain" fell, ushering in a 45-year period of strict Soviet control over the nations it (understandably) figured it needed as a buffer zone against another attack from the West.

Germany and its capital city, Berlin, were split between the four victorious Allied powers: France, Britain, the USA, and the USSR. While three of the allied sectors worked amicably together and became West Germany and West Berlin, the Soviet sectors fell behind the Iron Curtain. Southern Germany, or Bavaria, was the American sector, which may explain why America's clichéd image of Germany is Bavarian.

The United States, learning from the mistakes of World War I's Treaty of Versailles that a healthy Germany is safer than a wounded Germany, funded the rebuilding of Western Europe with a huge and effective aid program called the Marshall Plan. Western Europe's economy lurched and then boomed while Eastern Europe lagged under its

The Commie with the Coke. With the breakup of the Soviet Union, Western culture—and tourists—are flooding East.

controlled Soviet-style economy. The NATO (West) and Warsaw Pact (East) alliances were formed.

The Cold War began. The USSR blockaded West Berlin (1948). With the help of an American airlift, this island of the capitalist West remained free to provide a painful contrast to the bleak Eastern economies. (The West German government subsidized this contrast by providing many perks: tax breaks, cheap flights, draft deferments, and so on to anyone who would live, travel, and work in West Berlin.) The USSR, under the guise of a Warsaw Pact peacekeeping force, crushed revolutions in Hungary (1956) and Czechoslovakia (1968). To keep their people in, the East German government built in 1961 what it called the "anti-Fascist barrier"—what we called the Berlin Wall.

Caught between two superpowers and sitting on nuclear arsenals capable of destroying Europe's windmills, castles, pubs, and people many times over, Europe was tense. With many one-legged pensioners and tombstone-covered hills as reminders, Europe knew the reality of war. As "evil empire" rhetoric raged between the flagbearers of the planet's two most aggressive ideologies, many Europeans feared their homeland would be the fighting ground for World War III.

But in the 1980s, the Cold War began to thaw. The rise of the

Polish labor movement, Solidarity, under Lech Walesa made a powerful impression on workers across Eastern Europe. Then in 1985 came Mikhail Gorbachev, the first modern, truly post-Stalin, post–World War II Soviet leader. His reforms and personal charisma made him the man of the decade. "I 'heart' Gorby" pins were common across the Warsaw Pact countries as the Soviet leader ended the Brezhnev doctrine, saying, basically, if you want to split and do your own thing economically, good luck, but we'll need to maintain foreign policy control (as in Finland) for defensive purposes.

Driving an economic machine that didn't work and with its fuel tank on "E," the USSR fought and lost a war of economic attrition with the USA. While America was left deeply in debt, the Soviet Union collapsed (as it would have anyway, given time).

And, like dominoes, the tumultuous revolutions of late 1980s and early 1990s toppled Communist regime after Communist regime across Eastern Europe. East German Communist leaders were tried and convicted for abuse of power and corruption. The dictator of Romania and his wife were executed. A playwright became the president of Czechoslovakia. Agreeing on a "Velvet Divorce," Czech and Slovak split peacefully. Every time we turned around, another nation raised its grass-roots to the sky, tossed out its outdated Communist party, and threatened to join the Eurail club.

In Eastern Europe, a lifetime of pent-up entrepreneurial spirit has been unleashed, offering the visitor no shortage of tour guides, bed-and-breakfast places, and travel thrills. East Germany is being assimilated into the sleeker West (with typical German tenderness). Berlin, once again the capital of Germany, is shuffling itself back together with building projects that would have made Hitler proud. Prague, the best-preserved Baroque city in Europe, is the darling of East European tourism with as many tourist crowds as Salzburg or Edinburgh. Farther east (Bulgaria, Romania, Ukraine), things get more bleak and depressing. Despite their rich cultures and warm, curious people, these countries are in desperate times economically and the average traveler might not enjoy the challenge of traveling here. The five most accessible and livable cities of the former Soviet Union (St. Petersburg, Moscow, Tallinn, Riga, and Vilnius) are also the most enjoyable for visitors. Budget independent travel through these cities is far easier now than it was five years ago.

Meanwhile, in Western Europe, countries have been working out other problems. No European country has perfect homogeneity. Small nationalities without a nation are struggling for independence or survival. France, for instance, has the Basques, the Corsicans, and the Celtic people of Brittany, many of whom see themselves as un-French parts of a French empire ruled from Paris. The George Washingtons and Nathan Hales of these small, neglected nationalities are making news in Europe. Terrorism filled headlines throughout the 1980s and 1990s, and there's no reason to think that patriots will stop regretting that they have only one life to give for their countries.

A silent victim of modern times, the environment, gained attention in the 1980s. The Green party, whose platform was primarily environmental, raised issues many chose not to see in spite of the diseased forests, dead rivers, and radioactive reindeer in their midst. Nuclear accidents, acid rain, ozone problems, and chemical spills are awakening a continent notorious for treating its Mediterranean Sea like its own private cesspool. Even politicians suckling the teats of big business are beginning to realize that you can't exploit the poor on an uninhabitable planet.

Modern Art: Reflecting a World in Turmoil

Why is modern art so bizarre? Better to ask: Why is the modern world so bizarre? The world changed by leaps, bounds, and somersaults during the last century. Strange as some art might seem, it's often an honest representation of our strange world.

The world wars devastated Europe. No one could have foreseen the extent of the slaughter. People, especially artists, were shocked, disgusted, and disillusioned. As old moral values were challenged by the horror of war and our rapidly changing society, so were artistic ones.

Modern art is such a confusing pile of styles and theories that only one generalization can be made: little of it looks like the real world. But you can't judge art simply by how well it copies reality. Artists distort the real world intentionally. Especially in modern art, some of the messiest and least-organized-looking works ("My four-year-old coulda' done that!") are sophisticated, based on complex theories requiring knowledge of many art styles. If you don't understand it, you can't judge it. Learn about art first, understand the artist's purpose, and then you can appreciate or criticize with gusto.

Modern artists portray the "real" world in two different ways, expressive or abstract. Expressive art is like van Gogh's. It depicts the real world but distorts things to express emotion. Abstract art abandons the visible world altogether, making basic lines and patches of

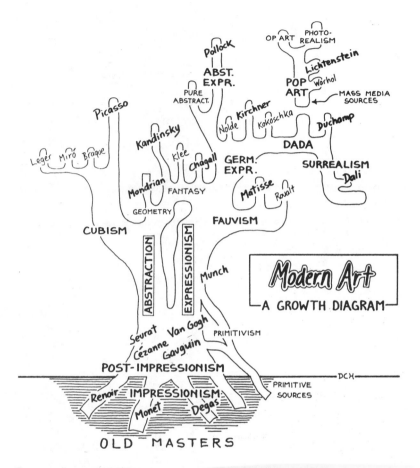

color that reflect not real objects but a more fundamental beauty. Other modern styles such as Cubism, primitivism, and the combo style of abstract expressionism, are variations on these two basic themes.

Expressionism

The best example of the "expressive" distortion of reality is called expressionism. This style carries van Gogh's emotionalism to the extreme. In _The Scream,_ Norwegian artist Edvard Munch ("MOONK," 1863–1944) bends and twists everything into a landscape of unexplained terror. We "hear" the scream in the lines of the canvas rising up from the twisted body, through the terrified skull, and out to the sky, echoing until it fills the entire nightmare world of the painting.

We can appreciate the power of modern art by comparing *The Scream* to an earlier work, Gericault's *Raft of the Medusa* (see page 216). Both are a terror on canvas. But while Gericault's terror arises from a realistic portrayal of a grotesque event, Munch simply distorts the appearance of an everyday scene so we see it in a more powerful way, from a different emotional perspective.

Expressionism flourished in Germany from 1905 through 1935. Artists showed the horror and injustice of the war years they experienced. The garish colors, twisted lines, and mask-like faces stress emotion over realism.

Munch, **The Scream**, *1893 (Edvard Munch Museum, Oslo). Norwegian Munch led the way into the artistic movement aptly called "expressionism." These artists distorted reality to express the horror of the modern world. The Munch Museum in Oslo is excellent.*

Abstract Art

The second strain of modern art, "abstraction," is less understood than the "expressive" distortion employed by Munch and van Gogh. Abstraction is simplification.

Since a tree, for instance, can never be painted with all its infinite details, all art is to some extent an abstraction, or simplification, of the real world. For so many generations, artists had denied this fact, trying to make their two-dimensional canvases look as real as the three-dimensional world they painted. But by the 20th century, the camera had been accepted as the captor of reality. Artists began to accept the abstract and artificial nature of paintings. In fact, they emphasized and enjoyed this abstraction to the extent of neglecting the subject itself. They were free

Abstract pondering

From Realism to Abstraction

Here is a progression of realism to abstraction based on Cézanne's post-Impressionist painting (top), which is more or less realistic. Below left: The figures are flattened, the canvas reduced to a composition of geometric shapes. The subject matter is still apparent. Below right: Simplified into a jumble of puzzle pieces, the card players are barely recognizable. The blocks of line and color themselves become the subject.

Cézanne, **The Card Players**, *1892*

Van Doesburg, **Card Players**, *1916*

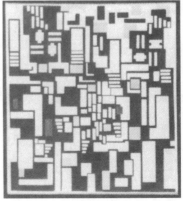

Van Doesburg, **Card Players**, *1917*

to experiment with the building blocks of realistic art: lines, colors, and shapes. Not concerned with representing the real world, this art is called "nonrepresentational."

Abstract artists are free, like children with a set of brightly colored building blocks. Rather than use the blocks to build a house or some recognizable object, children are fascinated by the blocks themselves. Like children, abstract artists spend hours organizing patterns that are pleasing for their own sake, not because they add up to something else. But unlike children, abstract artists generally have years of training with which to plan the best arrangement of the "blocks."

To appreciate and judge modern art, the viewer needs to know the rules, especially if the art can't be compared to reality.

Abstract Art = Visual Music

It's helpful to compare abstract art to pure instrumental music. Some music is designed to imitate a sound heard in nature, such as a storm or a bird's call. Other music is intended to express an emotion, such as the sadness caused by the death of a friend. But most music is the perfect audio equivalent of abstract visual art. It simply plays with the beautiful "shapes and colors" of sound, the harmonious relationship of tones. Our ears don't demand to know what the sounds are supposed to represent. Our ears are better than our eyes at accepting abstract beauty.

Abstract art explores the relationships of lines and colors. The rules of these relationships are visible to the trained eye just as the rules of music are audible to the trained ear. But to the average viewer (or listener), abstract art (or music) is to be enjoyed, not analyzed. Music is enjoyable even if you don't understand the meter and scale on which it's built. The same is true of visual abstract art—it's just plain nice to look at. (Notice the similarity between the titles of abstract artworks and musical compositions: *Composition with Red, Yellow and Blue,* "Sonata for Piano and Violin No. 1.")

Abstract artists have

Kandinsky, **Composition 238: Bright Circle,** *1921. Reality is tossed out the window as the artist calls on us to enjoy more basic shapes and colors. We hope this is right side up.*

been criticized for avoiding reality—for playing with their building blocks and making patterns that only they can understand. Artists such as Piet Mondrian, Paul Klee, and Wassily Kandinsky have replied that what they paint is reality, not the fleeting reality of the visible world that changes and passes away, but the eternal and unchanging world of geometrical relationships. The abstract artist simplifies the world into timeless shapes and colors. Are your eyes as open-minded as your ears?

Primitives and Wild Beasts

"Primitivism" is a return to the simplified (and therefore abstract) style used in prehistoric cave paintings and stylized, early Greek art. Primitivists tried to paint the world through the eyes of primitive people, with a calculated crudeness.

Rousseau, **War**, *1894 (Orsay Museum, Paris)*

Paul Gauguin was their inspiration. Gauguin rejected the sterile, modern, industrial world (and its sterile art) for the expressive and magical power of primitive images.

The Fauves (French for "wild beasts," pronounced "foavs") shocked the modern-art world with their exuberant use of elements of primitive

art: strong outlines; bright, barbaric colors; and two-dimensional flatness. The Fauves distorted the visible world so we could see it through more primitive eyes.

Their leader was Henri Matisse (mah-TEES, 1869–1954), a master of simplicity. Each of his subjects is boiled down to its essential details and portrayed with a few simple lines and colors.

Matisse simplifies reality so we can see it better through primitive eyes. The two-dimensional flatness shows Gauguin's influence.

Even though Matisse's work looks crude, his classical training is obvious. The "flat," primitive look is actually carefully planned 3-D. The bright colors that seem so bizarre are purposely placed to balance the composition. And despite the few lines, his figures are accurate and expressive.

Picasso and Cubism

Pablo Picasso's long, prolific career spans several art styles. Picasso (1881–1973), an innovator, provides us with prime examples of many things characteristic of modern art.

When he was 19, Picasso moved from Barcelona to Paris to be where the artistic action was. (An exciting collection of his early work is displayed in his house in Barcelona.) Picasso's early paintings of beggars and other social outcasts are touching examples of expressionism done with the sympathy and understanding of an artist who felt, perhaps, as much an outcast as his subjects. These early works were from his Blue Period (around 1905), so called because their dominant color matches their melancholy mood.

Picasso was jolted out of his Blue Period by the abstract methods of the Fauves. Fascinated but not satisfied with the Fauvist 2-D treatment of 3-D, Picasso played with the "building blocks" of line and color to find new ways to reconstruct the real world on canvas.

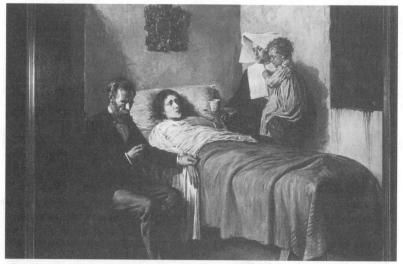

Picasso, **Science and Charity,** *1897 (Picasso Museum, Barcelona). As a teenager, Picasso painted realistically.*

Picasso, **The Frugal Meal,** *1904 (Museum of Modern Art, New York). He then explored beyond what the eye sees, evolving through several stages. This stage was melancholy, a style of expressionism called Picasso's "Blue Period."*

In about 1910, after an orgy of artistic exploration, Picasso and his friend Georges Braque found a new way to portray their world. This was Cubism, so called because the painting looks as though it was built with blocks. Cubism is like breaking a vase and arranging the broken pieces on a flat surface. In Picasso's work, chunks of light and shadow seem to stand out in 3-D, like shards of broken glass reflecting light.

Picasso was still tied to the visible world. The anatomy might be jumbled, but it's all there. Picasso shattered the real world, then pieced it back together on canvas in his own way.

In his monumental mural *Guernica,* Picasso blends the abstract and the expressive. In the 1930s, Nazi-backed Spanish Fascists destroyed the Spanish town of Guernica. Picasso captured the horror of the event, not through a realistic portrayal but through expressive images.

The ambiguous, abstract nature of *Guernica* elevates the painting to a statement about all wars. There are some clearly recognizable images of the agony of war: the grieving mother with her dead child (a modern *Pietà*); the dying

Picasso, **Seated Nude,** *1909 (Tate Modern, London). During a frenzied period in Paris with painting buddy Georges Braque, Picasso jumbled realism into a new art style, "Cubism."*

Picasso, **Guernica**, *1937 (Reina Sofia Museum, Madrid). This masterpiece combines Cubism, surrealism, and abstractionism in black, grey, and white to show the terror of the Fascist air raid on a defenseless town during the Spanish Civil War. Today it is a virtual national monument of Spain and a comment on the futility and horror of war in general.*

warrior clutching a broken sword; the twisted horse's head. But the real power of the work comes from the disjointed anatomy typical of early Cubist works, as if the bombs had shattered every belief and decimated every moral principle, leaving civilization in a confused heap of rubble.

Guernica, Spain's national work of art, spent the Franco years in exile. Today it's the powerful centerpiece of the Reina Sofia Museum in Madrid, a few blocks from the Prado museum.

Dada

The Jazz Age of the 1920s, when Europe tried to drown the memory of the war in wine and cynicism, produced Dadaism. The name was intentionally nonsensical and childish to poke fun at the pompous art styles, theories, and -isms of prewar times. The one rule of the Dada theory is that there are no rules. The *Mona Lisa* with a mustache, a snow shovel signed by the artist, a collage of shredded paper dropped on a canvas—these were the Dadaists' contribution to Art, a summation of the rebelliousness and disgust of the Roaring Twenties.

If a snow shovel is art, what is art? With mass production, the lines began to blur. Handmade art became an economic dinosaur as it became possible for rich people to buy beautiful objects and furnishings right off the production line. Artists found themselves on the outside of an industrial society that was interested more in utility and affordability than in aesthetics and uniqueness.

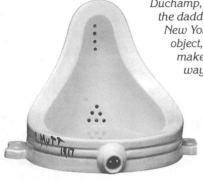

Duchamp, **Fountain,** _1917. Marcel Duchamp, the daddy of Dada, placed this urinal in a New York exhibit. By taking a common object, giving it a title, and calling it art, he makes us think about the object in a new way._

Without patrons to please, modern artists had no one to please but themselves and fellow artists. They turned to subjects interesting to the highly educated—studies in color, brushwork, and textures. Originality and innovation became more important than beauty.

Modern artists face the same challenge as Michelangelo's successors: to be original at all costs. If you can't please the public, shock it.

Surrealism and Beyond

Dada's successor for shock value was surrealism. (The name implies "beyond realism," as if reality isn't weird enough already.) Inspired by the psychiatric theories of Sigmund Freud, surrealism explores the inner world of the subconscious mind. The canvases of Salvador Dali are primal, troubling "dreamscapes." In dreams, objects appear in weird combinations, constantly changing in shape and meaning. A woman becomes a cat, the cat has a train pass, the cat is the train....

Marc Chagall (shuh-GAWL, 1887–1985), although not a surrealist, used the same scrambling of images. Raised in Russia, Chagall mixed a rich borscht of Russian folk images, Jewish motifs, and Christian messages. His

Chagall, **Self-Portrait with Seven Fingers,** _1912 (Stedelijk Museum, Amsterdam)_

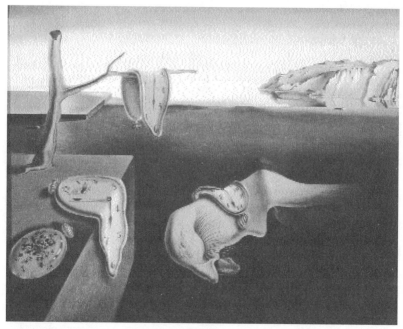

Dalí, **The Persistence of Memory,** *1931 (Museum of Modern Art, New York). This first-ever look at "flex time" sums up the surrealists' attempt to shock us by taking familiar objects and placing them in an unfamiliar context.*

colorful paintings are a stimulating fantasy of mostly weightless images. The Chagall museum in Nice, designed by the artist himself, is a delight.

While surrealists painted recognizable objects (though often in a twisted or unusual setting), other artists produced purely abstract works. As Europe struggled to rebuild and recover after World War II, the focus of art shifted to the United States.

Pop Art

Pop Art of the 1950s and 1960s, like Dada of the Jazz Age, challenges the old rules of what constitutes art. The everyday toothpastes, soup cans, comic books, and advertisements of commercial society are displayed as art. The viewer sees these objects in a new way, reflecting on the value our society places on them.

Modern artists experiment with modern materials. From initial experimentation with Cubist collages, artists began replacing paint with all kinds of things. The resulting mixed-media creations stimulate

Lichtenstein, **Whaam!**, *1963 (Tate Modern, London). A child's comic book becomes a 70-square-foot piece of art: Pop Art. What would Raphael think?*

all the senses—in some cases, even smell—and fuse the mediums of painting and sculpture.

Painting has been the most dynamic of the visual arts in this century, but sculpture followed some of the same trends. The primitivism of the Fauves influenced Constantin Brancusi, whose sculptures are the equivalent of Matisse's "minimal" paintings. Brancusi altered the shape of the original stone only slightly.

Author Gene Openshaw "getting into" modern art (Pompidou Center, Paris)

Modern Art Sights

- *Guernica*, Reina Sofia Museum, Madrid
- Picasso Museum, Barcelona, Spain
- Dalí Museum, Figueres, Spain
- Picasso Museum, Paris
- Pompidou Center, Paris
- Grimaldi-Picasso Museum, Antibes, France
- Marc Chagall National Museum, Nice, France
- Foundation Maeght, St. Paul, French Riviera
- Many galleries on the French Riviera
  (Matisse, Chagall, Picasso)
- Wallraf-Richartz Museum, Köln, Germany
- Stedelijk Museum, Amsterdam
- Kröller-Müller Museum, near Arnhem, Netherlands
- Tate Modern, London
- Guggenheim Gallery, Venice
- Louisiana Museum, north of Copenhagen, Denmark
- Munch Museum (Expressionism), Oslo, Norway
- Kunst Museum (lots of Paul Klee), Bern, Switzerland
- Art of the Criminally Insane (Collection de l'Art Brut),
  Lausanne, Switzerland
- Modern Art Museum, Stockholm, Sweden

Anywhere in Europe: Commercial galleries sell contemporary art. Temporary exhibits abound; often, one wing of a museum is reserved just for temporary exhibits. Check local periodical entertainment guides, tourist information offices, and posters around town.

Dalí,
Metamorphosis of Narcissus

Modern Architecture

"Form follows function" was the catchphrase of early 20th-century architecture. While painters and sculptors have to concern themselves primarily with how good their artwork looks (its form), architects must also be concerned with how their buildings work (function).

At the beginning of the 20th century, the ready availability of steel frames, reinforced concrete, and high-quality, mass-produced glass gave architects the tools to build almost any style of building they wanted. Architects began stripping buildings down to their barest structural elements, letting the function dictate the form.

The international style that developed in the 1920s followed the lead of the Bauhaus, a German art school. This blocky building emphasized industrial design and functionalism in architecture. Rectangular outlines, flat roofs, no ornamentation, white walls, and lots of glass were Bauhaus favorites. When the Nazis closed the Bauhaus, its director moved to the United States. And tall, boxlike, steel-and-glass skyscrapers soon dominated the standard U.S. urban skyline.

Contemporary European architecture has branched in several directions. An extreme example of form following function is the Pompidou Center in Paris. This huge, exoskeletal structure drapes its "guts" on the outside. All plumbing, heating ducts, and wiring are brightly color coded and in full view, freeing the interior space for its expansive modern art museum.

Le Corbusier, who said "a house is a machine for living in," was a major force in 20th-century European architecture. An innovative leader in city planning, he popularized putting buildings on pillars to create space below. After Le Corbusier, governmental buildings were no longer built to look like neoclassical temples. One church he designed, in Ronchamp, France, has become a pilgrimage site for students of architecture.

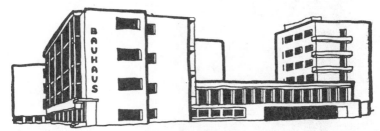

Gropius, **Bauhaus**, 1925, Dessau, Germany. Modern architecture focused on function over good looks. This purely geometric building set the style for almost every skyscraper since.

Le Corbusier,
Chapel, 1954,
Ronchamp, France.
A far cry from
Gothic, this highly
expressive church
(located atop a hill
in the Vosges
Mountains) is one of
the gems of modern
architecture.

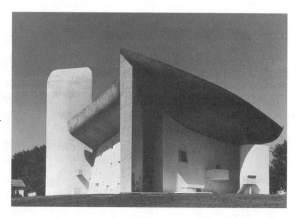

Munich's buildings for the 1972 Olympic Games are an interesting experiment in tent forms. Across the street, the BMW headquarters and museum occupy a futuristic, cylindrical, glass skyscraper.

Scandinavian architects such as Alvar Aalto from Finland developed their own style based on simplicity and clean lines. These traits carry over into the Scandinavian furniture and lighting designs popular in America today.

Europe is continually balancing the need to preserve what's old and to accommodate what's new. Choosing preservation over traffic circulation, Rome plans to eventually close the busy street that bisects its richest architectural ruins. Amid Barcelona's bustling fast-food stands, Gaudí's Sagrada Familia cathedral is still lovingly being built, long after his death. In Paris in 1990, I. M. Pei plopped a glass pyramid in the courtyard of the stately Louvre. Below the pyramid is an underground complex of shops, eateries, and services that skillfully turn the aging Louvre into a thriving, modern building.

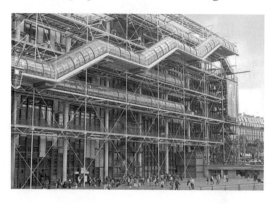

Pompidou Center,
b. 1977, Paris. With its
guts color-coded and
draped on the outside,
the interior of this
Parisian cultural
center is filled with
modern art galleries
and exhibits.

Modern Architecture Sights

- Temppeliaukio Church, Finland, Helsinki
- Tapiola (planned suburb), Finland, Helsinki
- Works of Alvar Aalto (museum), Jyvaskyla, Helsinki
- Vallingby and Farsta (planned suburbs), Stockholm, Sweden
- The "Cube" at La Defense, Paris
- Forum/Les Halles shopping mall, Paris
- Pyramid Entrance to Louvre and attached mall, Paris
- Pompidou Center, Paris
- Chapel at Ronchamp, France
- Guggenheim Bilbao, Bilbao, Spain
- Termini Train Station, Rome
- Berlin housing projects (Kreuzberg district), Berlin
- Hundertwasser Haus, Vienna
- Rotterdam, the whole city, Netherlands

**I. M. Pei's Pyramid** entry to the Louvre, 1990, Paris

The streets of Europe's cities are becoming "people places." Most large cities (such as Copenhagen, Florence, and Munich) have traffic-free pedestrian areas full of shops and cafés, providing perfect opportunities for that great European pastime—people watching.

Faced with ever-dwindling space, rising populations, and dynamic societal changes, European architects and city planners have come up with some creative ideas. Today's architecture is—as it has been from the cave dweller to Egypt and from Rome to the Renaissance—a product of available materials and technology, climate, and the needs of the people.

A United Europe

As Europe grapples with problems concerning the environment, terrorism, refugees, politics, and competition in a global market, it has recognized the growing necessity of speaking, trading, and legislating with one voice. Today's European Union is the result of efforts started years ago.

In 1948, Belgium, the Netherlands, and Luxembourg (BeNeLux) united economically to compete with the bigger countries. Later, the European Coal and Steel Community (founded by Germany, France, Italy, and the BeNeLux nations) quickly showed that the free trade concept was a winner.

In 1957, these six countries expanded their agreement to include agricultural products, further linking their economies. This affiliation became known as the Common Market.

The Common Market was joined by Great Britain, Ireland, Denmark, Greece, Spain, and Portugal. In the mid-1990s, Austria, Sweden, and Finland became members, while Norway voted against membership. Today this European Union (EU) bustles with 15 states and over 370 million producer/consumers.

In 1992, all commercial borders between EU nations were dissolved. In the mid-1990s, passport controls for citizens and tourists were eliminated as well. Today the EU has one common passport and one uniform driver's license.

Most of the EU now has a common currency, the euro. Still in its infancy, the euro turns into bills and coins in 2002—when schillings, marks, lire, and francs turn into souvenirs. The euro is good news for American travelers. We won't lose money at exchange offices at every border. We can comparison shop without fancy calculations throughout the 11 European countries that have adopted the Euro. And, for your shopping convenience—as long as the euro roughly equals a dollar in value—you can leave your currency converter at home. Throughout Euroland, menus and signs that list prices in euros are, in essence, listing prices in dollars.

The economic success of the EU, the demands of continental problems like acid rain that know no borders, and the pressure to compete in a global market against the Americas and Asia convinced most Europeans that unification is a good—or at least necessary—idea.

The EU has a number of problems to tackle, such as establishing a unified defense force. This became apparent during the unrest in former Yugoslavia.

The countries of the EU, mostly run by liberal governments, are also

AIDS poster. *Uniting, but with caution, Europe looks to the future.*

struggling with a small but disturbing far-right movement. The far right, which builds its support on the fear that a flood of immigrants threatens quality of life, has a high profile in France (National Front party) and more recently, in Austria (Freedom party). Far-right parties consistently score at least 15 percent in national elections and polls in Germany, Norway, Switzerland, and even freewheeling Denmark.

The more established "foreigners," many of whom were born in Europe, are families of guest workers invited by Germany and Switzerland in the 1970s and '80s to do menial labor. The recent arrivals pouring into Europe are political or economic refugees from war-torn lands and former colonies. Unification, which erases borders, makes it easy for immigrants to enter Europe.

A growing number of Europeans resent the newcomers for taking away jobs or living on welfare. Fearful of another Hitler, Europe wonders whether it's better to suppress far-right groups or let them spout off . . . while foreigners increasingly find themselves the targets of racism and even violence.

The opening of the English Channel Tunnel (the Chunnel) in 1995 shows that Europe is growing together physically—in ways unimaginable just a decade ago. The world's longest tunnels are under construction as Norway tames its rugged environment. Huge bridges lace together Sweden's and Denmark's islands. And bullet trains crisscross the ever-smaller continent. Europe is charging confidently into an age where there are only neighbors. Assuming everyone finds a way to live together, the physical, political, and economic

In 2002, Europe's new currency, the Euro, puts the mark, franc, and lira out of business.

David C. Hoerlein

unification of Europe is great news for Europeans and tourists alike.

Free trade throughout Europe is obviously worth pursuing, but just how far should unification go? What about the foreign policy of a united Europe? What impact will a freer Eastern Europe have, with its pent-up capacity to consume and produce? What about the reunification of Germany, which has in itself created a new superpower?

The wealthy countries of the European Union are leery of the economic drag that southern and eastern countries might bring to a united Europe. Poorer countries don't want to be shut out.

Many expect the unification of Europe to include a series of widening circles, with a core union functioning almost as a single country, a second circle containing Great Britain, a wider circle containing Scandinavia and Switzerland, and an outermost circle letting Turkey and Eastern Europe in on some of the trade fun. Sadly, the fate of Russia is still an unknown.

Many worry that unification will cause a homogenization of the cultures. But as Europe unites, regions become less of a threat to nations. These days the endangered cultures of Europe—those ethnic groups without their own country—will meet less resistance, thereby causing fewer problems. As the political relevance of Madrid and London wanes, Catalunyan flags will wave freely in Barcelona and Celtic children will learn their own language. For the first time in 300 years, London has allowed the Scottish parliament to meet. It's reason to hope that the cultural diversity which makes Europe so great will not only survive unification—it will thrive because of it. *Vive la différence!*

The Superpower Bowl		
Region	*Population*	*Rough GNP*
EU	370 million	5 trillion
U.S.	260 million	6 trillion
Japan	125 million	2.5 trillion

As you feel the fjords and caress the castles, remember that Europe is alive—coping, groping, and more interested in its future than in its past. As visitors, we often forget that quaintness, cute thatched-roof houses, and yodeling are not concerns of the average European. Sure, it's exciting to find odd remnants of Europe's Old World that somehow missed the 21st-century bus. But much of what we see touted as the "real thing" culturally is actually a cultural cliché kept alive for the tourists. As you travel, seek out contemporary Europe as well as its past. Educate yourself about the concerns and issues of today.

As the world hurtles toward 100 trillion McDonald's hamburgers served, western-style prosperity is changing Europe. It seems that when all the wrinkled old ladies in black are gone, they are destined to be replaced by Coca-Cola, skyscrapers, fast food, computers, and the global pop culture.

The most encouraging aspect of our future is that as the world grows smaller, more people will travel and rub shoulders. As this happens and we begin to view our globe as the home of 6 billion equally precious people, we'll all feel a little less American, British, Japanese, French, or whatever, and a little more like a member of humankind.

The lessons of history apply even today. It's easy to think that we are in a grand new age with no precedent, one that follows no rules. But every generation has thought that of their era, and we're just the latest in a long line of "pioneers."

History is happening now, and plenty of excitement awaits. If we see ourselves in historical perspective, grasp how yesterday shaped today, and learn less from the news media and more from our travels, we will better understand and shape the events of tomorrow.

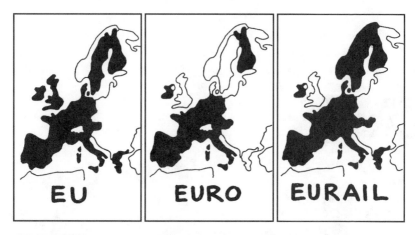

EU: *The European Union consists of Austria, Belgium, Denmark, Finland, France, Germany, Great Britain, Greece, Ireland, Italy, Luxembourg, Netherlands, Portugal, Spain, and Sweden.*

Euro: *The euro is the common currency of most of the EU, known informally as Euroland. Exceptions are Britain, Denmark, Sweden, and Greece.*

Eurail: *To travelers with a railpass, Europe isn't the EU or Euroland—it's Eurail country. All aboard!*

Part II

Country Specifics

While we tried to tell the complete story of Europe from the
pyramids to Picasso in one raucous sweep, certain regions—
such as Britain, Ireland, Iberia (Spain and Portugal), and
Turkey—simply demand special treatment. The body of this
book dealt with the core story. Now we offer a few country-
specific history sweeps of regions which evolved a little apart
from the mainstream of Europe.

Britain

Ancient Britain

The Isle of Britain was a mysterious challenge to General Julius Caesar as he prepared for his invasion. Curtained in mist, separated from the civilized Continent by an arm of the ocean, peopled by strange, savage tribes who painted themselves blue and sacrificed human beings to their gods—this was nearly all that was known of merry olde England when Caesar set sail in 55 B.C. to conquer it.

The 45-year-old general had conquered Gaul (modern France) but wanted one more conquest to impress the folks back home so that when he returned to Rome they would invite him to rule the empire. His invading ships approached Dover to find the cliffs lined with screaming, war-painted, spear-carrying Britons. After beaching, Caesar led a swift charge, driving the Britons back. The Romans huddled near the coast and waited for reinforcements, which were delayed by stormy weather. They were harassed by daring native soldiers driving war chariots, who would dash up to the camp balanced on the yoke, wreak havoc, and ride away.

As soon as new ships arrived, a weary Caesar packed up and returned to Gaul. His conquest of 200 meters of beach was hailed as a triumph in Rome; the Senate proclaimed an unprecedented twenty days of public thanksgiving.

The next year, better prepared, Caesar tried again, this time marching inland as far as modern London. He won battles, took hostages, exacted tribute, and made treaties. He left England having brought the mysterious land into its first contact with "civilization."

Celts (500 B.C.–A.D. 43)

The Celtics (pronounced KELL-tiks, except in Boston) Caesar found weren't as barbarous as he had expected. There were perhaps 100,000 Britons scattered in small, isolated tribes. A number of towns had 500 people; present-day Colchester, with 1,000, was the largest. Still, most were rural farming/hunting/herding tribes united under a local chieftain. People didn't travel or trade much and most buildings were small and made of wood.

The Celts (who included Gaels, Picts, Scots, and many smaller tribes) migrated to England and Ireland from the Continent beginning around 500 B.C. They conquered and blended with the prehistoric inhabitants (those even-more-mysterious people who built Stonehenge with huge rocks quarried 100 miles away) and traded goods as far as ancient Greece. The Celtic language survives today in modern Gaelic (Scotland), Erse (Ireland), Welsh (guess), and Breton (Western France). About half of present-day Great Britain is of Celtic-Pictish blood.

The Celts' nasty reputation in the Roman mind came from the Druids. These witch-doctor priests presided over rituals to appease the gods, spirits, and demons that inhabited the countryside. There were ghosts and spirits everywhere; one could feel them in the gloom of a dark forest or in the power of a rushing waterfall. The Druids, painted blue, sacrificed and decapitated animals and occasionally humans, offering the head to a local god or to one of the more powerful fertility or war gods. Then they tore the body apart, using the disposition of the guts to predict the future. They also practiced voodoo magic, cursing someone by making a statue of the person and then mutilating it.

The Romans, tolerant as they were, drew the line at Druidism. Because the Druids were also tribal aristocrats trying to preserve tradition, they posed a political threat to the Romans. The Druids maintained power for a century after Caesar's brief invasions.

Roman Britain (A.D. 43–500)

Then, in A.D. 43, the Emperor Claudius ordered a massive invasion that overwhelmed the courageous but outmatched Celts. Claudius personally rode north from Rome for the victory procession through Colchester, accompanied by the Praetorian Guard, a host of Roman aristocrats, and the imperial elephant corps to impress the natives. The Romans had arrived.

Claudius left after two weeks with the simple order, "Conquer the rest." It took 40 years, but finally all the lowland areas of England and Wales, plus lower Scotland, were in Roman hands, where they would remain for four centuries. The fiercely independent herdsmen of the Scottish highlands, though nominally Roman, never were assimilated into "civilized" Roman society (and, some would say, have yet to be assimilated into British society).

Queen Boadicea, _who led the charge against Roman invaders, still whips her horses today in the shadow of London's Big Ben._

The conquest wasn't without resistance. In A.D. 60, after a dispute at modern-day Colchester, Roman soldiers took the Celtic palace, flogged the queen, raped her daughters, and seized the royal treasury. The outraged Celts banded together under Queen Boadicea and set out burning and looting Roman towns. The rebels took "Londinium" (London), burned it to the ground, and offered the Romanized inhabitants as human sacrifices to the Celtic god of war. Blood hungry with success, the rebellion spread. It took months for the Romans to quiet the Celts. The winter was a bleak one for Britain as the Romans wreaked violent revenge. To escape reprisal, Boadicea and her family took poison. (Boadicea is honored with a statue across the street from Big Ben, in London.)

The Romans learned a lesson, however, and instituted policies to keep the Celts happy. Government was in the hands of a Roman, but he allowed local chieftains to retain power as long as they cooperated with him. Local customs and religious practices were generally accepted.

Around their forts, the Romans planned towns in the familiar Roman pattern: a rectangular street plan with the forum (marketplace) and basilica (courthouse) in the center, temples, baths, and a piped water system. Later, earthwork walls were built, defining their growth limit through the Middle Ages. Some towns such as Corinium (today's Cirencester) and Aquae Sulis (modern Bath) grew to have over 1,000 inhabitants.

To connect towns and forts and to facilitate trade and communication, the Romans built roads, many of which still stand. Latin was taught, and soon it was as popular (in urban centers) as Celtic. When marriage was legalized for Roman soldiers, they often married local girls, and their sons grew up to join the ranks.

The line between "Roman" and "Briton" grew fuzzier and fuzzier. By A.D. 200, the urban centers of southeast England were as "civilized" as any part of the empire. The population of Roman Britain grew to 2 million.

Londinium was the Roman center of the country, the capital, trade center, and the hub of the road system. It was surrounded by a stone wall (parts of which are still visible near the Tower of London). From here, Britain traded with the Continent, exporting wool, metals, hunting dogs, corn, and oysters. In return, they got all the luxuries of the Roman world: pottery, wine, glassware, lamps, jewelry, silverware, furniture, and the latest clothing fashions.

The northern tribes of Scotland weren't very impressed with what the Romans had to offer, preferring independence to the niceties of Latin culture. Roman soldiers had to protect their settlements from periodic raids by the Highlanders. They conquered as far north as the present border of Scotland and then built a wall.

Hadrian's Wall (built while Hadrian was emperor, around A.D. 130) stands 20 feet high and 8 feet thick (wide enough for a chariot to drive upon), stretching from coast to coast across northern England. It was manned by 20,000 soldiers in forts spaced one mile apart ("mile castles") all along the wall. For more than three centuries it kept the Scots at bay, and much of it stands today, a tribute to Roman military engineering. (Hadrian's Wall is worth a visit. The best-preserved section is in Northumberland near the town of Hexham. A youth hostel called Once Brewed is just a short walk from Housesteads Fort, a Roman mile castle with the best museum about the wall.)

Christianity arrived with the Romans. Rome, generally tolerant of local religions, accepted many of the local Druid gods, giving them new Latin names. (The superstitious Roman soldiers, assigned to a distant outpost near a dreary forest, were careful not to offend any fierce spirits that might have dwelled there.) The sterile Roman religion with its abstract gods and reverence for the state didn't really do it for the locals, so the Britons, like many Romans throughout the empire, turned to

Eastern religions such as Mithraism, the Cult of Isis, and Christianity.

Legend has it that Christianity was brought by Joseph of Arimathea, the man who paid for Jesus' burial, and that he converted the Britons with a miracle: he planted his staff in the ground and it took root, becoming a thorn tree in Glastonbury that was said to bloom every Christmas.

Christianity became a powerful force—probably the number-one religion during the Roman occupation. But Celtic, Roman, and Eastern religions were also a part of Roman Britain. As late as A.D. 400, Celtic temples were built; many Druidic rituals survived among the peasants until modern times.

As Rome fell, so fell Roman Britain. The combination of internal decay and external enemies that caused Rome's collapse forced the Romans to slowly withdraw troops and administrators from Britain. Over the centuries, even the Roman governors and generals had become Britonized and drifted away from Rome. Some generals went so far as to secede from the empire, declaring themselves kings of Britain. Without Rome's strength and organization, the island was easy prey for invaders. In A.D. 409, the emperor in Rome was forced to completely abandon Britain.

The Anglo-Saxons (A.D. 400–800)

The invaders came from Germany and Denmark, tribes called Angles, Saxons, Jutes (and worse names by the Britons). They came not as conquerors but as refugees, leaving behind crowded, bleak homelands for the fertile farmlands of Britain. As early as A.D. 250, small groups in long-boats began arriving on the northeast coast. The Roman Britons fought them off when they could and tolerated them when they couldn't. As Roman support waned, the invasion/migrations increased. The sixth century saw the Anglo-Saxons pushing the Celts and Romanized Britons westward. This is the period of the real King Arthur, most likely a Christian Romanized British general valiantly fighting the invading tribes.

By 600, the southeast part of the island was "Angle-land" (England), the land of the Angles. The Roman world slowly crumbled; the towns dwindled, and the roads fell into disuse. The invaders were a rough, savage people compared to the Romans, with no central government or economy. Each tribe had its own chief and council of elders. The society was bound by a code of hierarchy and personal loyalty similar to that of the later medieval feudal system.

England had entered the Dark Ages. The economy was weak, life was harsh, and justice was severe. The "wergild," a system worked out to financially compensate relatives for people murdered in feuds, gives us a look at the value placed on human life in those harsh times. If a noble was killed, the murderer's clan had to pay the victim's clan 1,200 shillings; a knight was worth 300; a free peasant, 200; killing a serf required no recompense at all. Women of equal position were worth less than their male counterparts. Hmmm.

The Anglo-Saxon pagan religion replaced Christianity in many places. Some of these Norse gods are familiar to us today: Tiw, Woden (King of the Gods), Thor (with his hammer), Frig. Not familiar? How about "Tiw's-day," "Woden's-day," "Thor's-day," and "Frig's-day." They also celebrated a spring festival to the goddess Eostre (Easter).

Christianity reentered England with missionaries from both Ireland and Rome. When the Saxon King Aethelbert of Kent was converted (around 600), the tide was turned. Within a hundred years, England was again mostly Christian, though not by much. Pagans continued to rule in many kingdoms throughout the Dark Ages.

One of the Christian kings, Offa (around 780), brought some stability to the warring Anglo-Saxon tribes. The time of peace brought a renaissance of learning, and the English language took its earliest form. The poem *Beowulf,* written in England but incorporating Norse mythology, was written at this time. (You can see a manuscript in the British Library, London.) Offa printed coins with his portrait on them, advancing the notion that the many Anglo-Saxon tribes were part of a single nation. He also built a trench to separate England from the Celtic Welsh. Offa's Dike, running the length of the English-Welsh border, is a popular hike.

Only Two Invasions to Go (A.D. 800–1066)

True unity didn't come until after another set of invasions—this time from the Vikings, the Anglo-Saxons' distant cousins from Denmark. The two groups warred, made peace, and mingled during the next few centuries. This was the period of rulers with names such as Harold Harefoot, Eric Bloodaxe, Edgar the Peacock, Ethelred the Unready, and Edward the Confessor (Edward commissioned Westminster Abbey).

The stew of peoples that make up present-day England was nearly complete—from prehistory to the Celts, the Romans, the Anglo-Saxons, and finally the Danes. Next came the Normans, from northern France (present-day Normandy). William the Conqueror invaded from across the channel, defeating Saxon King Harold at the Battle of Hastings (1066). This battle marks England's escape from the Dark Ages and her entry into the High Middle Ages.

English Kings and Queens

"For God's sake, let us sit upon the ground and tell sad stories of the death of kings...."

Shakespeare, _Richard II_

The history of England's royalty is full of violence, corruption, treason, sex, scandal, power, and greed. Remarkably, the country survived its rulers.

England's Alfred the Great

Alfred (849–899), an enlightened and compassionate ruler, is considered the first king of a united "England." He rallied the scattered Anglo-Saxon tribes of England to ward off the Viking invaders. After establishing peace, he turned to matters closer to his heart. Having had an older brother, he never expected to become king, so he studied poetry and Latin. He even visited Rome in his teens.

When he became king, he reformed the government and built schools that taught English as well as Latin. Alfred deserves his reputation as the model English king—strong, learned, and kind.

French Kings: The Normans

William the Conqueror crossed the channel from Normandy and defeated the Saxon forces at Hastings. He was crowned king of England on Christmas Day 1066, in London's Westminster Abbey, where future kings and queens would be crowned. A harsh but efficient ruler, he united the British lords and established a feudal society. (Construction of the Tower of London, where so many leaders were later executed, was begun during William's reign.)

William and his Norman successors were never very popular with the common people. They were foreign invaders who spoke French and followed French customs.

The Tower of London, b. 1077–1097. The prison and execution site for those accused of crimes against the monarchy. Admission tickets include a very informative and entertaining tour by a Beefeater. (Executions by reservation only.)

His son William II, called "Rufus" (the Red) because of his ruddy complexion, was even less well liked. A vain, arbitrary tyrant, he made no attempt to mix with the English people. He died in a hunting accident—an arrow in the back. His brother Henry just happened to be in the hunting party, behind him. Henry immediately rode to Winchester, seized the treasury, and was crowned king the next day.

More French Kings: Angevins

The French kings expanded their empire. Henry II, who took power in 1154 at the age of 21, is the first of the Angevin kings. Through family inheritance and his marriage to Eleanor of Aquitaine, Henry II amassed a great deal of land, called the Angevin Empire, stretching from Scotland to northern Spain. His long and hard-fought rule consolidated the empire.

Henry was a good soldier and a fair diplomat, plus he was well read (for a king) and possessed of restless energy and a violent temper. The beginning of his reign was marked by optimism. He and his wife Eleanor, a beautiful and accomplished lady of the time, established a court where chivalrous knights, ladies, troubadours, and scholars met (for more information on this Camelot, see page 91). Henry built numerous castles throughout the empire.

But then things went bad, and it seemed as though everyone in the world was fighting Henry. He waged war with the Welsh, the Scots, and French rebels. He quarreled with English barons over taxes. His sons, supported by Eleanor, tried to overthrow him. Perhaps the most painful betrayal was that of his close friend and adviser, Thomas Becket, whom he had appointed Archbishop of Canterbury. When Becket's strong, independent policy threatened the king's power, Henry's knights murdered Becket in Canterbury Cathedral. Becket became an instant martyr to the English people, and the cathedral became a popular pilgrimage site.

Henry II died a broken man, and his son Richard the Lionhearted assumed power. Richard was the model of a chivalrous knight—a good soldier, a poet, a musician, and a handsome, valiant Crusader. He was also a Frenchman. He hated England. (He once said, "I would sell London if I could find a buyer.") During his 10-year reign, he spent only six months in the country he ruled.

Everyone hated Richard's successor, his brother John Lackland. Everyone. He is unanimously considered the worst king England ever had. Devious and weak, he had an uncanny ability to make enemies of everyone—barons, popes, the English, and the French. He murdered his own nephew in a drunken rage. He waged war in France and lost miserably. The Angevin Empire collapsed under his rule. He overtaxed and bullied the English barons. All in all, he was very much the evil King John of the Robin Hood legend—perhaps the one true character in the myth.

John's place in history was assured by fixing his seal to the Magna Carta (Great Charter) forced on him by unhappy barons. This was the first step of many in English history to limit the power of kings and increase that of the nobles and common people. (The Magna Carta is on display in the British Library, London.)

Royalty on the Rocks: The Troublesome Centuries (1200–1400)

The next two centuries gave Shakespeare enough regicide, rebellion, and treason for eight plays. In that time, four kings were murdered, two died in battle, civil wars were rampant, and two family lines of kings were overthrown.

Edward II, a tyrant, was opposed by Roger Mortimer, his wife's lover. Edward was captured and murdered in a manner so brutal that to describe it would exceed this book's standard of good taste. Well, okay, if you insist. Suffice it to say that a red-hot poker, Edward's backside, and a thrusting motion were involved. Ooh.

His son Edward III (reigned 1327–1377) avenged his father's death in a relatively civilized manner, by merely having Mortimer hanged, drawn, and quartered. Edward's good rule (aided by his chivalrous son, the famous "Black Prince") included early victories in the Hundred Years' War with the French, in which England initially conquered, and then slowly lost, France.

The next monarch, Richard II (reigned 1377–1399), ruled poorly and was finally overthrown by an upstart baron who locked Richard in the Tower of London. The long line of French-English kings came to an end.

The House of Lancaster

Henry IV, the Usurper (reigned 1399–1413), of the house of Lancaster, was the first completely English king—the son of English parents who spoke no French. Handsome, athletic, a musician and scholar, he invited poet Geoffrey Chaucer to his court. Yet like so many others, when he died he was bitter and broken, worn out by years of opposition and civil war.

His son, the "Prince Hal" of Shakespeare's plays, was said to have lived a misspent youth, carousing, gambling, and thieving with commoners and prostitutes. Whether true or not, when he became Henry V, he was cold, stern, and very capable. His victory at the Battle of Agincourt (1415) put most of France back under English rule.

All of Hal's gains became losses in the weak hands of Henry VI, whose attempts to hold France were foiled by a young French peasant woman, Joan of Arc. She claimed to hear voices of saints and angels who told her where to lead the French armies. She was eventually captured and burned as a witch by the English, but not before the French had gained an upper hand in the war.

War of the Roses

The inept Henry VI of the Lancaster family was opposed by the York family, and a long civil war broke out—the "War of the Roses," named for the white (York) and red (Lancaster) roses that the families used as their symbols. Edward IV, a York, locked Henry in the Tower of London, later executing him. Edward died young, at the age of 40, reportedly worn out by his sexual excesses.

Two of Edward's excesses survived him, but not by much. His sons, the heirs to the throne, were kidnapped and murdered in the Tower of London by Richard III (Edward's own brother), and both houses decided the bloody war had to end. When a petty noble from the house of Tudor defeated Richard's armies and killed him in battle, all of England was prepared to rally round him as the new king. Henry VII was crowned, a diplomatic marriage was arranged, and England was united.

Tudor Rule, 1485–1603

Henry VII (reigned 1485–1509) was shrewd and efficient; he was England's first "modern" chief executive. He united the country and built up a huge treasury. (To protect himself from traitors, he established a royal bodyguard, the Beefeaters.) His 18-year-old son inherited a nation that was solvent, strong, and at peace.

Henry VIII (reigned 1509–1547) was the English version of a Renaissance prince—tall, handsome, athletic, a poet and musician, and well read in secular learning and theology. He was charismatic but could also be arrogant, cruel, gluttonous, erratic, and paranoid.

The most notorious event of Henry VIII's reign was the break with the Catholic church (and his establishment of the nearly identical Church of England). This arose over the Catholic church's refusal to grant him a divorce from his first wife, Catherine of Aragon (the daughter of Ferdinand and Isabella of Spain) and to sanction his subsequent marriage to the beautiful and lively Anne Boleyn. Henry was determined to get a wife who could give him a son. For whatever reasons—love, desire for an heir, diplomacy, or sheer lust—Henry went through six wives, divorcing, imprisoning, or beheading them when they no longer served his purpose.

Henry faced enemies in England over his break with Catholicism, and he dealt with them characteristically—with the ax. Among those beheaded at the

Henry VIII, _by Hans Holbein_

Tower for holding fast to their convictions was Thomas More, Henry's chancellor and author of the famous political tract, "Utopia."

While the Reformation wars raged on the Continent, England was having religious troubles of its own. After the brief but weak reign of Henry's long-awaited male heir, the stage was set for Henry's daughters.

Mary I (reigned 1553–1558), the daughter of his first wife, Catherine, had her mother's fanatic Spanish Catholic devotion (the same kind that gave us the Inquisition). She was convinced her mission was to

return England to the Roman church—come Hell or high water. Neither came, but in her zeal, she ordered burned at the stake over 300 men, women, and children. She ordered the execution of the innocent, 17-year-old Lady Jane Grey (a rival for the throne) in 1554. Compared with the tens of thousands killed in other countries it seems like nothing, but it shocked the English enough that they turned their backs on Catholicism for good and nicknamed their queen "Bloody Mary."

Mary's successor, Elizabeth I (1558–1603), Henry's daughter by the fiery Anne Boleyn, had

Elizabeth I, 1558–1603

absorbed the lesson of religious fanaticism. She was a Protestant with a broad Renaissance education. Her tolerant policies and prudent nature brought peace at home and victory abroad, making England a true European power for the first time. Among other conquests, Elizabeth subdued Ireland, beginning that country's centuries of struggle for independence.

The English navy defeated the famed Spanish armada and soon ruled the waves. Explorers and traders probed the New World and Asia, bringing back spoils and luxury goods. (Sir Walter Raleigh introduced tobacco from America to a skeptical Queen Elizabeth.)

Elizabeth was golden haired, prudent, and a "Virgin Queen," but her cousin Mary, Queen of Scots, was dark, lively, and a lover of dance, music, and men. Mary (not "Bloody Mary"), a Catholic from the Stuart family, represented the opposition to Elizabeth and the Protestant regime. After Mary was implicated in an anticrown plot, Elizabeth imprisoned her for 19 long years. But Mary never bowed. Fat, wrinkled, and wearing a wig to cover her balding head, she was finally led to the execution block.

The Elizabethan era was England's High Renaissance, especially in literature. Shakespeare, Raleigh, John Donne, Christopher Marlowe, and many others shaped the course of English literature and the English language itself. (The British Library in London has letters and manuscripts by England's great writers.)

The Stuarts and Civil War

When Elizabeth died, presumably still a virgin and definitely without an heir, the Tudor throne passed to the Stuarts—to James, son of Mary, Queen of Scots. James I (reigned 1603–1625) was vain and arrogant, a "foreigner" (from Scotland), and a Catholic to boot, who succeeded in alienating both the English people and Parliament.

James insisted that he ruled by "divine right" and was therefore above Parliament and human laws. The one lasting achievement of his reign was the King James version of the Bible, a landmark translation in both theology and literature, the culmination of the Elizabethan Renaissance.

It's said that James steered the ship of state toward the rocks and then left his son to wreck it. Throughout the 17th century, the haughty Catholic Stuart kings were at odds with Parliament until Parliament got fed up, rebelled, and established a "constitutional monarchy" that limited, by law, the king's power.

Charles I (reigned 1625–1649) was his father's son in every way, but even more so: he was pompous, vain, anti-Protestant, and anti-Parliament. When Parliament refused to grant him more money, he dissolved the body for over 10 years. Parliament (which was made up mostly of nobles) responded by raising its own army and declaring war on the king. Their leader, Oliver Cromwell, vowed, "We will cut off the King's head with the crown on it." Civil war had begun.

Parliament defeated the troops loyal to the king, deposed him, and set up a Commonwealth ruled by itself. Charles was executed as Cromwell had promised.

Cromwell, a Puritan gentleman-farmer elected to Parliament, soon assumed the powers of a dictator. He was very capable and religiously tolerant, and he kept a steady hand in a troubled time. However, he himself suspended Parliament, à la Charles, when it disagreed with him.

When Cromwell died, in order to prevent another civil war in the struggle for power, Parliament invited Charles II to reign—on the condition that he follow the rules it set out.

(The French experienced a similar cycle 130 years later. The royalty abused its power; Parliament took matters into its own bloody hands, beheading the king. After a dictator's enlightened but harsh rule, the king was invited back and allowed to rule with constitutional or parliamentarian limitations.)

Charles II and Restoration

The "Restoration" of the monarchy (1660) was reason to celebrate in England. After decades of civil war and Puritan rule (with all the negative things "puritan" implies), it was nice to have the pomp, ceremony, luxury, and even decadence of the Stuart kings. Charles II (1660–1685) had spent his exile in the magnificent court of Louis XIV. He returned to London with the latest fashions.

Charles had a series of dazzling mistresses who shocked the Puritan Parliament and titillated the public. (There were so many, most of them Catholics, that one of them took to identifying herself: "I'm the Protestant whore.")

During Charles' reign, London was devastated by a plague and burned to the ground in the Great Fire of 1666. The rebuilding, lead by architect Christopher Wren, reflects Charles' Baroque influence (from Versailles).

Charles' brother, James II, lived up to the Stuart name by persecuting Protestants and plotting against Parliament. He was thrown out in the "Glorious Revolution." Parliament invited James' daughter and her husband to rule again, according to the dictates of Parliament. William and Mary were succeeded by the unremarkable Queen Anne.

The House of Hanover

In 1714, the Stuart line was exhausted and so were the English people, worn out by religious strife. Parliament chose the king least likely to stir up trouble, George I (reigned 1714–1721) of Germany. George was 54 years old, spoke no English, and had no interest in politics. His chancellor, Sir Robert Walpole, essentially ran the country. George II (1727–1760) was the sequel to this bland state of affairs.

George III (1760–1820) was the first truly English ruler in 50 years. He took the throne with high hopes and then ran right into the American Revolutionary War, the French Revolution, and Napoleon. The world changed too fast for him, and in 1810, he slipped into madness. England was left with "an old, mad, blind, despised, and dying king" (as the poet Shelley put it).

But England was changing rapidly, the Industrial Revolution was creating a whole new society, and England's monarchy knew it would meet the same fate as its French counterpart if it didn't modernize.

Victoria

Fortunately, along came Queen Victoria (reign 1837–1901), the first of England's modern figurehead monarchs. She had little interest and less influence in government. Her husband, Prince Albert, took some part in promoting science and industry (especially in organizing the Great Exhibition of 1851), but after his death things were run by Parliament and prime ministers (Disraeli and Gladstone).

Victoria was under five feet tall but radiated a regal aura. She was strong, bearing nine children, whom she married off to other European royal houses. (Kaiser Wilhelm and Tsarina Alexandra of World War I fame were her grandchildren.) She hated Georgian excesses and was notoriously prudish (hence, our word "Victorian").

The Victorian period saw England rise to its zenith. Its colonial empire was the largest in the world and its technology was the envy of Europe, yet its pockets of poverty were worse than those of many of its colonies.

Victoria's son, Edward VII (reign 1901–1910), was born and raised in the lap of Victorian luxury but never quite grew up, assuming the throne as a "child" of 60. The Edwardian period before World War I was the last golden (though fading) age of English optimism and civility. The horrors of the Great War shattered that forever.

The House of Windsor

Edward's son, George V of Windsor, ruled in the "modern" style (subservient to law and Parliament) until 1936, when he was succeeded by his son, Edward VIII. Edward (the Duke of Windsor), in the most-talked-about action of modern royalty, abdicated the throne to marry a commoner, twice-divorced American Mrs. Wallis Warfield Simpson. Edward's brother, George VI, ruled until his popular daughter, Elizabeth II, took the throne in 1952 with her husband, Phillip Mountbatten, Duke of Edinburgh. Charles, Prince of Wales (of _National Enquirer_ fame), waits to be our generation's entry in the parade of English kings and queens.

As you travel through England, you'll hear plenty of news about Charles, his royal rug rats, and the British royalty of today. If you're alert and even if you're not, there's a good chance you'll get at least a fleeting glimpse of England's busy first family. Although their kings and queens don't come cheap and are only figureheads, most British seem to thoroughly enjoy having a royal family.

Victorian London

"It was the best of times, it was the worst of times...."
Charles Dickens, _A Tale of Two Cities_

Dickens' words best describe his own city of London in the 1800s. With 4 million people, it was the world's largest. It was the busiest, the richest, the most productive; it was the hub of the most industrialized nation on earth and the capital of a colonial empire that covered nearly a quarter of the world's land surface. But the seamy underside of London was like a Third World country—dirty, poor, disease ridden, and dangerous.

This contrast was everywhere. You could buy any commodity in the world on London's docks and lose it to a thief just as quickly. It was the center of industrial growth, yet it was choked with coal dust and industrial filth. London hosted the lavish social life of Prince Edward as well as the squalid existence of thousands of homeless urchins begging, stealing, and sleeping in the streets. Palaces and townhouses contrasted with sagging tenements; well-lit cafés opposed seedy pubs where the poor indulged in one of their few affordable pastimes, drunkenness.

This was the Victorian period—that is, it occurred within the time of Queen Victoria (1837–1901). Victoria's husband, Prince Albert of Germany, was handsome, intelligent, progressive, and extremely proper. Victoria adored him. He was the quintessential gentleman.

The Great Exhibition and London's Growth

It was one of Albert's projects that spurred London's remarkable growth. He was fascinated with science and technology and proposed a Great Exhibition "uniting the industry and art of all nations"—in other words, a World's Fair. Held in 1851 in Hyde Park, it was the talk of Europe.

More than 6 million visitors jammed London's streets. The main attraction was the amazing Crystal Palace, an iron-and-glass structure with 300,000 windowpanes, covering 19 square acres—the symbol of the new and glorious Industrial Age. The Exhibition was a smashing success, and many visitors returned to settle down in London.

The Victorian Age was a building time: the Houses of Parliament, the Law Courts on the Strand, railroad stations (to accommodate a revolutionary form of transportation), churches, office buildings, and townhouses went up. Unfortunately, this abundance of building was not accompanied by a similar abundance of good taste. Most were designed in a rather bland neo-Gothic or neoclassical style. The one truly Victorian style was the use of ornamental ironwork, inspired by Joseph Paxton's Crystal Palace. There was wrought iron everywhere; everything had a railing, whether needed or not.

On a typical business day, London traffic moved as fast as the narrow streets would allow. Double-decker buses—horse drawn in those days—were as vital as their big red cousins of today. Efficient, two-wheeled, horse-drawn cabs sped recklessly through the streets. And the bicycle brought new mobility. On the streets— along with bobbies, pickpockets, lamplighters, and rostitutes—were merchants of all kinds, many of whom sang songs to advertise their wares: the quack doctor hawking his Elixir of Life and the popular muffin man, ringing his bell to attract children at tea time.

The British Empire of the 19th century was the biggest, richest, and most powerful in history. Here, **John Bull** *(the British Uncle Sam) is selfishly holding his swollen colonial empire.*

The Rich

On the busy streets, London looked like a real melting pot of humanity, but Victorian society was rigidly hierarchical: rich, middle class, and poor. The rich spent part of their time on their country estates, coming to London only for "the season," an annual period of socializing and parties. The main purpose of these events was to pretend to have fun while arranging marriages for the children. Most marriages were business deals involving large dowries.

Every rich family had servants. The husband and wife each had personal attendants to dress them, advise them, and keep their social calendar. Besides these, there were the cooks and maids. Cleanliness, like godliness, was a priority.

The Middle Class

The middle-class families, while trying to keep up with the wealthy, were strongly influenced by the example of Victoria and Albert. The royal couple was the model of domestic happiness—proper, hardworking, and devoted to their many children. So it was throughout middle-class London. The wife was lord and master of the house; the husband was lord and master of the wife. He came home from work to find his slippers and velvet jacket warming by the fire. After dinner he'd play with the kids, do some reading aloud, listen to his wife play the piano, and go to bed early.

One of the characteristics of the Victorian Age was the advance of the middle class. They lived in nice homes equipped with that newfangled invention, the toilet. They were well educated and infected with Albert's interest in science and the arts. The popularity of Dickens' works attests to this; his novels were serialized in pulp magazines that reached literally millions of people.

The Poor

Progress did not trickle down to London's wretched lower classes, however. The upper classes were oblivious to the lifestyle of the urban poor. The lower class lived in a different world, one that the upper class didn't care to know about. In the East End, people lived in decaying, crowded buildings crawling with rats. While a middle-class family of 10 (most Victorians had large families) lived in a spacious, 10-room house, the poorest lived 10 to a single room. Human waste lined the streets.

The gas lighting hardly cut through the dark on foggy nights in narrow alleyways where cutthroats lurked. Brothels, gambling dens, and pubs were these districts' major businesses.

Work was scarce. A man might haul garbage, shovel coal, or make deliveries, but that was about it. Women and children labored in the factories for pennies. For those in debt, there was the workhouse, which was much like a prison work camp. For some, the alternatives were drunkenness or the Queen's Army. Recruiting sergeants stood outside the pubs with shillings in their hands as bait for the down-and-out.

Private charities did little good. It wasn't until major government reforms at the end of the century that the slums got some relief. The reforming spirit got a boost from the writings of Dickens, a poor boy who made good but never forgot his roots.

But all the classes in Victorian London had one thing in common—a spirit of optimism. There was a vitality to the city that even the poor felt. There was a sense that technology could bring about a better life for all, that hard work and right living would be rewarded just as surely as laziness and vice would be punished. London was a busy, hard driving, shrewd city that maintained an outer face of gentility, grace, and good cheer.

Architecture in Britain

From Stonehenge to Big Ben, travelers are storming castle walls, climbing spiral staircases, and snapping the pictures of 5,000 years of architecture. Let's sort it out.

The oldest ruins—mysterious and prehistoric—date from before Roman times back to 3000 B.C. The earliest sites, such as Stonehenge and Avebury, were built during the Stone and Bronze Ages.

Iron Age people (600 B.C. to A.D. 50) left desolate stone forts. The Romans thrived in Britain from A.D. 50 to 400, building cities, walls, and roads. Evidence of Roman greatness can be seen in lavish villas with ornate mosaic floors, temples uncovered beneath great English churches, and Roman stones in medieval city walls. Roman roads sliced across the island in straight lines. Today, unusually straight rural roads are very likely laid directly on ancient Roman roads.

As Rome crumbled in the fifth century, so did Roman Britain. Little architecture survives from Dark Ages England, the Saxon period from 500 to 1000. Architecturally, the light was switched on with the Norman Conquest in 1066. As William earned his title "the Conqueror," his French architects built churches and castles in the European Romanesque style.

English Romanesque is called "Norman" (1066–1200). Norman

Late Gothic fan vaulting mixes structural support with decoration.

churches had round arches, thick walls, and small windows; Durham Cathedral and the Chapel of St. John in the Tower of London are typical examples. The Tower of London, with its square keep, small windows, and spiral stone stairways, is a typical Norman castle. You'll see plenty of Norman castles—all built to secure the conquest of these invaders from Normandy.

Gothic architecture (1200–1600) replaced the heavy Norman style with light, vertical buildings, pointed arches, soaring spires, and bigger windows. English Gothic is divided into three stages. Early English (1200–1300) features tall, simple spires, beautifully carved capitals, and elaborate chapter houses (such as the Wells Cathedral). Decorated Gothic (1300–1400) gets fancier, with more elaborate tracery, bigger windows, and ornately carved pinnacles, as you'll see at Westminster Abbey. Finally, the Perpendicular style (1400–1600, also called "rectilinear") goes back to square towers and emphasizes straight, uninterrupted vertical lines from ceiling to floor with vast windows and exuberant decoration, including fan-vaulted ceilings (King's College Chapel at Cambridge).

Through this evolution, the structural ribs (arches meeting at the top of the ceilings) became more and more decorative and fanciful (the most fancy being the star vaulting and fan vaulting of the Perpendicular style).

As you tour the great medieval churches of England, remember that nearly everything is symbolic. For instance, on the tombs, if the figure has crossed legs, he was a Crusader. If his feet rest on a dog, he died at home; but if the legs rest on a lion, he died in battle. Local guides and books help us modern pilgrims understand at least a little of what we see.

Wales is particularly rich in English castles, which were needed to subdue the stubborn Welsh. Edward I built a ring of powerful castles in Wales, including Caernarfon and Conwy.

Gothic houses were a simple mix of woven strips of thin wood, rubble, and plaster called wattle and daub. The famous black-and-white Tudor, or half-timbered, look came simply from filling in heavy oak frames with wattle and daub.

The Tudor period (1485–1560) was a time of relative peace (the War of the Roses was finally over), prosperity, and renaissance. Henry VIII broke with the Catholic church and "dissolved" (destroyed) the monasteries, leaving scores of England's greatest churches gutted shells. These hauntingly beautiful abbey ruins surrounded by lush lawns (Glastonbury, Tintern, York) are now pleasant city parks.

Although few churches were built during the Tudor period, this was a time of house and mansion construction. Warmth was becoming popular and affordable, and Tudor buildings featured small square windows and many chimneys. In towns where land was scarce, many Tudor houses grew up and out, getting wider with each overhanging floor.

The Elizabethan and Jacobean periods (1560–1620) were followed

Tintern Abbey—*destroyed by Henry VIII in 1536—sits peacefully today in South Wales.*

by the English Renaissance style (1620–1720). English architects mixed Gothic and classical styles, then Baroque and classical styles. Although the ornate Baroque never really grabbed England, the classical style of the Italian architect Palladio did. Inigo Jones (1573–1652), Christopher Wren (1632–1723), and those they inspired plastered England with enough columns, domes, and symmetry to please a Caesar. The Great Fire of London (1666) cleared the way for an ambitious young Wren to put his mark on London forever with a grand rebuilding scheme, including the great St. Paul's and more than 50 other churches.

The celebrants of the Boston Tea Party remember England's Georgian period (1720–1840) for its lousy German kings. Georgian (English for neoclassical) architecture was rich and showed off by being very classical. Grand ornamental doorways, fine cast ironwork on balconies and railings, Chippendale furniture, and white-on-blue Wedgewood ceramics graced rich homes everywhere. John Wood Jr. and Sr. led the way, giving the trend-setting city of Bath its crescents and circles of aristocratic Georgian row houses.

The Industrial Revolution shaped the Victorian period (1840–1890) with glass, steel, and iron. England had a huge new erector set (so did France's Mr. Eiffel). This was also a Romantic period, reviving the "more Christian" Gothic style. London's Houses of Parliament are neo-Gothic—just 150 years old but looking 700, except for the telltale modern precision and craftsmanship. Whereas Gothic was stone or concrete, neo-Gothic was often red brick. These were England's glory days, and there was more building in this period than in all previous ages combined.

The architecture of our century obeys the formula "form follows function"—it worries more about your needs than your eyes. England treasures its heritage and takes great pains to build tastefully in historic districts and to preserve its many "listed" buildings. With a booming tourist trade, these quaint reminders of its—and our—past are becoming a valuable part of the British economy.

Ireland

Irish History

One surprising aspect of Ireland is the richness of its history. While the island is not particularly well endowed with historic monuments, it is soaked in history. Here's a thumbnail overview.

The story of Ireland can be broken into four sections:

500 B.C.–A.D. 500	Iron Age
500–900	"Age of Saints and Scholars"
900–1900	Age of invasions and colonization
20th century–present	Independence and the question of a united Ireland

The Celtic people left the countryside peppered with thousands of ancient sights from the Iron Age. While most of what you'll see are little more than rock piles and take a vigorous imagination to reconstruct (ring forts, wedge tombs, monumental stones, and so on), it's evocative simply standing next to a megalith that predates the pharaohs while surrounded by lush Ireland. A rich bounty of the finest gold, bronze, and iron work of this period is in the National Museum in Dublin.

The Romans called Ireland Hibernia, or "Land of Winter"; it was apparently too cold and bleak to merit an attempt to take over and colonize. The biggest nonevent in Irish history is that the Romans never invaded. While the mix of Celtic and Roman contributes to what makes the French French and the English English, the Irish are purely Celtic. Latinized France and England have boules and cricket. Untamed Ireland has hurling. This wild Irish national pastime (like airborne hockey with no injury timeouts) goes back to Celtic days, 2,000 years ago.

Celts worshiped the sun. Perhaps St. Patrick had an easy time

Throughout the Middle Ages, Ireland was a society based on monastic communities such as this settlement of **St. Kevin's at Glendalough.** *When barbarians threatened, the monks scampered up their round tower (left of steeple) and pulled up the ladder.*

converting the locals because they had so little sun to worship. Whatever the case, a former Roman slave boy, Patrick, helped Christianize Ireland in the fifth century. From this period on, monks established monastic centers of learning that produced great Christian teachers and community builders. They traveled, establishing monastic communities all over Ireland, Britain, and Europe. One of the monks, St. Brandon, may have even sailed to America.

While the collapse of Rome left Europe a mess, it meant nothing to Ireland. Ireland was and remained a relatively cohesive society based on monastic settlements rather than cities. While Europe was rutting in the Dark Age mud, the light of civilization shone brightly in Ireland through a Golden Age lasting from the fifth through the ninth centuries. Irish monks—such as those imported by Charlemagne to help run his Frankish kingdom in A.D. 800—actually carried the torch of civilization back to Europe. The greatest art of Dark Age Europe is the manuscripts (such as the ninth-century *Book of Kells,* which you'll see in Dublin) "illuminated," or richly illustrated, by Irish monks.

Viking invasions of the ninth century wreaked repeated havoc on the monasteries and shook Irish civilization. Vikings established trading towns (such as Dublin) where before there were only Celtic settlements and monasteries.

The Normans, who invaded and conquered England after the Battle of Hastings (1066), were Ireland's next uninvited guests. In 1169, the Anglo-Normans invaded Ireland. These invaders, big-time organizers, ushered in a new age in which society (government, cities, and religious organizations) was organized on a grander scale. Individual monastic settlements (the basis of Irish society in the Age of Saints and Scholars) were eclipsed by monastic orders just in from the Continent, such as the Franciscans, Augustinians, and Cistercians.

The English made a concentrated effort to colonize Ireland in the 17th century. Settlers were "planted," and Irish society was split between an English-speaking landed gentry and the local Irish-speaking landless or nearly landless peasantry.

During the 18th century, Ireland thrived under the English. Dublin was Britain's second city. Over time, greed on the top and dissent on the bottom required more repressive colonial policies. The Enlightenment provided ideas of freedom, and the Revolutionary Age emboldened the Irish masses. (Even the non-Catholic Dubliner, Jonathan Swift—dean of St. Patrick's cathedral in the early 18th century—declared "Burn all that's British, except its coal.")

To counter this Irish feistiness, English legislation became an out-and-out attack on the indigenous Gaelic culture. The harp, symbol of Irish culture, was outlawed. Written and unwritten laws made life for Catholics and Irish-speakers very difficult.

The potato famine of 1845–1849 was a pivotal event in Irish history. The stature of Ireland and its language never recovered. In a few years, Ireland's population dropped from 8 million to 5 million (3 million either starved or emigrated). Ireland's population has not grown since. Britain's population, on the other hand, has grown from 12 million in 1845 to around 60 million today. (During this period, Ireland's population, as a percent of England's, has dropped from 65 percent to 8 percent.)

While the English are likely to blame the famine on overpopulation (Ireland's population doubled in the 40 years leading up to the famine), many Irish say there actually was no famine—just a calculated attempt by a threatened England to starve down the local population. In fact, there was plenty of food grown on the island for export. It was only the potato crop that failed . . . and that happened to be what the Irish subsisted on.

The average farmer grew fancier export products for his landlord and was paid in potatoes which, in good years, he grew on the side. (If this makes you mad at the English landlords, consider American ownership of land in Central America where the landlord takes things one step further by not growing the local staple at all. He devotes all the land to more profitable cash crops for export and leaves the landless farmer no alternative but to buy his food—imported from the United States—at plantation wages, in the landlord's grocery store.)

The famine was a turning point in Irish history. Before the famine, land was subdivided—all the boys got a piece of the family estate (which grew smaller and smaller with each generation until there wasn't enough land to feed a family). After the famine, the oldest son got the estate and the younger siblings, with no way to stay in Ireland, emigrated to Britain, Australia, Canada, and the United States. Today there are 40 million Irish-Americans.

After the famine, Irish became the language of the peasant. English was for the upwardly mobile. Because of the huge immigration to the United States, Ireland began to face west, and American influence increased. (As negotiations between Northern Ireland and the Irish Republic continue today, American involvement in the talks is welcomed and considered essential by nearly all parties.)

The tragedy of the famine inflamed the nationalist movement. Uprising after uprising made it clear that Ireland was ready to close this thousand-year chapter of invasions and colonialism. Finally, in 1919, Ireland declared its independence. While the northern six counties (the only ones without a Catholic majority) voted to stay with Britain, the independent Republic of Ireland was born.

Northern Ireland

Northern Ireland consists of the six counties (with a Protestant majority) that opted for British rule.

In the Republic of Ireland, with 94 percent Catholic and only 6 percent Protestant, there is no question who is dominant. But in Northern Ireland, the Catholic minority is a sizable 35 percent that demands attention. In the past, discrimination was considered necessary to maintain the Protestant status quo in the North and that led to "The Troubles" that have filled headlines since the late 1960s.

It is not a fight over Catholic and Protestant religious differences. It's whether Ireland will be free or part of Britain. The indigenous Irish, who generally want a free, united, and independent Ireland, happen to be Catholic. The British Protestants "planted" so long ago have developed their own powerful attachment to that green and soggy land . . . as well as an allegiance to Britain.

When Ireland won its independence (a 1921 treaty gave it dominion status within the British Commonwealth—like Canada), the issue of unity with the North had to be dealt with. It was uncertain what the final arrangement would be. In the North the long-established Orange Order and the newly mobilized Ulster Volunteer Force (UVF) worked to defend the union with Britain. The UVF became the military muscle of the "Unionists." This would be countered on the Catholic side by the Irish Republican Army (IRA). With the Republic's neutrality and the North's enthusiastic support of the Allied cause

Political wall murals are the art which decorates sectarian neighborhoods in Belfast. Here, in a Protestant district, the Union Jack comes with a stubborn bulldog. The message: Northern Ireland will stick with Britain.

in WWII, Ulster won a spot close to London's heart. After WWII the split seemed permanent, and Britain invested heavily in Northern Ireland to bring it solidly into the United Kingdom fold. (While Euro-aid to the Republic has softened the contrast, travelers today notice that the North has better roads and feels like part of a wealthier country.)

With the Civil Rights movement of the 1960s, Irish rights needed to be addressed. Extremists polarized issues, and demonstrations became violent. As Protestants and Catholics clashed in 1969, the British Army entered the fray. They've been there ever since. In 1972, a watershed year, combatants moved from petrol bombs to guns. A new, more violent IRA emerged. In the most recent 25-year chapter

Terminology

Ulster consists of nine counties in the north part of the island of Ireland. Six of those make up Northern Ireland (three counties remain part of the Republic). Unionists want the North to remain with Britain. Republicans want a united and independent Ireland ruled by Dublin. The political wing of the Irish Republican Army (IRA) is Sinn Fein, led by Gerry Adams. Orange, and the red, white, and blue of the Union Jack, are the favored colors of the Unionists. Green is the color of the Republicans. Everyone drinks Guinness.

When a Rick Steves' tour visited Derry (a.k.a. Londonderry), the mayor welcomed the group with a private tour of city hall and more than a wee dram of Irish whiskey in his office.

in the struggle for an independent and united Ireland, more than 3,000 people have been killed.

A 1985 agreement granted Dublin a consulting role in the Northern Ireland government. Unionists bucked this and violence escalated. In that same year, the Belfast City Hall draped a huge and defiant banner under its dome proclaiming "Belfast Says No."

In 1994 the banner came down. With Ireland's recent membership in the European Union, the fastest growing economy in Europe, and the weakening of the Catholic church's influence, the consequences of a united Ireland are less threatening to the people of the north. There is a strong movement toward peace.

In 1994 the IRA declared a cease-fire. The Protestants followed suit and talks are still underway. The Republicans want British troops out of Ireland and political prisoners released. The Unionists want the IRA to turn in its arms and figure their prisoners are terrorists and jail is where they belong. Optimists hail the signing of the Good Friday Accord in 1998.

Major hurdles to a solid peace persist (such as the IRA's latest refusal to disarm). But the downtown checkpoints are history, "bomb damage clearance sales" are over, and summer camps are teaching Catholic and Protestant children to shed their clan baggage and live happily together.

From a traveler's point of view, no trip to Ireland can be called complete without a look at both the Republic and the North.

Ireland's best sight: its people.

Iberia

The cultural landscape of modern Spain and Portugal was shaped by the various civilizations that settled on the peninsula. Iberia's sunny weather and fertile soil made it a popular place to call home.

The Greeks came to Cadiz around 1100 B.C., followed by the Romans, who occupied the country for almost 1,000 years, until A.D. 400. Long after the empire crumbled, the Roman influence remained, including cultural values, materials, building techniques, even Roman-style farming equipment, which was used well into the 19th century. And, of course, wine.

Moors (711–1492)

The Moors—North Africans of the Moslem faith who occupied Spain—had a huge cultural influence on Spanish and Portuguese history. They arrived on the Rock of Gibraltar in A.D. 711 and moved north. In just seven years, the Moors completely conquered the peninsula.

Compared to Dark Age Europe, Iberia under Islamic control was an intellectual center. Islam was more tolerant than medieval Christianity of other religions. In Spain, both Christians and Jews were allowed freedom, relative equality (for a fee), and the opportunity to rise to positions of wealth and power. The interaction among the three cultures sparked inquiry and debate, producing some of the Middle Ages' finest scholars. In 950, the library at Cordoba in Spain held some 600,000

Court of the Lions, Alhambra, Granada, Spain

*Capping a hilltop, the **Alhambra**—the last Moorish stronghold in Spain—
reminds visitors of Granada's Moslem glory days.*

manuscripts. In the same year, there were only 5,000 manuscripts in
all of France.

Islamic countries, like the Byzantine Empire, helped keep Greco-
Roman learning alive. From the Middle East to North Africa to Spain,
Islam fostered science and literature while Europe was still groping
for the light switch.

Rather than brutal subjugation, the Moorish style of conquest was
to employ their sophisticated culture to develop whatever they found.
For example, they encouraged wine making, although for religious
reasons they themselves weren't allowed to drink alcohol.

Throughout the seven-century reign of the Moors, feisty enclaves
of Christianity remained. Local Christian kings fought against the
Moors whenever they could, whittling away at the Moslem empire,
gaining more and more land. After a sustained push, the last Moorish
stronghold, Granada, fell to the Christians in 1492.

The slow, piecemeal process of the *Reconquista* (Reconquest) split
the peninsula into the independent states of Portugal and Spain. In
1139 Alfonso Henriques conquered the Moors near present-day Beja
in southern Portugal and proclaimed himself king of the area. By
1200, the Christian state of Portugal had the borders it does today,
making it the oldest unchanged state in Europe. The rest of the peninsula was a loosely knit collection of smaller kingdoms. Spain's major
step toward unity was in 1469, when Ferdinand II of Aragon married

Monument to the Discoverers, _1960, Belém, near Lisbon. With Henry the Navigator at the lead, these explorers expanded Europe's horizons and made Portugal a superpower 500 years ago._

Isabella of Castille. Known as the "Catholic Monarchs," they united the other kingdoms under their rule.

The Golden Age (1500–1650)

The expulsion of the Moors set the stage for the rise of Portugal and Spain as naval powers and colonial superpowers. During this Golden Age, Spain and Portugal dominated the economy of Europe. Through exploration (and exploitation), tremendous quantities of gold poured in from their colonies in the New World, Asia, and Africa, making the Iberian Peninsula the most powerful corner of Europe. The aristocracy and the clergy swam in money. Art and courtly life flourished.

It was Ferdinand and Isabella who financed Columbus' expedition to seek a new western trade route to Asia. The Spaniards, fueled by the religious fervor of the _Reconquista_, were also interested in spreading Christianity to the newly discovered New World. Wherever they landed, they tried to Christianize the natives—with the sword, if necessary.

The Portuguese expansion was motivated more by economic concerns. Their excursions overseas were planned, cool, and rational. They colonized the nearby coasts of Africa first, progressing slowly around Africa to Asia and South America.

When Vasco da Gama sailed around the southern tip of Africa to

India in 1498, he opened a profitable new trade route with the East, breaking Italy's monopoly on trade with the Orient. The states on the Atlantic seaboard—Portugal, Spain, Holland, and England—emerged as the superpowers of trade.

From that point on, Italy stagnated, becoming an economic backwater and a political pawn of the stronger nations that took the lead economically as well as culturally. The Prado collection, chock-full of Italian masterpieces bought with New World gold, testifies to Spain's wealth. The focus of European civilization shifted farther west.

Slow Decline

The dazzling, fast money from the colonies blinded Spain and Portugal to the dangers at home. Great Britain and the Netherlands, which had become strong naval powers, defeated the Spanish armada in 1588.

During the centuries when science and technology in other European countries developed as never before, Spain and Portugal were occupied with their failed colonial politics. The Portuguese imported everything, stopped growing their own wheat, and neglected their fields.

In the 18th century, Spain was ruled by the French Bourbon family. Major sights of the era, such as Madrid's Royal Palace and the nearby La Granja Palace, are French in style.

Endless battles, wars of succession, revolutions, and counterrevolutions weakened the countries. In this chaos there was no chance to develop democratic forms of government. Dictators in both countries made the rich richer and stifled the underprivileged masses.

Art

The "Big Three" in Spanish painting are El Greco, Velázquez, and Goya.

El Greco (1541–1614) exemplifies the spiritual fervor of much Spanish art. The drama, the surreal colors, and the intentionally unnatural distortion have the intensity of a religious vision. For more on El Greco, see pages 303–4.

Diego Velázquez (1599–1660) went to the opposite extreme. His masterful court portraits are studies in realism and cool detachment from his subjects. See also pages 182-3.

Goya (1746–1828) matched Velázquez's technique but not his detachment. He let his liberal tendencies shine through in unflattering portraits of royalty and in emotional scenes of abuse of power. He unleashed his inner passions in the eerie, nightmarish canvases of his last, "dark" stage. For more information, see pages 218-9.

Not quite in the league of the Big Three, Murillo (1618–1682) painted a dreamy world of religious visions. His pastel, soft-focus works of cute baby Jesuses and radiant Virgin Marys helped make Catholic doctrine palatable to the common folk at a time when many were defecting to Protestantism.

You'll also find plenty of foreign art in Spain's museums. In painting during the Golden Age, Italian Renaissance style was the rage—the Prado's vast collection makes it clear. Spanish painters, caught in the grip of the medieval Inquisition and the holy war against the Moors, concentrated on religious scenes. Secular art had to be imported. During its Golden Age, Spain's wealthy aristocrats bought wagon loads of the most popular art of the time—Italian Renaissance and Baroque works by Titian, Tintoretto, and others. They also loaded up on paintings by Rubens, Bosch, and Brueghel from the Low Countries, which were under Spanish rule.

In modern times, Pablo Picasso (don't miss his _Guernica_ mural in Madrid), Joan Miró, and surrealist Salvador Dalí have made their marks. Great museums featuring all three artists are in or near Barcelona.

El Greco

El Greco's (1541–1614) painting fused Italian Renaissance technique with the Spanish religious passion. Born in Greece (his nickname means "The Greek"), trained in Venice, and caught up in the devout fervor of Spanish mysticism, El Greco combined Greek iconography, Venetian color, and Spanish Catholicism to create an individual style.

El Greco's people have unnaturally elongated, slightly curved bodies, like flickering flames. The serene faces look like those of saints on a Byzantine icon. Yet it is obvious from the natural, personal details of his portraits that El Greco learned Renaissance realism.

El Greco is often called the first "modern" painter because he deliberately chose to tamper with realism to emotionalize a painting. By now, nature and realism had been mastered. Artists set about busily exploring new realms.

If you fall in love with El Greco at Madrid's Prado, then you must visit his hometown, Toledo, which is dotted with his works. Toledo, the historical and cultural capital of Spain, is a great place to gain an appreciation of the Spanish Renaissance. A tour of Toledo's cathedral, with masterpieces from the greatest Spanish artists of each era from Gothic to

El Greco, **Pentecost** *(detail), 1604 (Prado, Madrid). The faces flicker like flames. From El Greco's time on, artists were free to go beyond naturalism.*

Baroque, will prove Italy didn't have a monopoly on artistic genius. Local pride shines through as your guide shows you what was going on in Spain while Michelangelo was busy painting the Sistine Chapel.

Architecture

The two most fertile periods of architectural innovation in Spain and Portugal were during the Moorish occupation and in the Golden Age.

The Moors brought Middle-Eastern styles with them, such as the horseshoe arch, minarets, and floor plans designed for mosques. Islam forbids the sculpting or painting of human or animal figures ("graven images"), so artists expressed their creativity with elaborate geometric patterns. All over Spain and Portugal, but especially in Cordoba and Granada, you'll see impressive Moorish buildings. The ornate stucco of Granada's Alhambra, the elaborate arches of Sevilla's Alcázar, and decorative colored tiles are evidence of the Moorish sense of beauty. Mozarabic art (by Christians under Moorish rule) and Mudejar art (by Moors after the Christian reconquest) blended the styles of East and West.

As the Christians slowly reconquered the country, they turned their fervor into stone, building churches both in the heavy, fortress-of-God

Churches built during Spain's Golden Age were decorated in the "Plateresque" style—like intricate silver filigree.

Romanesque style (Lisbon's cathedral and Santiago de Compostela) and in the lighter, heaven-reaching, stained-glass Gothic style (Barcelona, Toledo, Sevilla). Gothic was an import from France, trickling into conservative Spain long after it swept through Europe.

The money reaped and raped from Spain's colonies in the Golden Age (1500–1650) spurred new construction. Churches and palaces were built using the solid, geometric style of the Italian Renaissance (El Escorial) and the more ornamented Baroque. Ornamentation reached unprecedented heights in Spain, culminating in the Plateresque style of stonework, so called because it resembles intricate silver filigree work.

Portugal's economic boom also triggered a cultural boom. Portugal's highly ornamented answer to Spain's Plateresque is called Manueline, named after a king from that period. The Manueline style in both art and architecture is an exuberant combination of Gothic and Renaissance forms decorated with shells, anchors, and ropes. These nautical motifs are a tribute to the source of the money that made this art possible: the lucrative sea trade. You can see fine examples of this Portuguese Renaissance style in the Lisbon suburb of

The cloisters of the **Jeronimos Monastery** in Belém near Lisbon are a textbook example of Manueline architecture. Vasco da Gama and company prayed here before sailing away to make history.

*Lisbon's **Belém Tower** was the last sight Portuguese explorers saw when setting sail, and the first they saw upon returning home.*

Belém, particularly the Belém Tower and the cloisters of the Jeronimos Monastery, the most impressive in Iberia.

After the Golden Age, innovation in Spain and Portugal died out, and most buildings from the 18th and 19th centuries follow predictable European trends. Spain's major contribution to modern architecture is the Art Nouveau work of Antonio Gaudí (1852–1926).

Antonio Gaudí and Modernista

The *Renaixenca* (Catalan cultural revival) gave birth to *Modernista* (Catalan Art Nouveau) at the end of the 19th century. Barcelona is the capital of *Modernista*—meaning "a taste for what is modern." This free-flowing organic style broke with tradition and experimented with glass, tile, iron, and brick. Decoration became structural.

Antonio Gaudí is the most famous *Moderniste* artist. From four generations of metalworkers, a lineage of which he was quite proud, he incorporated his ironwork into his architecture and came up with novel approaches to architectural structure and space. Most of his "cake-left-out-in-the-rain" buildings, with asymmetrical designs and sinuous lines, can be found in Barcelona (see page 227).

The 20th Century and Beyond

During World War I, Portugal fought on the Allied side and Spain stayed neutral. In World War II both countries were neutral, uninterested in foreign policy as long as there was quiet in their own states.

From 1936 to 1939, Spain suffered a bloody and bitter civil war between Fascist and democratic forces, won by the Fascist dictator Francisco Franco. During the war, the Nationalists (Franco's fascist Falange party) were supported by Hitler and Mussolini abroad and the army, police, and civil guard at home. The (Spanish) Republicans were

Picasso, **Guernica** *(detail), Reina Sofia Mueum, Madrid.* Guernica *was inspired by the Nazi devastation of that town in 1937.*

befriended by idealists, writers, workers' groups, intellectuals, socialists, and the like. Russia supported them until Stalin got fed up with their ideological independence. Volunteers from many countries formed the International Brigades about which Ernest Hemingway wrote.

This was the first modern war. Hitler enjoyed trying out World War II–style bombing. Guernica, the town flattened by Fascist bombs, was immortalized by Picasso's famous painting (which was moved into Spain only after Franco's death). The war was brutal, with brothers killing brothers, entire villages being slaughtered, and half a million dead.

It's a wonder that the ragtag Republicans held out against Franco and his well-disciplined and well-stocked Nationalists for three years. Franco's 1939 victory was followed by more bloody reprisals. Franco ruled Spain until his death in 1975.

The many victims of Spain's civil war are commemorated by the Valley of the Fallen outside Madrid. A 450-foot-tall concrete cross marks the giant mausoleum carved into a hillside outside Madrid. Dug mostly by Republican prisoners, the mausoleum displays Franco's tomb as its centerpiece.

Franco was succeeded by King Juan Carlos, who opened Spain up to the democracy it enjoys today.

Democracy in Spain and Portugal is still young. After an unbloody revolution, Portugal held democratic elections in 1975. After 41 years of dictatorship, Spain finally had elections in 1977.

Today, moderate Socialists are in power in both countries, trying (with moderate success) to fight the problems of unemployment and foreign debts. Portugal, which as recently as a few years ago felt poor and left behind, is enjoying a boom time fueled by Euro-aid. Spain, a latecomer to the European Union, is also booming. Since the events of 1992 (the World's Fair, Olympic Games, and 500th anniversary of Columbus' "discovery" of America), *Viva España* is sung *con gusto*.

Turkey

Anatolian History for Beginners

Anatolia is the timeless term for the geographical baklava known today as Turkey. In Turkish, "Anatolia" means "land of mothers." This fertile land has nourished civilizations for thousands of years. The oldest city in the world—dating from 7500 B.C.—is thought to be Çatalhoyuk, near modern-day Konya.

Hittites in Anatolia, 2000–1180 B.C.

Anatolia, which quietly coasted through the Neolithic and Bronze Age, was easily conquered in 2000 B.C. by the Hittites, an Indo-European people. The Hittites introduced writing to Anatolia, and their records indicate an advanced legal system. By uniting all of Anatolia, the Hittites created a superpower that rivaled (and invaded) Egypt. In 1180 B.C., just when they reached their peak, they abruptly—and mysteriously—fell.

This Turkish history in a pistachio shell was written by Turkish tour guide Mehlika Seval.

After the Hittites, 1180–334 B.C.

Anatolian unity passed with the Hittites, and the land was filled with small, unrelated, and relatively unimportant groups.

The Lycians lived in city-states fringed along Anatolia's southern coast. The Phrygians (frij-ee-ans) settled in the middle of Anatolia. Their King Midas was endowed with the touch of gold (in legend only). The Phrygians were known for their bravery, artistic talents, and intricately designed tombs. The Lydians, known for their creativity, invented numerous musical instruments such as the lyre and harp. More significantly, they invented coinage. During this period, Greek city-states such as Symrna (Izmir) hugged Anatolia's western coast— an area the Greeks called Iona. These cities existed as separate entities, united only by their Greek culture.

Then, in around 600 B.C., the Persians swept in from the east. Cyrus the Great conquered all of Anatolia and solidified a 300-year reign of Persian rule.

Hellenistic and Roman Anatolia, 334 B.C.–A.D. 300

Alexander the Great, a Macedonian, conquered Greece politically in the late fourth century B.C. This ended the Golden Age of Greece under Athenian rule. But Alexander, who had great respect for the Greek culture, proceeded to build an empire that was basically Greek in culture. This was the Hellenistic period. Alexander beat back Persia and conquered Anatolia in 334 B.C. As a result, Greek "Hellenistic" culture dominated Anatolia. Trade and prosperity increased, and new cities sprang up throughout the region.

After Alexander's death in 323 B.C., his generals fought over an empire that stretched from Italy to India. Anatolia got chopped up, and the biggest chunk was called Pergamon. The Pergamon kings struck up an alliance with Rome, and in 133 B.C., the last Pergamon ruler bequeathed his kingdom to Rome. Eventually Rome took over most of Anatolia, and over the next 300 years, Rome's "Province of Asia" prospered.

Between A.D. 47 and 57, the apostle Paul made three missionary journeys to Anatolia. Several books of the New Testament are letters he wrote to struggling Christian congregations at Ephesus (Ephesians), Colossea (Colossians), and Galatia (Galatians). Christianity was an upstart new religion, and Paul's work helped strengthen its hold.

Byzantine Empire, A.D. 300–1453

When Constantine became the Roman emperor, he moved the capital of his kingdom from a declining Rome to a more strategic, powerful posi-

Istanbul's **Hagia Sofia** mosque, built as a church in the 6th century A.D. during the reign of Justinian, was in its day the biggest domed-building in the world.

tion in the east. He chose Byzantium, a city that linked Europe and Asia. In A.D. 330, Constantine declared Byzantium to be the New Rome. With modesty characteristic of an emperor, he renamed it Constantinople.

Thus began the Byzantine Empire—a synthesis of Greek culture, Roman politics, and Christian religion—which would survive for a thousand years. Constantine kicked things off by converting to Christianty. In 380, Theodosius I established Christianity as the state religion. In churches, beautiful Byzantine mosaics glorified Christian themes. (You'll see fine examples in Istanbul's Chora Church.) During the reign of Justinian (527–565), the Byzantine Empire was at its peak, encompassing the Balkans, Italy, Eygpt, and North Africa.

The slow and steady decline of the Byzantines (800–1453) came about partly because of their own political mistakes (such as over-taxation, which strangled the economy) and partly because of another up-start religion.

The Selcuks, 1037–1243

Mohammed heard the voice of God, and the Arab and Turkish worlds listened. In 1037, Selcuk Turks from Central Asia rode a wave of Islam into Baghdad, where they established a Selcuk kingdom among fellow Moslems. After taking over modern-day Iran and Iraq, the Selcuks fought Byzantine forces, winning control of nearly all of Anatolia but leaving Constantinople to the Christians. The Selcuks created a wealth of beautiful architecture, ornate tiles, and poetry.

In the 13th century, the Selcuk's greatest philosopher was born. A religious leader and mystic, Mevlana started an Islamic sect in Konya known for its whirling dervishes. Mevlana's words were simple and profound. He said, "Love lies out of the reach of dogma. In all mosques,

Rather than depicting images of people, places, or things, Islamic art consists mainly of calligraphy—in this instance, an embellished phrase from the Koran.

temples, churches, I find one shrine alone. The lovers of God have no religion but God alone."

Meanwhile, Constantinople limped along as its rulers fought over succession. From 1202 to 1204, during the Fourth Crusade, crude Crusaders sacked the Christian city and carried off its wealth. With friends like these, the Byzantines hardly needed enemies. But look out . . .

Ottoman Empire, 1326–1919

The Mongols trampled through Anatolia in 1243, scattering the Turks and ending the era of Selcuk rule. The Turks formed small principalities, or city-states. Osman was one of the rulers. According to custom, his subjects took his name and called themselves Osmanli. The Europeans mangled the pronunciation of "Osmanli" into "Ottoman." Over the years, Osman's principality grew in size and power, taking over Bursa as its capital. Eventually, the Osmanli gang grew strong enough to challenge Constantinople, the eastern stronghold of Christendom. In 1453, Mehmet II conquered the city and renamed it Istanbul.

In the mid-1500s, the Ottoman Empire reached its peak during the reign of Suleyman the Magnificent. He triggered an explosion of architecture (such as Istanbul's grand Suleymaniye Mosque, known popularly as the Blue Mosque) and expanded his territory as far east as Hungary and as far south as North Africa. Central Europe's primary worry was this powerful Ottoman Empire which "knocked at the door of Vienna."

The titles of Suleyman's successors, men such as Selim the Sot and Ibrahim the Mad, tell a story of decay. The Ottoman Empire died a lingering death over several centuries, forfeiting much of its territory. Rotten from within, stifled by palace intrigues and infighting, the Ottoman Empire became known as "the sick man of Europe."

The eager vultures of Europe (France, Britain, Italy, Greece) could hardly wait for the feast to begin. Anatolia was a strategic east-west trade route between Asia and Europe and a north-south link between the Black Sea and Mediterranean.

In World War I, a clueless Ottoman Empire stumbled by siding with Germany. Even worse, the Turks nearly wiped out the Armenian civilization in a series of brutal campaigns, leaving a black mark on Turkish history. After World War I ended, the victorious Allies drew up a treaty which carved up Turkey among the French, Italians, and Greeks. But it wasn't quite that easy...

Ataturk and the Turkish Republic, 1919 to the present

An astonishing man, Ataturk almost single-handedly created modern-day Turkey. He had risen to prominence in Turkey for his success and bravery at the World War I battle of Gallipoli. After World War I, when the fate of his country was up for grabs, Ataturk quickly asserted control. In 1919, with lightning speed, he gathered an army. Over a three-year period, he chased out French and Italian troops and repelled a Greek invasion.

In 1923, Ataturk established the Turkish republic and set into motion a series of reforms. Rarely in history has anyone exerted such power with such effect in so short a time. In less than 10 years, Ataturk:

- separated religion and state (by removing Islam as the state religion and upholding civil law over Islamic law)
- aligned Turkey with the West rather than the East
- adopted the Christian calendar
- decreed that Turks should have surnames, similar to Western custom
- changed the alphabet from Arabic script to Roman letters
- changed the language spoken in the mosque from Arabic to Turkish
- distanced Turkey from the corrupt Ottoman Empire by abolishing the sultanate and caliphate, and outlawing the fez and veil

- abolished polygamy
- emancipated women (by comparison, Swiss women received the vote in 1971)

Ataturk could not have accomplished all that he did without the support of his people. Still highly revered throughout Turkey, he is the subject of virtually every statue and public portrait. Whether seen as a savior, a revolutionary reformer, or a benevolent dictator, he earned the name his parliament bestowed upon him—Ataturk, which means "Father of the Turks."

Modern Turkey

After Ataturk's death in 1938, Turkey foundered as it searched for a leader and experimented with democracy. Its military has a constitutional obligation to defend the separation of mosque and state. During several times of crisis, the military has taken control of the country, each time returning control to the people.

Turkey's neighbors include Iran, Iraq, Syria, Georgia, Azerbaijan, Armenia, Bulgaria, and its traditional adversary, Greece. Surrounded by potential powder kegs, Turkey strives for neutrality in politics and moderation in religion.

The major problems facing Turkey today are its weak economy (troubled by inflation and devastating earthquakes), a Kurdish minority in the southeast clamoring for autonomy, and a constant Moslem fundamentalist threat to the constitutionally ordained separation of mosque and state.

Part III
Art Specifics

Art Appreciation

"Only through art can we get outside ourselves and know another's view of the universe."

—Marcel Proust

To Know Art Is to Love Him

Getting to know art is like getting to know another person. First impressions mean a lot, but true understanding takes time. And you're more likely to become friends if you have an open mind.

In art, as with people, "Don't criticize what you can't understand." Learn about it first. Then you can really run it into the ground.

Most works of art show two things: the physical subject and the mood or message the artist is conveying. Artists can change or distort reality (the actual subject matter) to enhance the mood. When we

know why reality is distorted, we can see the world through the artist's perspective.

Knowing a little something about artists' lives makes their art more interesting and sometimes easier to understand. Find out where the artist was and what the inspiration was for a certain painting. A simple painting of crows in a wheat field takes on new meaning when you know that, shortly after painting it, van Gogh shot himself.

Techniques

Artists know what catches your eye. They use this knowledge to punch the right emotional buttons to get their message across. (Modern advertisers have made a science of this.) Here are some of the techniques used to attract your attention and produce an emotional response.

Composition

Composition, the layout of the main figures, is the skeleton of the work. Imagine a painter planning out a scene on grid-lined graph paper, calculating how big the main characters will be and where to place them. Let's say the artist decides to arrange the figures into a geometrical pattern, say a pyramid like this:

It doesn't look like much in rough form, but flesh out this skeleton composition with neat lines and real-life colors and you have Raphael's *La Belle Jardinière*. The geometrical composition is what makes the picture so harmonious and pleasing to the eye.

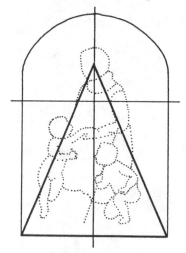

Raphael's **La Belle Jardinière**

Look at the skeleton pattern. Notice how much forethought went into the composition, how orderly and pleasing the shapes are. Imagine the rough shapes colored in. It would look something like modern art, no? Abstract art uses the same rules of composition, line, and color, but doesn't portray real-life subjects.

Line

The eye will naturally follow the curve of a line until it's broken by a line running in another direction. The artist uses this eye movement to create movement and rhythm in the scene which, in turn, creates a mood of tension or rest in the viewer. At their own pace, trained artists guide you from one figure to the next.

In the Isenheim altarpiece, Grünewald directs all the motion toward Christ's face. From John's pointing finger, your eye travels to the face, up Christ's arm to the crossbar, out to the end, down to the grieving figures at the left, down their slanted bodies to the kneeling Mary, and up her arm, pointing again to Christ's head. Grünewald moves our attention full circle, always returning to the central figure of Jesus, where the lines intersect.

 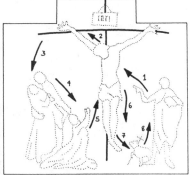

Grünewald's **Isenheim Altarpiece**

Perspective

Lines are governed by the laws of perspective—the science of painting three-dimensional objects on a two-dimensional surface. When you draw receding lines to turn a square into a 3-D box, you've followed the laws of perspective. If the lines of the box were continued, they'd eventually converge on the horizon at what is called the "vanishing point."

Da Vinci's **Last Supper**

Using perspective and the vanishing point, an artist can place the viewer of a painting right in the middle of the action. Think of the picture frame as a window through which you are viewing the painted scene. Where are you in relation to the main figures? The artist lets you know, subconsciously, with the vanishing point.

The vanishing point is also the compositional center of the work. In Leonardo's famous *Last Supper,* the lines converge at the center of the canvas, which is the emotional focus: Christ's head. All the linear motion flows to and from this center of calm.

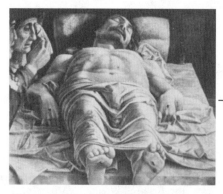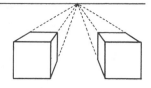

Mantegna, **Dead Christ,** *1466 (Pinacoteca di Brera, Milan). This Renaissance experiment in extreme foreshortening brings the viewer right to the scene of the action. The psychological effect of seeing the body from this intimate viewpoint is exciting.*

Color

Color is the flesh on the compositional skeleton, bringing the figures to life. It too plays a role in bringing order to art. The artist can make the picture peaceful by using harmonious colors or tense by using colors that clash.

Red, yellow, and blue are the primary colors; we get the rest by blending these three. Red is associated with passion, action, intensity, and (as designers of fast-food menus know) hunger. Yellow is warmth, the sun, peace. Blue is melancholy, thoughtful, the sea and sky. Some colors complement each other (red and green), while others contrast (yellow and orange). The various combinations and moods available to the artist are endless.

Some painters make outlines of figures, then fill them in with smooth color (like a coloring book). Giotto demonstrated this technique. Monet, however, used almost no outlines whatsoever. His paintings are more like a mosaic of minute patches of color applied by quick strokes of the brush.

Understanding Is Appreciation

When people, admitting their ignorance of art, say, "But I know what I like," they usually mean, "I like what I know." It's easier to like something that's familiar and understood. Baseball is the most boring game in the world if you don't understand the rules or players. Good wine is best appreciated by people who've made a point of understanding the art of wine making. You can't appreciate the classic lines of a '56 Chevy if you don't know a Volvo from an Edsel. If you like what you know, you can usually increase your liking by simply increasing your knowing.

When you understand an artist's intention and techniques, you can appreciate the work even if you don't like the result. In baseball, you can appreciate a well-turned double play even if you don't like it (it made your team lose). In art, you may not like what was painted—it might be an unusual, startling, or bland scene—but you might appreciate the artist's composition or use of line and color.

Learn as much as you can about art history, artists, styles, theories, and so on, but remember that the best aid to art appreciation is simply an open mind.

Check out an art book with nice color prints from the library. Relax in your favorite chair. Light a fire. Pour a glass of wine or stoke up your pipe. Then, alone or with a friend, leaf slowly through the book.

Art—like the Vigeland statues filling Oslo's Frogner Park—can be playful.

Don't bother much with names, dates, or commentary. Just look for a painting or two you like. Play a game where you pick your favorite from each chapter, and then compare notes with a friend.

Once you find a painting that speaks your name, ask yourself why you like it. Is it the bright colors? The story it tells? The emotional effect on you? Does it make you feel good? Or sad? Or angry? Any reason for liking art is a good one. Just try to recognize what it is. Look for other works by an artist you like. If you like a similar work, maybe that means you like that style. What do the two works have in common?

Assume that the artist put a lot of thought and sweat into the artwork and is happy with the result. Try to understand why.

Museum-going

Europe is a treasure chest of great art. Many of the world's greatest museums will be a part of your trip. Here are a few hints on how to get the most out of these museums.

Pre-trip studying makes the art more fun. It's a waste to visit Rome or Greece or Egypt with no background in the art of those civilizations. I remember touring the National Museum of Archaeology in Athens as an obligation and being quite bored. I was convinced that those who looked as if they were enjoying it were actually just faking it. Two years later, after taking a class in ancient art history, that same museum was a fascinating trip into the world of Pericles and Socrates, all because of some background knowledge.

A common misconception is that great museums have only great art. A museum such as Paris' Louvre is so big (the building was, at one time, the largest in Europe), you can't possibly cover everything properly in one visit, so don't try. Be selective. Use a guide, audioguide, or guidebook to take you through the best two hours of viewing in a museum. Brief guide pamphlets recommending a basic visit are available in most of Europe's museums. With this selective strategy, you'll appreciate the highlights while you are fresh. For me, museum-going is the hardest work I do in Europe, and I'm good for two, maybe three hours. Assuming that's your limit too, we've written *Mona Winks* (John Muir Publications, 1998), a collection of two-hour self-guided tours through Europe's 20 greatest museums.

Mona Winks: Self-Guided Tours of Europe's Top Museums. *By Rick Steves and Gene Openshaw.*

If you are especially interested in one piece of art, spend a half-hour studying it and listening to each passing tour guide tell his or her story about *David* or *Mona Lisa* or whatever. The guides do their own research and each one comes up with different information to share. There's really nothing wrong with this sort of tour freeloading. Just

Throughout Europe, technology is making museum-going more interesting. "Audioguides" like this enable visitors to wander through a gallery and punch in the numbers of any piece of art for a full description.

don't stand in the front and ask a lot of questions. Many museums offer fine (and often free) tours, either of the general collection or with a particular focus. Call the museum in advance to learn what's scheduled. Most museums also have fine coffee shops or cafeterias to punctuate longer visits.

Before leaving, thumb through a museum guidebook index or look through the postcards to make sure you haven't missed anything of importance to you.

Most museums are closed one day during the week. Your local guidebook or tourist information should know when. Free admission days are usually the most crowded. It may be worth the entrance fee to avoid the crowds. While arriving late can be a fine way to avoid the summer heat and crowds, many museum ticket offices close 45 minutes before the museum does. If you'll be in a museum till the very end, visit the extremities first; these are the places likely to be shut down early as the museum staff begins sweeping the art lovers out.

Art Patronage

It's only recently that artists have claimed the right to paint just what they want, just how they want it. In ancient times, artists had a low social status and were expected to do as they were told. Anyone who worked with his hands was simply a common laborer, like a bricklayer. The ancient Egyptians, with their need for funerary art, encouraged painters and sculptors and paid them well for their services but never gave them any special respect. Architects had higher social status; they worked with their heads, not their hands. Imhotep, who designed the first pyramid in 2600 B.C., was actually deified.

In early Greece, most artists were slaves. Gradually artists gained respect. By the Golden Age, they had begun to sign their works, rising above the level of the anonymous craftsman. Still, even the great sculptor Phidias was criticized for vanity when he tried to include his self-portrait (and that of Pericles) in one of his works on the Acropolis.

By the time of Alexander the Great (about 300 B.C.), however, artists were freer to express their individual tastes. For the first time private patrons financed artists to make works that were merely pleasing to look at. Artists became respected and admired in the community. Alexander showered wealth and favors on his favorites. He was so pleased with a painting that he once offered the great artist Apelles one of his own mistresses.

The more practical Romans thought their artists should be paid but not pampered. As Seneca put it, "Art should be enjoyed; artists should be disdained." Nevertheless, their society gave artists plenty of work: government buildings, temples, monuments to emperors and conquerors, coins, household goods, graven images of gods, and portraits. Roman artists were treated as anonymous skilled craftsmen who couldn't compare with the classical Greeks. Rich Romans were most interested in buying copies of Greek masterpieces.

With the fall of Rome and the resulting economic and cultural decline, there were no strong states and few wealthy individuals. What little art remained was in the hands of the church. Monks illustrated manuscripts of the Bible and sacred writings. Virtually the only market for a lay artist was in churches and monasteries. "Lodges" of journeymen masons, carvers, sculptors, and the like traveled from town to town building religious structures.

Artists fought for economic security against the unstable patronage of the Middle Ages by forming guilds. Half union, half co-op, guilds trained artists, regulated quality standards (as well as moral standards), and served as middlemen between the artists and prospective buyers. In a sense, the guild often was the artist's patron: it told him where and when to work and gave him his percentage of the fee when the completed product was approved. As late as 1570 in Italy, artists were required to be members of a guild.

The guild underlined the artist's role as craftsman. In Holland, the Guild of St. Luke included painters, carvers, and goldsmiths as well as plumbers, slate layers, printers, and lantern makers. Most commissions were collaborations between guild members: one covered the walls, another painted a design on them, another carved the ornaments, and so on.

As Europe prospered, so did artists. Individual artists were in high demand, and art flourished. We see the same pattern throughout history: a culture prospers by economic or military expansion, creating a class of patrons with a taste for decoration. In ancient Egypt this class was the ruling kings and priests, who used art to maintain the political and religious status quo. Greece and Rome added a new class of wealthy people who appreciated art apart from its propaganda purposes. (Rome, however, was still very much into art as propaganda, as you see by all its commemorative statues and triumphal arches.) In the early Middle Ages, the church was virtually the only patron, producing art only for its limited, spiritual purposes.

During the Italian Renaissance, all three patrons—church, state, and private individuals—used their growing wealth to compete for a few artists. This climate of healthy competition not only made artists wealthy, famous, and respected, but it also, for the first time in history, allowed them freedom to create art on their own terms (within the structure of their commission), not solely according to the patron's specifications. With Michelangelo, the modern idea of the artist as a divinely inspired genius had arrived. Self-portraits were becoming more common.

Patronage and artist prestige reached its height during the Baroque period. Rubens and Bernini lived like princes, courted by kings, cardinals, and intellectuals alike.

In the Northern European countries, a large middle class of merchants and bankers controlled the wealth. Steady patronage by the church and monarch was not available because the North was Protestant and more democratic. Rather than pro-king and pro-church art, northern artists had to turn to easygoing, nonpreachy scenes that would interest the buying public: landscapes, domestic scenes, humorous incidents. They still did some made-to-order works, but more and more they began to complete works for display at trade fairs, hoping to find buyers. This set the precedent for modern patronage.

In the time of absolute monarchs, such as Louis XIV of France, artists were compelled to work for the king alone. Louis established the Royal Academy to train young artists for his service. They had less independence than their counterparts in free-market Holland and England but more formal training and financial security. France soon became the center of European art.

The Modern, Independent Artist

The French Revolution was the symbolic if not final end of the Old Regime of church, state, and aristocrats which had financed most of Europe's great art since the Middle Ages. Artists became more and more independent. They turned away from the propaganda art of church and kings, and even from so-called lovers of freedom such as Napoleon.

In the 19th century, art retreated into the museums and galleries. Artists didn't wait for a specific commission to decorate a particular palace, church, or public square. Instead, they created what they wanted, then looked for a place to exhibit it. The Impressionists had to arrange their own exhibitions when the conservative galleries refused their controversial work. Some artists (such as Cézanne) rejected all outside patronage or official schooling by financing themselves or by simply refusing to sacrifice their artistic principles to the demands of the buying public. The bohemian artist, starving but not selling out, was born.

Of course, some forms of official patronage have filled the vacuum. Churches still commission artists and architects (the church at Ronchamp, France, by Le Corbusier is one modern example). And governments offer some of the steadiest sources of support for an artist.

Patronage is moving away from art for art's sake; large corporations fund the arts for public relations purposes and tax write-offs. Art buying has also become a major investment area for businessmen with no interest in the art itself.

As you enjoy Europe's art, wonder who paid for it and why. One thing is for sure: it wasn't designed to embellish a museum. Some person or organization probably employed that artist for a particular self-serving purpose. Today, happily, the greatest art of our civilization fills Europe's great museums, and that art serves the public.

Common Subjects and Symbols in Art

In a quick jaunt through any church, palace, or museum, you're bound to see many of the same subjects painted and sculpted in different ways by different artists. A little knowledge (a dangerous thing, but we'll trust you) of these common themes helps you appreciate the art much more.

The inspiration for most European art comes from the Bible and Greek/Roman mythology. For general background, read the Book of Matthew in the New Testament (about 35 pages long) and a children's book of Greek myths. (The following "Christian Themes and Symbols" section was written by Mike McGregor.)

Christian Themes and Symbols

Jesus of Nazareth (c. 4 B.C.–A.D. 29)

The life of Jesus is the most popular source of material for artists. Here's a thumbnail sketch.

Born in a stable under miraculous circumstances, Jesus was visited by shepherds and Wise Men. His religious mission had earlier been announced to his mother, Mary, by the angel Gabriel. He was raised to be a carpenter, but even at an early age he proved his teaching powers.

At 30, he left home to preach the word of God, choosing 12 disciples, or apostles. He preached, performed miracles, healed people, and antagonized the religious establishment.

On a visit to Jerusalem, Jesus celebrated Jewish Passover with his disciples. Later that night he was arrested by the Roman and Jewish authorities, betrayed by one of his own followers. Arraigned before the Jewish elders and the Roman governor, Pilate, and mocked and

Medieval: This 14th-century crucifix concentrates on the agony of Christ—His twisted, body and drooping head.

Renaissance: Masaccio's Christ is solid, serene, and triumphant—part of a majestic architectural setting presided over by God the Father.

Baroque: Rubens captures the drama and human emotion of the moment with the expression on Christ's face and the rippling energy of the surrounding figures.

Modern: Rouault breaks the scene into its basic geometrical "abstract" forms. The heavy outlines and blocks of color are almost a return to medieval stained glass.

whipped by Roman soldiers, he was given a crown of thorns and sentenced to die by crucifixion. They made Jesus carry his own cross to the execution site.

Crucifixion was a Roman specialty. The victim often hung for days before dying. The Romans stabbed Jesus in the side for good measure. Above the cross were the Roman initials I.N.R.I. for Jesus of Nazareth King (Rex) of the Jews. Mary was comforted at the foot of the cross by John, one of the disciples. After Jesus' death, his body was taken down and placed in a tomb.

After three days, Jesus came alive again and visited his friends and disciples. Then he ascended into heaven.

Popular Bible Topics in Art

Old Testament

The Old Testament tells the history of the Israelite people, from the creation of the world to the coming of Jesus. Of the following Biblical events, Michelangelo painted nine of the first ten on the ceiling of the Sistine Chapel at the Vatican in Rome:

- **God divides light from darkness** (Gen. 1:3–5).
- **God creates the sun and moon** (Gen. 1:14–18).
- **God separates water from earth** (Gen. 1:9–10).
- **Creation of man** (Gen. 2:7).
- **Creation of woman** (Gen. 2:21–22).
- **Original sin**—A serpent convinces Eve to eat the one fruit God told her not to, and she in turn convinces Adam to have a bite. This is the first sin, and Adam and Eve are banished from the garden (Gen. 3:1–24).
- **Cain and Abel**—Adam and Eve have two sons. Abel becomes a keeper of sheep and Cain, a farmer. Both make sacrifices to God, but God accepts only Abel's sacrifice. Cain becomes angry, kills his brother, and is banished forever (Gen. 4:11–12).
- **The Flood**—Upset with His creation, God causes a flood to destroy virtually all of humankind (Gen. 6:5–7, Gen. 7:11–24).
- **Noah's sacrifice**—After surviving the flood, Noah builds an altar and offers a sacrifice to the Lord (Gen. 8:20).
- **Noah's drunkenness**—Noah's sons respectfully cover their naked father (Gen. 9:20–23).
- **Abraham sacrifices Isaac**—God makes a pact with the wanderer Abraham, promising him many descendants even though he is old and his wife is childless. Abraham believes God, and his faith is rewarded

by the birth of his son, Isaac. But then God tests Abraham's faith by asking him to sacrifice Isaac. Abraham intends to obey, but God stops him just before he kills Isaac. Isaac becomes the father of the Jewish nation; one of his descendants is Jesus (Gen. 22:1–18).

• **Exodus from Egypt**—The people of Israel are captives of the Egyptians, but Moses rises up to lead them to freedom. Inspired by God, Moses parts the Red Sea to allow his people to escape quickly from the Egyptians (Exodus 14:16–30). The Jews are promised a new land, but because they disobey God, they are first forced to wander in the desert for 40 years (Exodus 1–19).

• **Moses and the Ten Commandments**—In order to tell the people of Israel how He wants them to live, God calls Moses to Mt. Sinai and gives him 10 "thou-shalt-nots" written on tablets of stone (Exodus 20:1–17).

• **David and Goliath**—The people of Israel are challenged in battle by the Philistines, who have a mighty giant warrior, Goliath. Of all the Israelis, only a young shepherd boy named David is bold enough to fight him. David uses rocks and a slingshot to bring Goliath down, then cuts off the giant's head. David later becomes king (1 Samuel 17:1–51).

New Testament

• **Annunciation**—The angel Gabriel announces the birth of a son, Jesus, to Mary (Luke 1:26–38). This scene usually includes a dove, symbolizing the Holy Spirit coming down to Mary.

• **Madonna and Child**—Mary and the baby Jesus (Luke 2:6–7).

• **Holy Family**—Mary and Jesus with Mary's husband, Joseph, mother Anne, or others. When two children are shown, they're usually Jesus and Johnny the Baptist.

• **Adoration of the Magi**—Three wise kings follow a bright star from the East and bow down to worship the baby Jesus (Matt. 2:1–12). Tradition says that one king was from Ethiopia; he is usually depicted having black skin.

• **Flight to Egypt**—Mary's husband, Joseph, is warned to flee from King Herod. The king, based on the prediction that a newborn boy (Jesus) would become greater than himself, has ordered all male infants killed. Joseph and Mary take Jesus to Egypt (Matt. 2:13–23).

• **Slaughter of the Innocents**—King Herod kills the children in and around Bethlehem, where Jesus was born (Matt. 2:16–18).

• **Baptism of Jesus**—John the Baptist pours water over Jesus in the Jordan River as a symbol of cleansing. God the Father is represented in the scene as an eye or a voice, and God the Holy Spirit is represented as a dove (Matt. 3:13–17).

- **Resurrection of Lazarus**—Jesus raises his friend Lazarus from the dead (John 11:1–45).
- **Last Supper**—Jesus celebrates the Jewish festival of Passover by having one final meal with his disciples. That same night he was arrested (Mark 14:1–31, John 13:1–17, 26).
- **Garden of Gethsemane**—Jesus is arrested while praying in a garden (Mark 14:32–53).
- **Crucifixion**—Jesus is nailed to a cross and dies (Matt. 27:27–54, Mark 15:16–39, John 19:16–37).
- **Pietà**—Mother Mary with the dead body of Jesus (no clear reference).
- **Resurrection**—On the third day after his burial, Jesus rises from the dead and appears to many people, including his mother, his disciples, Mary Magdalene, and two men on the road to Emmaus (Matt. 28, Mark 16, Luke 24, John 20–21).
- **Ascension**—Jesus leaves the earth by rising into the clouds (ascending) to return to his rightful place beside his Father in heaven (Acts 1:9–11).
- **The Last Judgment**—Jesus returns to the earth to sort out the good people and the bad. Angels float the good to heaven and demons drag the bad to hell. Bodies rise from their graves to find out how they will fare (Revelation).
- **Assumption of the Virgin**—Angels hoist Mary up through the clouds to heaven (no Biblical reference).

The Saints

Holy people were venerated by the European faithful. Though we don't know what they really looked like, we can tell who's who by their symbols.

- **Peter**—The most important saint, a disciple of Jesus. The name Peter means "rock." Jesus said, "Upon this rock I will build my church." St. Peter's Basilica, in Rome, is built upon the grave of St. Peter. Usually shown in middle age with a bushy beard, keys, or an upside-down cross in hand, symbolic of his crucifixion.
- **Paul**—The second most important saint, Paul was primarily responsible for establishing

Peter was crucified upside down

Christianity through his missionary journeys. He wrote half of the books of the New Testament. Shown bald headed and bearded, gripping a sword and a book.

• **Matthew, Mark, Luke, and John (the Four Evangelists)**— Wrote the first four books of the New Testament, which chronicle the life of Christ. Symbols: Matthew, an angel with a book; Mark, a lion; Luke, a winged bull; and John, an eagle with a book.

• **John the Baptist**—Shown as an emaciated prophet dressed in animal skins, carrying a long cross, a lamb, and often a scroll bearing the words *Ecce Homo* ("Behold the man," referring to Christ crowned with thorns). Spent many years preaching that Jesus was coming into the world,

Martin Schongauer, **Temptation of St. Anthony,** *c. 1490 (National Library, Paris). This early Christian saint (c. 300) was legendary for his ascetic desert life and the temptations he endured.*

then eventually baptized him. After objecting to Herod's marriage to his own brother's wife, John was imprisoned by Herod. At the request of Herod's stepdaughter, John was beheaded (Matthew 14:3–12).

• **Mary Magdalene**—A prostitute whom Jesus forgave of her sins, she became a follower of Jesus and was at the cross when he died. Usually shown having long hair and carrying a jar of ointment.

• **Michael, the Archangel**—Shown in armor, with a sword, standing over or fighting with a dragon; also sometimes shown with a set of scales. The most important of the angels, Michael cast Satan out of heaven and will one day blow the waking trumpet and lead the forces of Good at the last great battle on Judgment Day.

• **Anne**—The mother of the Virgin Mary, the grandmother of Jesus, shown with the Virgin Mary and usually also with the baby Jesus.

• **Francis of Assisi**—A medieval friar noted for his vow of poverty and love of God. The most important friar of all time, Francis founded the Franciscan order and lived in Assisi, Italy. He is usually shown in brown Franciscan habit, on his knees, with a winged Christ in the sky sending down the stigmata (the wounds from Jesus' crucified body appearing on Francis' body).

• **Sebastian**—A soldier in the army of Roman emperor Diocletian. Diocletian loved Sebastian, but when he learned Sebastian was a Christian, Diocletian ordered him tied to a tree and shot with arrows. Legend says Sebastian survived to confront Diocletian . . . only to be beaten to death with clubs. Usually depicted naked, tied to a tree, and pierced by arrows.

• **George**—The subject of many legends, George saved a town from a dragon to which the townspeople were sacrificing their children. He was a chivalrous knight, usually

St. Sebastian is shown pierced with arrows, the symbol of his martyrdom.

Michelangelo, **The Last Judgment** *(detail). The Christian martyr St. Bartholomew was skinned alive. Here he bears the face of Michelangelo. (Sistine Chapel, Vatican Museum.)*

shown on horseback spearing a dragon while the king's daughter, Cleodolinda (who was in the sacrificial on-deck circle), looks on.

• **Jerome**—A hermit, he translated the Hebrew Bible into Latin producing the Vulgate, the standard text of the Catholic church through modern times. His symbols vary, but he is often shown with a lion, from whose foot he extracted a thorn.

• **Bartholomew**—A first century–A.D. missionary. Tradition says he was captured in Armenia and flayed alive, then crucified for being a Christian. Bartholomew is usually shown with a book and knife or holding his skin. He is sometimes depicted being skinned.

• **Denis**—Sent by the pope on a missionary journey to Paris, Denis became the first bishop of Paris and was eventually beheaded for his faith. You'll see him all over Paris holding his head in his hands.

• **Theresa**—In the 16th century, she reformed the Carmelite monastic order and wrote many religious works. Theresa is usually shown with her heart pierced by an angel's arrow, or in ecstasy while praising God.

• **Christopher (the patron saint of us pilgrims and travelers)**—A third-century man who went out in search of someone to serve, he wandered aimlessly for years and ended up ferrying people across a river while waiting for Christ to appear to him. Christ finally appeared as a child whom Christopher carried across the river. Shown as a giant carrying a child and holding a staff.

These stories are found in pictures and stained glass in churches throughout Europe. The masses were usually illiterate, so church paintings were their Bible.

Much Christian art is symbolic. During medieval times, every animal, fruit, flower, color, and number had some meaning. Apes symbolized man's baser nature; bees were a symbol of industriousness (busy as a . . .); a lamb was a sacrificial animal (like Jesus); a dolphin carried the soul of the blessed to heaven. Mythical beasts had meaning, too: dragons (Satan), griffins (power), unicorns (purity), and phoenixes (resurrection). Numbers had symbolic meaning: 7 was a lot, 77 was a heck of a lot.

It's interesting to compare two different paintings or stained-glass images of the same subject. There are literally thousands of crucifixions, but no two are the same. Some artists concentrate on Jesus' agony, some on his serenity. For some, it's a gruesome moment of defeat, for others, a glorious triumph over sin.

Jesus is portrayed in different ways to emphasize different virtues. In one picture he is the Good Shepherd, a handsome, kindly young man caring for people as a shepherd cares for his sheep. In another he is a wise teacher. Or he might be a king, crowned in majesty. He may even be a warrior. These differences tell a lot about how people viewed the Christian message at the time of the painting.

Jesus taught with parables and performed miracles, both of which are common features in works of art. Look for the Prodigal Son (Luke 15:11–32), the Good Samaritan (Luke 10:30–37), Jesus walking on water (Matthew 14:25–27), and Jesus changing the water into wine (John 2:1–11). Only Jesus is shown with a cross on his halo.

Catholic churches generally show 12 scenes ("Stations of the Cross") from the crucifixion. These are meant to help worshipers focus on the suffering of their savior as he died for their sins.

If you see a face in a crowd of saints, church fathers, and Bible figures that you don't recognize, chances are it doesn't really belong in such holy company, anyway. Patrons of works often insisted that they be included in the work praising the Virgin Mary or what have you. If money couldn't buy them a spot in heaven, at least it could put them in a picture of heaven.

The Stars of Greek and Roman Mythology

The Greek gods were bigger-than-life human beings. They quarreled, boasted, loved, and hated just as mortals do, yet they controlled the fates of humankind. Classical mythology tells how the gods dealt with each other and with the mortals who asked them for favors. (The Greeks must have enjoyed hearing their own weaknesses glamorized, just as we do through our Hollywood stars.)

Later, the Romans adopted most of the Greeks' gods and gave them new names. Still later, Renaissance artists revived them, using them as symbols of Christian virtues and vices. After centuries of painting the same old God, it must have been a great sense of freedom to paint new ones and a whole pantheon of them, to boot.

In your museum-going, you're likely to see Prometheus discovering fire, Hades capturing Persephone, Pandora opening the box, Jason and the Golden Fleece, Midas and his Goldfinger touch, the Battle of the Centaurs, the Battle of the Amazons, Leda and the Swan, and on and on. Here are the most important Greek gods and how to recognize them (Roman name in parentheses):

• **Zeus (Jupiter)**—Ruled as King of the Gods in their court on Mount Olympus. He divided up his realm among his sisters, brothers, and children. Bearded, sometimes carries a spear. Zeus had a nasty habit of turning himself into some earthly form to hustle unsuspecting females. You're just as likely to see him portrayed as a bull, a cloud, a swan, or a shower of gold as in his majestic human body.

• **Hera (Juno)**—Wife of Zeus.

• **Poseidon (Neptune)**—King of the Sea. Holds a trident.

• **Hades (Pluto)**—King of the Underworld. Bearded and sad, carries a staff.

• **Apollo**—Ruler of the Sun, God of Music and Poetry. Drives the sun's flaming chariot across the sky each day. Major symbol is the sun.

• **Hermes (Mercury)**—Messenger of the Gods. His helmet and shoes have wings. Delivers a lot of flowers these days.

• **Ares (Mars)**—God of War. Dresses in war garb and carries a spear.

• **Dionysus (Bacchus)**—God of Wine and college fraternities. Holds

Diana the Huntress *(Orsay Museum, Paris)*

grapes, wears a toga and a wreath of laurel leaves. Sometimes shown as a chubby little boy.
• **Athena (Minerva)**—Goddess of Wisdom. A virgin, born from the head of Zeus. Carries a spear.
• **Artemis (Diana)**—Goddess of the Moon and Hunting. Carries a bow and arrow.
• **Aphrodite (Venus)**—Goddess of Love and Beauty. Often shown partially naked, with Cupid nearby.
• **Eros (Cupid)**—God of Desire. Usually shown as a baby with wings, wielding a bow and aphrodisiac-tipped arrows.
Other characters and miscellaneous beasts:
• **Pan (Faun)**—A lesser god of shepherds. Top half man, bottom half goat. Carries a pan flute.
• **Hercules**—Son of Zeus born to a mortal woman. Strongest man in the world. Performed many feats of strength. Often wears a lion's skin.
• **Odysseus (Ulysses)**—Homer's *Odyssey* tells the story of Ulysses' 10-year journey home from the Trojan War.
• **Helen of Troy**—The most beautiful woman in the world. Her kidnapping started the Trojan War, the subject of the *Iliad*. Hers is "the face that launched a thousand ships."
• **Satyr**—Top half man, bottom half goat. Horny.
• **Centaur**—Top half man, bottom half horse. Wise.
• **Griffin**—Winged, lionlike beast.
• **Harpy**—Bird with female human head and seductive voice.
• **Medusa**—Woman with hair of snakes and a face that, when glimpsed, turns people to stone. Slain by Perseus.
• **Pegasus**—Winged horse.
• **Minotaur**—Beast with the head of a bull. Lived in the labyrinth in the palace on Crete.

Even if you know zero about art, if you know who's in a painting and what they're doing, your interest level jumps 50 percent. By learning about Christian symbolism and classical mythology, your museum-going will be more fun.

Historical Scenes

Modern artists, in search of new subjects, turned to famous scenes from history, trying to capture the glory or emotion of the moment. In the early 1800s, Romantic artists tapped the patriotic fervor of their audiences with scenes of heroics against oppressors. Goya's *Third of May, 1808* shows the murderous execution of Spanish nationals by Napoleon's troops. Delacroix painted a stirring battle scene from a French antimonarchy uprising. J. L. David, a neoclassicist, chronicled (and "romanticized") the French Revolution and reign of Napoleon.

Still Lifes

Scholars debate whether "art imitates life" or "life imitates art," but to a great extent, "art imitates art." Artists will often choose a subject already done by many previous artists in order to carry on and extend the tradition both to learn from earlier masters' versions and to try something new.

Claesz, **Still Life** *(Rijksmuseum, Amsterdam)*

Perhaps the best example is the "still life," a painting of a set of motionless, common objects: fruit, cups, a knife, a chair, curtains, and so on. It's a simple form, often undertaken by students practicing their drawing and simple composition, yet many great artists have shown their ingenuity by turning it into superb art. Each successive artist is challenged to make the old style and familiar items new again.

Landscapes

Certain artists, such as Canaletto and Constable, concentrated on paintings of places: landscapes, seascapes, domestic and rural scenes. The same place may be completely different in two different paintings, so it is interesting to compare each artist's approach.

Baroque artists often decorated churches with an appropriate

El Greco, **Landscape of Toledo**

landscape—heaven. Ceilings seem to open up to the sky, gloriously busy with angels, chariots, and winged babies (called *putti*).

Portraits

Portraits are, of course, supposed to be accurate renditions of the posers, but many try to glorify their subjects. Two particular types of portrait sculpture are the "bust" (neck and head only) and "equestrian" (riding a horse).

The "nude" is another kind of portrait, concerned more with the shape of the body than specific identifying features. A good nude does not necessarily have the most beautiful body. It's up to the artist to pose the body just right, reclining or standing, to capture the most interesting and harmonious lines.

A classical style, *contrapposto* (Italian for "counterpoise"), is a painting or sculpture of someone standing, resting their weight on one leg. (Michelangelo's *David* is *contrapposto*.) The faint S-like curve of the body attracts the eye as much as any individual body features.

Artists and Dates

Bernini (bayr-NEE-nee), 1598–1680: Baroque grandeur.
Blake, William, 1757–1827: Mystical visions.
Bosch, Hieronymous (bosh), 1450–1516: Crowded, bizarre scenes.
Botticelli, Sandro (bot-i-CHEL-ee), 1445–1510: Delicate Renaissance beauty.
Braque, Georges (brock), 1882–1963: Cubist pioneer.
Brunelleschi, Filippo (broon-uh-LES-key), 1377–1446: First great Renaissance architect.
Brueghel, Pieter (BROY-gull), c. 1525–1569: Netherlands, peasant scenes.
Caravaggio (car-a-VAW-jee-oh), 1573–1610: Shocking ultrarealism.
Cézanne, Paul (say-ZAHN), 1839–1906: Bridged Impressionism and Cubism.
Chagall, Marc (sha-GALL), 1887–1985: Fiddlers on roofs, magical realism.
da Vinci, Leonardo (dah VINCH-ee), 1452–1519: A well-rounded Renaissance genius who also painted.
Dalí, Salvador (DAH-lee), 1904–1989: Father of Surrealism.
Degas, Edgar (day-GAH), 1834–1917: Impressionist snapshots, dancers.
Donatello (doh-na-TELL-oh), c. 1386–1466: Early Renaissance sculptor.
Dürer, Albrecht (DEWR-er), 1471–1528: Renaissance symmetry with German detail; "the Leonardo of the north."
El Greco (el GREK-oh), 1541–1614: Spiritual scenes, elongated bodies.
Fra Angelico (frah an-JELL-i-co), 1387–1455: Renaissance techniques, medieval piety.
Gauguin, Paul (go-GAN), 1848–1903: Primitivism, native scenes, bright colors.
Giorgione (jor-JONE-ee), 1477–1510: Venetian Renaissance, mysterious beauty.

Giotto (JOTT-oh), 1266–1337: Proto-Renaissance painter (3-D) in medieval times.

Goya, Francisco (GOY-ah), 1746–1828: Three stages—frilly court painter, political rebel, dark stage.

Hals, Frans (halls), 1581–1666: Snapshot portraits of Dutch merchants.

Ingres, Jean Auguste Dominique (ANG-gruh), 1780–1867: Neoclassical painter.

Manet, Edouard (man-NAY), 1823–1883: Forerunner of Impressionist rebels.

Mantegna, Andrea (mahn-TAYN-ya), 1431–1506: Renaissance 3-D and "sculptural" painting.

Matisse, Henri (mah-TEES), 1869–1954: Decorative "wallpaper," bright colors.

Michelangelo (mee-kell-AN-jell-oh), 1475–1564: Earth's greatest sculptor and one of its greatest painters.

Mondrian, Piet (mahn-dree-ahn), 1872–1944: Abstract, geometrical canvases.

Monet, Claude (moh-NAY), 1840–1926: Father of Impressionism.

Picasso, Pablo (pee-KAHS-oh), 1881–1973: Master of many modern styles, especially Cubism.

Raphael (roff-eye-ELL), 1483–1520: Epitome of the Renaissance—balance, realism, beauty.

Rembrandt (REM-brant), 1606–1669: Greatest Dutch painter, brown canvases, dramatic lighting.

Renoir, Auguste (ren-WAH), 1841–1919: Impressionist style, idealized beauty, pastels.

Rodin, Auguste (roh-DAN), 1840–1917: Classical statues with rough "Impressionist" finish.

Rubens, Peter Paul (REW-buns), 1577–1640: Baroque, fleshy women, violent scenes.

Steen, Jan (steen), 1626–1679: Slice-of-life everyday Dutch scenes.

Tiepolo, Giovanni Battista (tee-EPP-o-lo), 1696–1770: 3-D illusions on ceilings.

Tintoretto (tin-toh-RETT-oh), 1518–1594: Venetian Renaissance plus drama.

Titian (TEESH-un), 1477–1576: Greatest Venetian Renaissance painter.

Turner, Joseph Mallord William, 1775–1851: Messy "Proto-Impressionist" scenes of nature.

Uccello, Paolo (oo-CHEL-oh), 1396–1475: Early 3-D experiments.

Van Eyck, Jan (van IKE), 1390–1441: Northern detail.
Van Gogh, Vincent (van GO, or, more correctly, van GOCK), 1853–1890: Impressionist style plus emotion.
Velázquez, Diego (vel-LAHS-kes), 1599–1660: Objective Spanish court portraits.
Vermeer, Jan (vayr-MEER), 1632–1675: Quiet Dutch art, highlighting everyday details.
Veronese, Paolo (vayr-oh-NAY-zee), 1528–1588: Huge, colorful scenes with Venetian Renaissance backgrounds.

Timeline of Artists

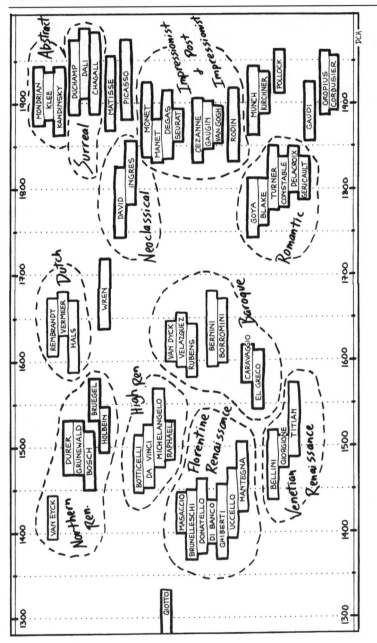

Music Appreciation

Music, like all art forms, is shaped by the cultural mood and environment of the time. It's easy to trace the course of musical history as it marches arm in arm with painting, architecture, philosophy, lifestyles, and sculpture from Baroque to neoclassical to Romantic to Impressionistic and into the no-holds-barred artistic world of our time.

As we trace the evolution of musical styles through post-Renaissance history, let's use this section as a review of the progression of art styles since the Baroque days of Louis, Bernini, and Bach.

The Baroque world was controlled exuberance, glory to man and his God-blessed accomplishments. Music, like art, was brilliant, bright, alive, and decorated with trills, flutters, and ornamentation like the powdered-wigged, perfumed, and elegantly gowned musicians who wrote and performed it.

But the frills rested on a strong foundation. While a two-part Bach invention, Handel's Messiah, or a Scarlatti sonata may sparkle with bright and happy ornaments, they are carefully based on a solid mathematical structure. An analysis of Bach's work shows many patterns, staircase-type series, and a grand plan, tying all the musical ribbons and bows together. Bach, Handel, and Scarlatti, all born in 1685, were the great musical masters of the Baroque period.

In the late 18th century, the neoclassical movement took art as well as music back to pure, clean basics. It was a stern reaction to the clutter of Baroque. Buildings were built with clean, true domes, circles, and squares. The age of reason had arrived, and beauty was simple. A good example of how music played along with the neoclassical movement is found in the art of Mozart. Neoclassical music is called simply classical. A classical composer, Mozart wrote pieces of powerfully simple beauty. Grand and frilly were out. The better a Mozart sonata is played, the easier it sounds. Classical music, like the dome on our Capitol, is a search for basic, pure beauty. Its beauty lies in its simplicity.

In the 1800s, reason and logic were dethroned and Nature and

*Classical concerts in historic settings, such as chamber music in Paris'
Sainte-Chapelle, make music appreciation easy.*

Emotion became a religion. Music's grand metronome had swung back
again. The Romantics were awestruck by the wonders of nature and
happy victims of its power and immensity. Grieg's fjord hideaway,
Verdi's nationalism, and Chopin's battered heart all inspired the masterpieces of this Romantic era. They expressed emotions—good and
bad—for the sake of emotions. Orchestras grew in size to add more
punch. A series of pieces by Chopin, Wagner, or Schumann can take
you through an emotional wringer. The pieces, often with names
reflecting their heartfelt stories (Ase's Death, Pleading Child, Raindrops
Prelude, Dreaming), want to strongly affect the listener rather than
merely entertain.

As painting reached beyond mere realism, we enter the Impressionist
era. While Monet and Renoir were catching sunbeams, leafy reflections,
and the fuzzy warmth of that second glass of wine, composers such as
Debussy and Ravel were doing the same thing on the keyboard or with
orchestras. Artists struggled to capture basic shapes, colors, and moods.
A blue moment, a fleeting rainbow, or an enchanted cathedral were targets of the artist's mind, the painter's brush, the composer's pen, and the
conductor's baton. Debussy is Monet for your ears. (And for the more
musical, Monet is Debussy for your eyes.)

Today's artists are abandoning reality, exploring new frontiers that
know no rules, and choosing personally stimulating works of artistic
esoterica over pleasing the people. Paintings are abstract, and music is
atonal.

Atonal music is freed from tonality and worry about what key are we in? There is no key, meter, or consistent beat pattern (such as 2/4 or 3/4 time). The only real rule is that artists should not be bound by the rules of others.

But atonality is as difficult for our ears as abstraction is for our eyes. We're taught to need art to portray something real, just as we need music to stick to a key. The great composer and pianist Franz Liszt knew the power of tonality. And so did his wife. To get him out of bed in the morning, she would play the first seven notes of a scale: do re mi fa so la ti . . . Sleepy Franz would toss aside the covers, run to the piano, and play that last necessary note . . . do. Liszt was a tonal guy. Good morning.

Appendix

Whose Story Is History?

The U.S., with 4 percent of the world's population, controls about one-third of its wealth. And, as they say in London (before stepping off the "tube"), "mind the gap." It's growing.

With all the chaos and suffering on this planet, its comforting to believe the rich got that way fair and square. Erik Dammann, Norwegian philosopher and author of *Future in Our Hands*, takes a campesinos view, arguing that the rich give history a comfortable spin.

When Columbus "discovered" America, the worlds biggest and one of its most beautiful and sophisticated cities was Tenochtitlan, present-day Mexico City. Built out over a large lake with a population of about half a million, it looked a lot like Amsterdam. There were goldsmiths, chemists, barbers, public baths, and bustling market-places. Pre-Columbian Mexico had a system of paved roads, aqueducts, suspension bridges, doctors (capable of performing skull surgery), police, a criminal code and court system, and a king elected by a council. Hernán Cortés, the Spanish conquistador who conquered present-day Mexico, wrote, "Discipline and high principles prevail everywhere. People are well educated and, as far as I can tell, the form of government resembles that of Pisa or Venice." This is the Mexico that the Europeans "discovered" and destroyed 500 years ago. Mexicans dont celebrate Columbus Day.

Many areas of Africa, Latin America, and Asia were just as morally, ethically, and technically developed as Europe before our culture expanded. In A.D. 400, while most of Europe was still in skins, Africans wore Indian cotton and Chinese silk. In 1500, the top industry in Timbuktu was books. Africa had intricate networks of roads, large cities, irrigation projects, and lots of trade. During these days, when European nations exchanged ambassadors with their African counterparts, they expressed much respect for African governments, crafts, and societies. By the 1800s, when artifacts from these same civilizations were brought to Europe, they were thought to be from

Atlantis or ancient Greece. By this time we had "learned" that Africans were incapable of creating objects of such quality. School books labeled Africa "the dark continent."

In 1498, Vasco da Gama discovered the route to India with the help of Arab sailors and African merchants along the way. The Indian Ocean already had a busy, well-balanced, and stable system of trade among Indians, Chinese, Arabs, and Africans. These people used boats much bigger than those the Portuguese had arrived in, and their boats were equipped with tools such as quadrants and compasses.

Europeans were usually received warmly. They saw incredible wealth and spent the next 400 years taking it. Entire cultures vanished as hundreds of millions were enslaved. Literate and stable societies were colonized, raped, and left illiterate with no basis for development. (Before Indonesia and Algeria were colonized by Europeans, their populations were 90 percent literate. When the Europeans were done with them, the colonies were left with their independence and 90 percent illiteracy.) Thousands of tons of gold were brought to Europe. All this gave Europe and the United States the resources, surplus wealth, land, and manpower to undergo the most rapid development in history—at the expense of the rest of the world. The inertia from this period still exists today, and the wealth continues to trickle up. In spite of lots of hardworking charities and well-meaning aid from rich countries, more money flows from the poor countries to the rich than vice versa, because of aggressive trade policies and interest payments on debts.

How did this happen? The Europeans were powered by greed and a love of gold. Exploration was a "for-profit" activity. And the cultures the Europeans met were just no match for Western tactics. For instance, African generals always left rear openings so their enemies could retreat if necessary. Battles were normally started in the afternoon so that the weaker side could retreat under the cover of darkness. Before the battle, opposing sides partied together.

In our culture, "all is fair in love and war." The first president of the United States won fame and a decisive victory by attacking on a Christmas Eve when his enemy was drunk and unprepared.

Within a few years of da Gamas famous voyage, Portugal controlled the Indian Ocean and had destroyed the 500-year-old cultures of East Africa. European memory of a destroyed civilization vanishes conveniently with that culture.

For the next nearly 400 years, the slave trade powered much of the European/American economy. A superprofitable triangular trade system brought slaves from Africa to America and minerals and natural wealth from America to Europe. This fueled Europes Industrial Revolution. Huge ports such as Liverpool grew up and boomed with the slave industry. During this period, the industrial basis of European/American economic power in modern times was established.

While only about 15 million slaves reached America alive, conservative estimates say Africa lost 50 million of its strongest young men through the European and American slave trade. For 400 years of demoralizing slavery, Africa received only the opportunity to buy European products.

African cultures crumbled and were comfortably forgotten. What was left had no confidence and almost no hope. (Some say that slave traders were only capitalizing on an existing institution of inter-African slavery. But slavery in Africa before the Europeans arrived was closer to feudal European serfdom. Only with European aggressiveness did slavery become big business.) In the 1800s, as slavery became unprofitable, the immorality of it was recognized.

Europes leaders met in Berlin and divided up Africa by drawing lines on the map. Cultural and linguistic boundaries were ignored. Looting Africa of its mineral wealth, colonial powers racked up annual profits of 50 to 500 percent.

Shortly after its discovery, Central America was given to Spain by Pope Alexander. The ensuing destruction of Mexico from 1519 to 1521 by Cortés and a handful of mercenaries is a fascinating story of greed and power.

According to pre-Columbian Mexican religion, their Messiah, Quetzalcoatl, was due to arrive wearing a beard and riding a horse (two things very unusual to these people) during the very year Cortés arrived, a bearded man on a horse. Thinking Cortés was Quetzalcoatl, the Mexicans warmly welcomed the Spaniard with 2,000 heavy pieces of gold. Montezuma, the Mexican leader, greeted Cortés, saying, "O Lord, our Lord . . . at last you have come to this land, to your own land and to Mexico your own city. Sit down on your mat, upon your throne which I have kept for you . . . Welcome to our land. Rest yourself now. Rest here for a while. Rest in our palace—together with your princes, your exalted companions, and all the others."

Cortés must have thought to himself, "This is really great!" He and his men were taken into the kings palace and were so impressed with all the gold and riches that they arrested Montezuma, destroyed the palace, and took all its riches.

Doubting the divinity of Cortés, the citizens asked him to leave and welcomed him to take their treasure with him. But Cortés wanted complete control, so the battle began and the Spaniards destroyed the civilization: 100,000 were killed, and the libraries, temples, art, and literature of this culture were lost forever. Today Montezuma is remembered for his "Halls" and as a kind of diarrhea.

Twelve years later, under the Spaniard Francisco Pizarro, gold-hungry Europe moved into South America. Europeans looted for 100 years before mining was even necessary. The Indians were beasts of burden. A hundred years of war and new diseases cut Mexicos population by 50 percent. As local populations shrank, Africans were imported to fill in. By 1800, about half of the populations of Venezuela and Brazil were Africans imported by European businessmen.

For 300 years, Spain milked Latin America until, in the early 1800s, independence was won. Then in 1824, British Foreign Minister Channing declared, "Latin America has won its freedom. If we play our cards right, this part of the world will be ours!" France, Britain, and the United States moved in, if not politically, then economically. Today, the outcome of a U.S. presidential election has a greater impact on the people of Central America than it does on the people of North America.

And the story continues. They say the wise learn from history. The value of what they learn depends on the quality of the history they study. Whose story is history?

A New Enlightenment through Travel

Thomas Jefferson said, "Travel makes you wiser but less happy." "Less happy" is a good thing. It's the growing pains of a broadening perspective. After viewing our culture from a coffeehouse in Vienna or a village in Tuscany, I've found truths that didn't match those I always assumed were "self-evident" and "God-given." And flying home gives me a healthy dose of culture shock in reverse. You know how I love Europe. But I haven't told you about my most prized souvenir—a new way of thinking.

The "land of the free" has a powerful religion—materialism. Its sophisticated priesthood (business, media, military, and political leaders) worships unsustainable growth. Contentment and simplicity are sins. Mellow is yellow. And evil is anything steering you away from being a good producer/consumer.

Yes, greater wealth could be wonderful. But for whom? The gap between rich and poor—both within our society and among humankind in general—is growing. Regulatory, tax, and spending policies in the United States since 1982 have caused the greatest trickle-up of wealth in our nation's history. And globally, the richest 358 people now own as much as the poorest 45% of humanity put together. Designer fortifications protect the wealthy in much of the world. In the U.S., the hottest things in the building industry are gated communities and prisons. The victims are the politically meek—those who don't or can't vote: the young, the poor, the environment, and the future. I've wandered the streets of Java, El Salvador, Puerto Rico, and south L.A. And I know being rich in a poor land means raising children behind deadbolts.

Whoa! What happened to me? The young Republican traveled. I saw countries less wealthy than ours (but with bigger governments) where everyone had a home, enough food, and health care. And, like the early astronauts, I saw a planet with no boundaries—a single, tender organism painted with the faces of 6 billion equally precious people. I unpack my rucksack marveling at how some politically active American Christians can believe that we're all children of God—while fighting against aid for the hungry and homeless.

A new Enlightenment is needed. Just as the French "Enlightenment" led us into the modern age of science and democracy, this new Enlightenment will teach us the necessity of sustainable affluence and peaceful coexistence with economic models other than unbridled capitalism, of controlling nature by obeying her and measuring prosperity by something more human than material consumption.

I hope your travels will give you a fun and relaxing vacation or adventure. I also hope they'll make you an active patriot of our planet and a voice for people at home and abroad who will never see their names on a plane ticket.

Rick Steves

Best of Europe Sightseeing Lists

Europe's Top Museums and Cultural Experiences

(Self-guided tours covered in our *Mona Winks* book)
In London: British Museum, British Library, National Gallery,
    Tate Britain, Westminster Abbey, and Westminster Walk
In Paris: The Louvre, Orsay Museum, Versailles, and
    Historic Paris Walk
In Amsterdam: Rijksmuseum and Van Gogh Museum
In Venice: St. Mark's Cathedral, Doge's Palace, and Accademia
In Florence: Uffizi Gallery, Bargello, and Renaissance Walk
In Rome: St. Peter's Cathedral, Vatican Museum, and A Walk
    Through Ancient Rome
In Madrid: The Prado

Rick's Favorite Works of Art

Garden of Delights, Bosch, Prado
Isenheim altarpiece, Grünewald, Colmar
Primavera, Botticelli, Florence
Guernica, Picasso, Madrid
Pietà, Michelangelo, Vatican
David, Michelangelo, Florence
Sistine Chapel (ceiling and *The Last Judgment*),
    Michelangelo, Vatican
School of Athens, Raphael, Vatican Museum
Virgin of the Roses, Schongauer, Colmar
Sainte-Chapelle church, Paris
St. John the Baptist, Donatello, Venice
Self-Portrait, Dürer, Prado
Hand of God, Milles, Stockholm
Rondanini Pietà, Michelangelo, Milan
Orsay Museum building, Paris
Temppeliaukio church, Helsinki

Gene's "Lucky 13" Picks
(with apologies to no one)

Isenheim altarpiece, Grünewald, Colmar
The Tempest, Giorgione, Venice
Head of Christ mosaic, Dafni, Greece
Interior of My Studio, Courbet, Louvre
Burial of Count Orgaz, El Greco, Toledo, Spain
School of Athens, Raphael, Vatican Museum
Moses, Michelangelo, San Pietro in Vincoli, Rome
Last Supper, Leonardo, Milan
Intrigue, James Ensor, Royal Museum, Antwerp
Descent from the Cross, Roger van der Weyden, Prado
Grande Odalisque, Ingres, Louvre
Jacob Wrestling with the Angel, Gauguin, National Gallery, Edinburgh
St. Francis in Ecstasy, G. Bellini, New York

Most Overrated Sights

Manneken-Pis, Brussels
Stonehenge, England
Atonium, Brussels
Athens, Greece
Glockenspiel, Munich (actually, glockenspiels in general)
The Little Mermaid, Copenhagen
Hitler's Bunker, Berlin
Spanish Steps and Trevi Fountain, Rome
Blarney Stone, Ireland
Land's End, England
Loch Ness Monster, Scotland
Cannes
Champs-Elysses, Paris' hamburger row

Most Underrated Sights

Ostia Antica, Rome's ancient port
Bath, England's finest city
Toledo Cathedral Sacristy, Spanish Renaissance
Chantilly château, near Paris
Vaux-le-Vicomte château, near Paris
Schatzkammer (Treasury), Vienna
Bern
Pisa Baptistery and Church (not Tower)

Most Underrated Museums

Vatican Museum (before the Sistine Chapel)
Unterlinden Museum (Isenheim altarpiece and more), Colmar
Chagall Museum, Nice
Groeninge Museum, Bruges
York Castle Museum, York
Costume Museum, Bath
Fitzwilliam Museum, Cambridge
Museo dell' Opera del Duomo (Donatello and Michelangelo), Florence
Museo de Santa Cruz (El Greco), Toledo
Kunstmuseum (modern, Klee), Bern
Kroller-Muller (van Gogh), Arnhem, Netherlands

Offbeat Europe

Paris sewers tour
A million skeletons in Paris Catacombs
Parco dei Mostri, cement monster park near Viterbo, Italy
L'Art Brut (art of the criminally insane), Lausanne, Switzerland
Legoland, Bilund, Denmark
Portmeirion (Italian city), Wales
Homage to Stravinsky fountain (next to Pompidou Center), Paris
Hundertwasser Haus, Vienna
Cappuccin crypts (bones), Rome and Palermo, Italy
Medieval Crime and Punishment Museum, Rothenburg, Germany

Favorite Festivals

Salzburg Music Festival, end of July through August
Edinburgh, late August through early September
Munich beerhalls, June 1 through May 31
Oktoberfest, late September to early October, Munich
Each country's national holiday (such as French Bastille day, July 14
    and Swiss Independence day, August 1)
Palio, Siena, Italy (July 2 and August 16)
Carnevale, Venice (early February)
Fasching, Germany (especially Köln), February
Kinderfest, Dinkelsbuhl, Germany (mid-July)

Favorite Churches

Charlemagne's chapel, Aachen
Sacré-Coeur, Paris

St. Peter's, Vatican
Toledo Cathedral, Toledo
Sainte-Chapelle, Paris
Orvieto, Italy

Best Evening Scenes

Flamenco and paseo street scenes, Sevilla
La Dolce Vita stroll, Via del Corso, Rome
Passeggiata/Paseo, almost any Italian/Spanish town in evening
Piazza Navona, Rome
Jazz clubs, Paris
"Pub Crawl," back streets of Venice
Empty St. Mark's Square at midnight, Venice
Tivoli, Copenhagen
Any Italian hill town after the tour buses leave
Breakwater, Vernazza, Cinque Terre, Italy

Musical Sights

State Opera Houses, Vienna, Milan, and Paris
Mozart's birth house, Salzburg
Musée Carnavalet (Chopin), Paris
Ringve musical history museum, Trondheim, Norway
Beethoven's birth house, Bonn
Europe's greatest organs: Passau (Germany), Haarlem (Holland),
    St. Sulpice (Paris)
Beatles Story, Liverpool
Grieg home, Troldhaugen, Bergen, Norway

Royal Jewels

Crown Jewels, Tower of London
Schatzkammer, Vienna and Munich
Apollo Gallery, Louvre, Paris

Cemeteries

Cappuccin crypts (oodles of bones), Rome and Palermo
Pére Lachaise (Chopin, Jim Morrison, Edith Piaf, Oscar Wilde), Paris
Central Cemetery (Beethoven, Brahms, Mozart, etc.), Vienna
U.S. cemeteries in Normandy (France) and Bastogne (Belgium)
Bone chapel, Hallstatt, Austria

Sports and Games Sights

Olympics museums, Innsbruck and Lausanne
Olympic Stadium, Berlin, Athens
Olympic Village, Munich
Ski jumps in Innsbruck, Garmisch
Ski museum, Holmenkollen ski jump, Oslo
Gaelic Athletic Association Museum, Dublin
Hurling match, anywhere, Ireland
Hang gliders and parasailers, throughout the Alps (especially Chamonix, Tegelberg near Füssen, and the Schilthorn)
Luge rides near Reutte, in Tirol (Austria) and Chamonix (France)
Autoworld museum, Brussels
Casinos in Baden-Baden (Germany) and Monte Carlo

Assorted Military Sights

The medieval armory (awaiting the Turkish hordes), Graz, Austria
Musée de l'Armee, Invalides, Paris
Medieval Crime and Punishment Museum, Rothenburg
Valley of the Fallen, near Madrid
Vasa, Swedish warship, Stockholm
Armory (medieval weapons), Doge's Palace, Venice
Gibraltar
Waterloo (fans only), Brussels, Belgium
Imperial War Museum, London

About the Authors

RICK STEVES (b. 1955)

Rick hosts and writes the public television series *Travels in Europe with Rick Steves,* publishes the *Back Door Travel Newsletter,* offers a generous Web site (www.ricksteves.com), lectures throughout the U.S. on independent travel, organizes and leads "Back Door" tours of Europe, and has written 22 travel guidebooks. His first book, *Rick Steves' Europe Through the Back Door,* started a cult of people who insist on washing their socks in sinks, taking showers "down the hall," and packing very, very light even when not traveling.

GENE OPENSHAW (b. 1956)

Gene is both an author and composer. After graduating from Stanford University, he promptly put his degree to work by writing joke books and performing stand-up comedy. He has written an opera entitled *Matter.* Seriously.

Send Us a Postcard

It's our goal to make this book the most helpful 300-plus pages on European history and art any traveler can read. Any suggestions, criticisms, or feedback from you would really be appreciated (send to Box 2009, Edmonds, WA 98020 or e-mail to rick@ricksteves.com). All correspondents will receive our *Back Door Travel Newsletter.* Thanks, and happy travels. —*Rick*

General Index

Geographical Index

A list of references by country, city, and region, for planning your trip

FREE-SPIRITED TOURS FROM

Rick Steves

Great Guides
Big Buses
Small Groups
No Grumps

Best of Europe ■ Best of Europe II ■ Eastern Europe ■ Turkey ■ Italy ■ Britain Spain/Portugal ■ Ireland ■ Eastern France ■ Western France ■ Village France Scandinavia ■ Germany/Austria/Switzerland ■ London ■ Paris ■ Rome

Looking for a one, two, or three-week tour that's run in the Rick Steves style? Check out Rick Steves' educational, experiential tours of Europe. Rather than seeing Europe as a spectator from a bus window, you'll be encouraged to dive into daily life. You'll have opportunities to meet the locals, see how local transportation and services work, and get comfortable wandering off on your own. By the end of the tour, you'll have the knowledge and confidence it takes to travel through Europe independently—which is what many of our tour members do before they return home.

Rick Steves' tours include much more in the "sticker price" than mainstream tours. Here's what you'll get with a Europe or regional Rick Steves tour...

Group size: Your tour group will be no larger than 26. **Guides:** You'll have two guides traveling and dining with you on your fully guided Rick Steves tour. **Bus:** You'll travel in a full-size 48-to-52-seat bus, with plenty of empty seats for you to spread out and read, snooze, enjoy the passing scenery, get away from your spouse, or whatever. **Sightseeing:** Your tour price includes all group sightseeing. There are no hidden extra charges. **Hotels:** You'll stay in small, characteristic, locally-run hotels in the center of each city, within walking distance of the sights you came to see. **Price and insurance:** Your tour price is guaranteed for 2001. Single travelers do not pay an extra supplement (we have them room with other singles). ETBD includes prorated tour cancellation/ interruption protection coverage at no extra cost. **Tips and kickbacks:** All guide and driver tips are included in your tour price. Because your driver and guides are paid salaries by ETBD, they can focus on giving you the best European travel experience possible.

Interested? Call (425) 771-8303 or visit www.ricksteves.com for a free copy of Rick Steves' 2001 Tours booklet!

Rick Steves' Europe Through the Back Door

130 Fourth Avenue North, PO Box 2009, Edmonds, WA 98020 USA
Phone: (425) 771-8303 ■ Fax: (425) 771-0833 ■ www.ricksteves.com

FREE TRAVEL GOODIES FROM

Rick Steves

EUROPEAN TRAVEL NEWSLETTER

My *Europe Through the Back Door* travel company will help you travel better **because** you're on a budget—not in spite of it. To see how, ask for my 64-page *travel newsletter* packed full of savvy travel tips, readers' discoveries, and your best bets for railpasses, guidebooks, videos, travel accessories and free-spirited tours.

2001 GUIDE TO EUROPEAN RAILPASSES

With hundreds of railpasses to choose from in 2001, finding the right pass for your trip has never been more confusing. To cut through the complexity, ask for my 64-page *2001 Guide to European Railpasses.* Once you've narrowed down your choices, we give you unbeatable prices, including important extras with every Eurailpass, *free:* my hour-long "How to get the most out of your railpass" video; your choice of one of my 16 country guidebooks and phrasebooks; and written advice on your one-page trip itinerary.

RICK STEVES' 2001 TOURS

We offer 16 different one, two, and three-week tours (160 departures in 2001) for those who want to experience Europe in Rick Steves' Back Door style, but without the transportation and hotel hassles. If a tour with a small group, modest family-run hotels, lots of exercise, great guides, and no tips or hidden charges sounds like your idea of fun, ask for my 48-page 2001 Tours booklet.

YEAR-ROUND GUIDEBOOK UPDATES

Even though the information in my guidebooks is the freshest around, things do change in Europe between book printings. I've set aside a special section at my website (www.ricksteves.com/update) listing *up-to-the-minute changes* for every Rick Steves guidebook.

> *Call, fax, or visit www.ricksteves.com to get your...*

☑ **FREE EUROPEAN TRAVEL NEWSLETTER**
☑ **FREE 2001 GUIDE TO EUROPEAN RAILPASSES**
☑ **FREE RICK STEVES' 2001 TOURS BOOKLET**

Rick Steves' Europe Through the Back Door

130 Fourth Avenue North, PO Box 2009, Edmonds, WA 98020 USA
Phone: (425) 771-8303 ■ Fax: (425) 771-0833 ■ www.ricksteves.com

AVALON
TRAVEL
publishing

BECAUSE TRAVEL MATTERS.

AVALON TRAVEL PUBLISHING knows that travel is more than coming and going—travel is taking part in new experiences, new ideas, and a new outlook. Our goal is to bring you complete and up-to-date information to help you make informed travel decisions.

AVALON TRAVEL GUIDES feature a combination of practicality and spirit, offering a unique traveler-to-traveler perspective perfect for an afternoon hike, around-the-world journey, or anything in between.

WWW.TRAVELMATTERS.COM

Avalon Travel Publishing guides are available
at your favorite book or travel store.

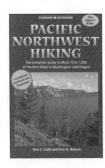

www.travelmatters.com

User-friendly, informative, and fun:

Because travel *matters.*

Visit our newly launched web site and explore the variety of titles and travel information available online, featuring an interactive *Road Trip USA* exhibit.

also check out:

www.ricksteves.com

The Rick Steves web site is bursting with information to boost your travel I.Q. and liven up your European adventure.

www.foghorn.com

Visit the Foghorn Outdoors web site for more information on the premier source of U.S. outdoor recreation guides.

www.moon.com

The Moon Handbooks web site offers interesting information and practical advice that ensure an extraordinary travel experience.

MOON HANDBOOKS

provide comprehensive coverage of a region's arts, history, land, people, and social issues in addition to detailed practical listings for accommodations, food, outdoor recreation, and entertainment. Moon Handbooks allow complete immersion in a region's culture—ideal for travelers who want to combine sightseeing with insight for an extraordinary travel experience in destinations throughout North America, Hawaii, Latin America, the Caribbean, Asia, and the Pacific.

WWW.MOON.COM

Rick Steves shows you where to travel and how to travel—all while getting the most value for your dollar. His Back Door travel philosophy is about making friends, having fun, and avoiding tourist rip-offs.

Rick's been traveling to Europe for more than 25 years and is the author of 22 guidebooks, which have sold more than a million copies. He also hosts the award-winning public television series *Travels in Europe with Rick Steves*.

WWW.RICKSTEVES.COM

ROAD TRIP USA

Getting there is half the fun, and Road Trip USA guides are your ticket to driving adventure. Taking you off the interstates and onto less-traveled, two-lane highways, each guide is filled with fascinating trivia, historical information, photographs, facts about regional writers, and details on where to sleep and eat—all contributing to your exploration of the American road.

"Books so full of the pleasures of the American road, you can smell the upholstery."
~ BBC radio

WWW.ROADTRIPUSA.COM

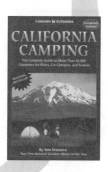